DNS For Dummies®

Cheat Sheet

Top-Level Domains

This list describes some of the more common top-level domains (TLDs), what they do, and whether they're unrestricted or restricted. Anyone can register a domain in an unrestricted TLD, but not in a restricted TLD.

.com	Commercial, for-profit entities (unrestricted)
.net	Network providers, such as ISPs and telecoms (unrestricted)
.org	Nonprofit organizations and entities (unrestricted)
.edu	Educational institutions (restricted)
.gov	U.S. government organizations (restricted)
.mil	U.S. military (restricted)
.xx	Country domains, where xx is the ISO-standard two-letter designation for the country. Some are restricted and some are not. The following four entries show examples.
.ca	Canada
.uk	United Kingdom of Great Britain
.au	Australia
.jp	Japan

DNS Record Types

- **Start of Authority (SOA):** The SOA record defines the zone as authoritative for the domain. The record contains TTL values and the master name server for the zone as well as a serial number.

- **Name Server (NS):** An NS record is added for each name server, master or slave, that is authoritative for the domain.

- **Mail Exchanger (MX):** MX records are used to direct e-mail to the correct mail server for the domain.

- **Host (A):** An A record maps a host name to an IP address.

- **IPv6 Host (AAAA):** The same as an A record except that it maps to an IPv6 address rather than to an IPv4 address.

- **Canonical Name (CNAME):** A CNAME record is used to alias a D? rather than to an IP address.

- **Pointer (PTR):** PTR records are used to map IP addresses to DNS around, as in an A record.

- **Text (TXT):** A TXT record is used to contain any information and is technical purposes.

- **Service Locator (SRV):** The SRV record is designed to allow DNS clients to find specific services rather than specific hosts on the network. This type of record is a key component of Microsoft Active Directory.

D1059965

For Dummies: Bestselling Book Series for Beginners

DNS For Dummies®

Cheat Sheet

Important NSLOOKUP Interactive Mode Commands

- ✔ **<name>:** By simply typing the fully qualified domain name to query, the A record is retrieved by default for that name. If you type a name that is not fully qualified (for example, `host` rather than `host.domain.tld`), the default domain set in your client configuration is appended followed by each search domain if that is unsuccessful. So if your computer is part of the `superstuff.edu` domain, an NSLOOKUP query for the host `stimpy` results in a search for `stimpy.superstuff.edu`.

- ✔ **Server:** The `server` command is used to configure which server is queried by `nslookup` when a query is specified. By default, your computer's configured DNS server is used.

- ✔ **Set type:** The `set type` command is used to set the query type. By default, A records are retrieved. The `set type` command can be used to select any record type (A, MX, PTR, CNAME and so forth) or ANY, which retrieves any record for the domain.

Zone Types

- ✔ **Master (primary):** A master zone is edited when changes are made to the domain. The master zone contains the master copy of the zone data. Typically, only the data in a single master zone is edited, saving you from having to edit the zone data on each DNS server and keep it synchronized. Multiple master servers are used sometimes, such as on the DNS servers of a Web hosting company.

- ✔ **Slave (secondary):** The slave zone is synchronized from the master zone data. Secondary zones are never edited, ensuring that the data on the slave DNS servers is always consistent, within reason, with the data on the master server.

My DNS Client Settings

DNS server 1 _____

DNS server 2 _____

DNS server 3 (optional) _____

Domain _____

Search domains (optional) _____

_____

_____

Key Troubleshooting Steps

Follow these steps to find the source of your DNS server problems. Although these steps can't cure all possible ills, they can help you find a resolution in most cases:

1. **Check your log files.** Many problems show up in the logs, making them simple to locate and repair.

2. **Check your data using a command-line DNS client, such as NSLOOKUP or DIG.** If you're having data problems with a zone or specific record, use one of these tools to attempt to locate the problem.

3. **Check your data by hand.** The last resort is to go through your zones and configuration by hand, looking for the problem with the specific zone or record.

How DNS Facilitates E-mail

These quick refresher steps show how DNS and SMTP servers work together to get your e-mail from Point A to Point B:

1. The client sends an SMTP message to an SMTP relay server.

2. The SMTP relay server locates the MX record for the domain in the e-mail address (`user@domain.tld`).

3. The SMTP relay server sends the message to the host specified by the MX record.

For Dummies: Bestselling Book Series for Beginners

DNS

FOR

DUMMIES®

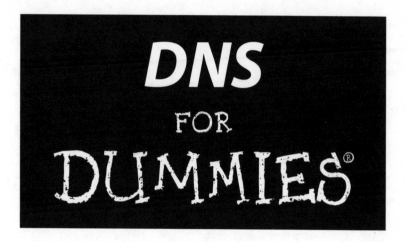

DNS FOR DUMMIES®

by Blair Rampling and David Dalan

WILEY

Wiley Publishing, Inc.

DNS For Dummies®

Published by
Wiley Publishing, Inc.
909 Third Avenue
New York, NY 10022

www.wiley.com

About the Authors

Blair Rampling is the Unix administrator at a mid-size resource company and is responsible for the administration of a number of Sun Solaris–based servers. His experience involves a wide array of systems, including Unix, Linux, and Microsoft Windows in both corporate and ISP environments.

David Dalan (CCDA, CCNA, MCSE, and B.S, Washington State University) has been employed as the technical trainer and training manager for a leading international technical support services call-center firm. He has also held the positions of field engineer, network analyst, and technical support manager for the software division of one of the world's largest publishers. He now enjoys working as a systems specialist for city government in his hometown. David's career has been focused on the development of technical training, providing networking design and analysis services for a range of clients, from small private schools to enterprise businesses. He also operates his own consulting firm, concentrating on network design and implementation projects in addition to authoring several books, including co-authoring *CCDA For Dummies,* with Ron Glister (Wiley Publishing, Inc.).

Author's Acknowledgments

Blair Rampling

Thanks to Greg Croy, for providing me with the opportunity to develop and write this book. Thanks to David Dalan and Rebecca Whitney, for developing my initial manuscript into the finished product you see today. Michael C. McPhee and David M. Sherwood provided technical input to ensure the book's accuracy. Finally, thanks to David Fugate, for providing the business sense and interaction that I can't. I want to thank everyone again who worked on this book, for their insight and patience.

David Dalan

I thank my loving wife and beautiful children for being the center of my life. I thank Rebecca Whitney, Blair Rampling, and Greg Croy for giving me the opportunity to play a small but hopefully meaningful part in this project and for putting all those long hours into this book.

Publisher's Acknowledgments

We're proud of this book; please send us your comments through our online registration form located at www.dummies.com/register/.

Some of the people who helped bring this book to market include the following:

Acquisitions, Editorial, and Media Development

Project Editor: Rebecca Whitney

Acquisitions Editor: Greg Croy

Technical Editor: Michael C. McPhee, David M. Sherwood

Editorial Manager: Carol Sheehan

Media Development Manager: Laura VanWinkle

Media Development Supervisor: Richard Graves

Editorial Assistant: Amanda M. Foxworth

Cartoons: Rich Tennant (www.the5thwave.com)

Production

Project Coordinator: Dale White

Layout and Graphics: Amanda Carter, Joyce Haughey, Stephanie Jumper, Michael Krizil, Jeremey Unger

Proofreaders: John Greenough, TECHBOOKS Production Services

Indexer: TECHBOOKS Production Services

Publishing and Editorial for Technology Dummies

Richard Swadley, Vice President and Executive Group Publisher

Andy Cummings, Vice President and Publisher

Mary C. Corder, Editorial Director

Publishing for Consumer Dummies

Diane Graves Steele, Vice President and Publisher

Joyce Pepple, Acquisitions Director

Composition Services

Gerry Fahey, Vice President of Production Services

Debbie Stailey, Director of Composition Services

Contents at a Glance

Table of Contents

Introduction

Welcome to *DNS For Dummies!* This is the book you have always wanted if you have ever needed to understand DNS or you need to set up and configure a DNS server and you haven't had the opportunity to learn the ropes yet.

Admittedly, DNS can be a daunting hill to climb. Traditional DNS documentation assumes that you're an expert on the Internet and its protocols, such as TCP/IP, and it uses lots of big words and technical jargon. In *DNS For Dummies,* we avoid that kind of intimidating language in favor of information that anyone can decipher.

About This Book

This book isn't meant to be a thorough technical overview of DNS, although it does that job admirably. If you just need to get your toes wet on the topic of DNS, you may be especially interested in Chapters 1–4 because they build a basis for exploring the more technical theory described in the following chapters. If you want, though, you can skip those chapters and jump right into our description of how to install and configure a DNS server.

When you need to perform a task with DNS as either a client or a server, you can pick up the book, turn to the section you need, and start from there. You don't need lots of knowledge to be able to jump into any section because the walk-through examples for each procedure are detailed.

How to Use This Book

This book is designed to be used as a practical guide to implementing and maintaining DNS on Windows-family servers and Unix-based servers. Additionally, if you're exploring the possibilities of building your own DNS server, this book contains information that demystifies the inner workings of DNS. As a working reference, this book contains the needed information that will help you configure your DNS server initially and continue supporting it long afterward. This text is a job aid, a handy and insightful reference you can use for answering DNS configuration- and maintenance-related questions in a hurry. In addition to its wealth of information, *DNS For Dummies* contains tips for getting additional information about particular topics related to DNS.

What You Don't Need to Read

A number of sections in this book are highly technical because DNS is a technical subject. You don't have to read anything that's in a sidebar or marked with a Technical Stuff icon to be able to use DNS clients or servers; reading those sections, however, can further your understanding of how DNS works behind the scenes.

In addition, several chapters are dedicated to the theory behind how DNS works. You get a better understanding of why DNS does certain things if you understand how the DNS process works. If you choose to skip Chapters 3 and 4 because of their technical nature, however, you won't miss the "meat" of working with DNS.

Foolish Assumptions

In writing this book, we have assumed that you're a somewhat technically literate user who is already familiar with the Internet to some extent. Although this book attempts to simplify DNS, it's still a technical subject at heart. Without a firm grasp of the basics of the Internet, you don't have much hope of understanding DNS. You should be familiar with terms such as WWW, e-mail, and IP address.

We have assumed also that you're somewhat comfortable with the operating system you're using — either Microsoft Windows or Unix/Linux. You should at least be able to navigate in Windows and use the basic configuration tools or be somewhat comfortable in a Unix shell and be able to view and edit files.

How This Book Is Organized

This book is organized into five parts. The parts separate the content of the book into activities such as working with clients or servers and configuring DNS zones. Each part is made up of a series of chapters, each divided into sections. You can start reading at any part or chapter in the book if you're interested in performing a certain task. The five parts are described next.

Part 1: How DNS Makes the Internet Go 'Round

You may or may not know that DNS is at the heart of the Internet. Almost every application on the Net uses DNS in one way or another. This part explains what DNS is, how DNS names are organized on the Internet, and how DNS works in theory.

Part II: Working with DNS Clients

Every system has DNS clients of some sort. Part II explains which DNS clients exist on your systems and how to use those clients. A chapter apiece is devoted to configuring DNS clients on your system and using those clients.

Part III: Working with DNS Servers

If you have ever wanted (or needed) to run your own DNS server, all the information you need is in Part III. One of its two chapters is devoted to installing and configuring a DNS server on Microsoft Windows; the other, to installing and configuring the BIND 9 DNS server on Linux or Unix.

Part IV: The Details: Setting Up Your DNS Zones

Every DNS server that isn't devoted purely to caching DNS entries has one or more zones. A zone contains all the information for a specific domain. If you need to add records to a zone, create a new zone, or even create a subdomain, Part IV is the place. It even explains how zones work and describes the major types of DNS records.

Part V: Security and Advanced DNS Tricks

If you want to do something extraordinary with your DNS server or you simply want to make it as secure as possible, Part V is for you. It covers the security problems faced by DNS and how to make sure that you aren't susceptible to those problems. This part also covers the advanced features in DNS servers and troubleshooting.

Part VI: The Part of Tens

Part VI talks about a variety of DNS-related subjects that may just tickle your fancy. From ten things even "experts" do to inadvertently trash their DNS servers to ten steps that can keep you chugging down the road to DNS nirvana, we give you all kinds of concise and relevant information. If you find yourself in need of a quick solution, this part of the book can be a life-saver.

Appendixes

The appendixes provide information beyond the normal scope of what you probably will do with your DNS servers. This information includes the use of the DNSCMD utility to administer your Windows DNS server from the command line, the use of Webmin to administer your UNIX DNS server graphically, and a list of available DNS server applications other than the Microsoft DNS Server and BIND, which are covered in this book.

Icons Used In This Book

Keep this information in mind while working with your DNS server. Although the information may not seem relevant in some situations, when you do need it, it's a life-saver.

You're delving into the deepest reaches of DNS server administration. Although this information isn't needed regularly in most cases, it does give you insight into the workings of the particular technology being examined.

This stuff is generally handy in the day-to-day operation of your server.

To visit DNS nirvana, avoid these common traps, shortcomings, or issues.

Where to Go from Here

DNS is a technical subject. By picking up this book, however, you have taken the first step to bridging the gap from Internet user to someone who truly understands the hows and whys of the Internet. Start anywhere you want in this book — just take a look at the table of contents or the index, and enjoy taking control of your Internet experience!

Part I
How DNS Makes the Internet Go 'Round

The 5th Wave   By Rich Tennant

"Daddy and I are going to give you all the love.com, care.com, and opportunities.com that we possibly can."

In this part . . .

Y ou may be familiar with DNS, or, like many users of the Internet and corporate networks, you may be blissfully unaware of what DNS is. Many users have no idea that DNS even exists.

The chapters in this part of the book introduce you to the basics of DNS, from how it works by itself (its internal processes, for example) to how it enables other applications to provide useful services to users. We even give you a step-by-step description of the processes that go on behind the scenes whenever you use an application that relies on DNS, such as a Web browser.

Chapter 1

The Basics of DNS

*U*nless you have been living in a cave, you have probably heard about the Internet. In homes and offices across the world, the Internet is fast becoming as ubiquitous as telephones and televisions. It has experienced rapid growth in large part because of a number of popular Internet-based applications, including the World Wide Web, e-mail, and instant messaging. One reason that a typical "nontechy" user can enjoy the Internet is that many of the details of connecting a computer to the Internet are hidden from general users. Almost anyone can browse the Web or send and receive e-mail without understanding anything about how the Internet works.

This ease of use is an important factor in our discussion of DNS in this book. Simply put, DNS allows people to use meaningful names, such as www.yahoo.com, to find Internet-based resources. In this way, DNS has allowed users from a wide range of educational backgrounds to makes use of the Internet. That wasn't always the case. In the beginning, the Internet was simply a method for government and educational institutions to talk to each other. At the time, only computer experts could use it because they possessed the knowledge needed to connect one computer to another on this "primitive" Internet.

Restricting use of the Internet to expert users wasn't good enough. Many hosts participating in the early Internet were located at, and supported by, staff members from, universities. Universities (notably, the University of California at Berkley) wanted to make use of this tool to help perform research and teach. Even though most users were computer specialists, the number of hosts added to the budding Internet would be too numerous to track manually. With the invention of a number of network protocols that worked behind the scenes to remove much of the manual interaction on the Internet, ease of use was greatly improved. These protocols included, among others, the Domain Name System, or DNS. DNS eliminated the need to manually remember IP addresses and replaced that system with human-readable names instead. DNS allows a name to be linked to an address and rather than have to remember a number of addresses, you need to know just the name of the system you want to contact. Although DNS plays quite a significant role in millions of users' daily Internet use, this ease of use is a side effect of the original intention of DNS. DNS was invented to solve the logistical problems that arose because too many hosts were on the Internet to be able to keep track of using a manual list of addresses.

A Short History of the Internet

The Internet, as we know it today, didn't start out with the intention of being a global communications medium for public use. Originally, what is now the Internet was simply a few educational and military computers that were interconnected. This network began with four nodes in 1969 and was known as ARPAnet, named for the Department of Defense Advanced Research Projects Agency (ARPA), which was in charge of developing the network that would provide a distributed communications system that could (among other things) survive a nuclear catastrophe.

ARPAnet originally used a protocol named Network Control Protocol (NCP) to connect participating hosts. Eventually, NCP no longer provided enough functionality to keep the budding network operating effectively. A new protocol, named TCP, was designed for ARPAnet that would eventually be expanded into the TCP/IP protocol now used on the Internet.

As ARPAnet grew, more and more applications were developed for it. Not surprisingly, the first "killer app" on ARPAnet was e-mail. Interestingly, the @ character as a means to separate the e-mail recipient and the server name was introduced in 1972, and the first emoticons were suggested on April 12, 1979. DNS was first introduced in 1984. The ability to dynamically map host names to IP addresses was particularly useful because approximately one thousand hosts were on the ARPAnet at that time.

As time passed, ARPAnet continued to grow in at an almost exponential rate. Although 1,000 hosts were on the Internet in 1984, that number grew to approximately 10,000 in 1987, and to more than 100,000 in 1989. In 1990, ARPAnet officially became the Internet. It took only another two years for another tenfold increase in the number of Internet hosts, to 1 million in 1992. More than 100 million hosts are now on the Internet. Note that this number refers to only registered A records in DNS and not to actual systems with only IP addresses.

Earlier in this chapter, we mention that the Internet uses the TCP/IP protocol suite to operate. Like the Internet, DNS depends on TCP/IP to operate. For that reason, we briefly examine the TCP/IP protocol suite in the following section.

1 Introduce Thee to TCP/IP

Transmission Control Protocol/Internet Protocol (TCP/IP) is the primary *protocol suite* on which the Internet now runs. Most often, networks can be described as being layered entities, and the Internet isn't any different. Each layer has its own protocols and processes designed to deal with particular segments of the network communications process. The lowest layers encompass the actual physical network connection on which the network is running. These layers are handled by the network hardware — such as routers and switches, the network cards in computers, and the physical network cabling — so the Internet on those layers is *agnostic* (it doesn't matter what type of media or protocols are running on those layers as long as each node can talk to every other node with which it needs to communicate). In fact, the Internet runs on a wide variety of physical networks, such as phone lines, T-carrier lines (such as T1 and T3), optical carrier lines (such as OC-3 and OC-12), in addition to older technologies, such as X.25 and ISDN. As long as a node can talk to a neighbor through some method, that node can become part of the Internet.

The International Standards Organization (ISO) has built for network communications a specification known as the Open Systems Interconnect, or OSI, model. This layered model specifies which processes any specific protocols (residing within the various layers) must be capable of handling. For example, protocols of the Sessions layer (Layer 5) are concerned with maintaining a communications session between two hosts.

At the highest layers of the network lie the applications. *Application protocols,* including HTTP and FTP, are what allow you to *do* anything on the Internet. They're the protocols that run the World Wide Web, e-mail, and everything else. A variety (an almost endless variety) of these application protocols exist, and although they're technically part of the TCP/IP protocol suite, don't be concerned about them here.

Linking the applications at the highest layer of the network to the physical links at the lowest layer are the TCP/IP protocols. Although TCP/IP is usually referred to in singular form, it's a combination of a number of protocols, typically including TCP or UDP and IP, which is always present. IP, a network layer protocol, interfaces with the lower layers of the network to enable data transmission across the physical network. At the layers below IP, only raw data is passed. The IP protocol also implements the addressing for each node — hence, the term IP address. An IPv4 address consists of a 32-bit binary number (although typically notated in decimal, IPv6 also uses a 128-bit address) that expresses a host and a network. Each node on an IP network must have a unique IP address. These addresses are how the nodes contact each other.

TCP sits above IP in the protocol *stack* and is known as a *transport layer protocol*. Although IP implements addressing and data transmission, TCP implements higher-level data-transmission features, such as flow control and error correction, to ensure that a connection is reliable. In other words, every packet that is sent reaches its destination.

In addition to TCP, another transport layer protocol is in the TCP/IP suite: the Unreliable Datagram Protocol (UDP). UDP, unlike TCP, doesn't concern itself with reliability. Packets may be sent, but you have no guarantee that the packets will be received or that they will be correct when they're received. UDP is a faster transport protocol than TCP, but it moves the onus for data reliability to the application layer protocols. This arrangement is sometimes favorable for performance reasons.

The OSI model

As we mention in the preceding section (refer to the Technical Stuff paragraph), a standard model for networking protocols is the Open Systems Interconnect (OSI) model. The OSI model, made all-powerful by the International Standards Organization (ISO), was designed primarily to support a developer's ability to change the elements within any of the individual layers, without having to modify components in the other six layers, as long as certain standards are followed. This functionality exists because components at any of the seven layers are concerned with only two issues: how to send data to adjacent layers and what to expect from adjacent layers. For example, Layer 5 cares only about communicating with Layer 4 and Layer 6. As far as Layer 5 is concerned, all layers other than 4 and 6 may as well not exist.

How does the OSI model relate to the TCP/IP suite of protocols? The *OSI model* is a system of seven layers designed to compartmentalize the different functions of intersystem communication, such as when two computers on a network are transferring data (see Figure 1-1).

TCP/IP is a protocol suite, not just a single protocol. It includes a number of protocols, each residing on one of the seven layers, such as TCP, IP, UDP, DNS, HTTP, and even FTP. The seven layers of the OSI model are often referred to by their number: Layer 1 or Layer 2, for example. They also have "friendly" names, such as Application and Transport, that sort of describe the function of the protocols defined at that particular layer. These layers aren't concrete items; more precisely, they're a way of conceptualizing the process of communications between two systems.

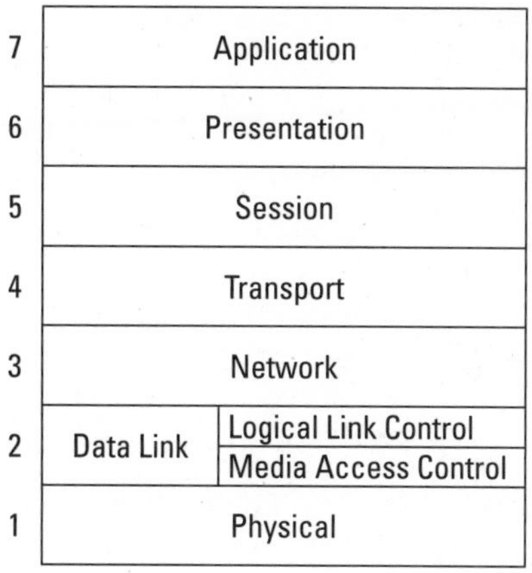

7	Application
6	Presentation
5	Session
4	Transport
3	Network
2	Data Link — Logical Link Control / Media Access Control
1	Physical

Figure 1-1:
The OSI
model.

This list describes the layers of the OSI model and the kind of functions expected at the particular part (layer) of the communications process:

✔ **Layer 7, Application:** On this layer, the applications for a protocol suite reside. It's where you use applications such as FTP to transfer files and HTTP to browse the Internet if you're running TCP/IP. Layer 7 is the furthest "away" from the network hardware. The Application layer protocols are responsible for getting the data from users and injecting it into the network protocol stack, and for receiving data from the network protocol stack and forwarding it to the user.

✔ **Layer 6, Presentation:** This layer ensures that the data transferred to and from the application layer is in the correct format for the process operating at the Application layer. Presentation layer protocols are uncommon, especially when using TCP/IP, but at one time, multiple character-encoding schemes were used, such as ASCII (the current standard) and EBCDIC (on older IBM systems). A presentation layer protocol was implemented to ensure that the network data was readable regardless of the encoding scheme of the system.

✔ **Layer 5, Session:** The processes operating on this layer are responsible for establishing and then ending network communication sessions between hosts. The Remote Procedure Call (RPC) protocol is a an example of a session layer protocol. RPC is used in one form or another by a variety of operating systems, from Windows .NET to RedHat Linux. RPC is used to establish the connection with the remote system, and then other protocols are used to *do* something with that connection.

✔ **Layer 4, Transport:** This layer is one of the most important in TCP/IP because practically all applications that make use of the TCP/IP stack use a Transport layer protocol. Transport layer protocols are responsible for managing a process known as flow control. *Flow control* involves the management of the rate at which packets flow so that the receiving system can receive the stream of data without errors. In other words, flow control keeps a sending computer from sending data faster than the receiving computer can handle it.

Transport layer protocols are also responsible for error correction (incorrect or missing packets are resent) and *segmentation*, where data too large to fit in the network layer packet is split into smaller chunks. The Transport layer protocol on the receiving end then reassembles the data. TCP/IP has a few Transport layer protocols, including TCP, UDP, and ICMP. ICMP is used for network management (the ping utility uses ICMP), TCP is a reliable protocol that does error correction, and UDP is a faster but unreliable protocol that doesn't do error correction. Note that although UDP doesn't do error correction itself, higher-layer protocols can use UDP and do their own error correction.

✔ **Layer 3, Network:** The real action happens here. This layer is responsible for the actual network addressing and establishing the connection with the remote system. For example, your (and everyone else's) IP address is defined at this layer. Routing also typically happens at the network layer because most routing equipment is configured to understand network layer protocols. In the TCP/IP stack, IP is the Network layer protocol. IP is used to provide the logical address that one system or application can use to refer to another system. Layer 3 is typically the last layer abstracted from the network hardware — in other words, it runs on any hardware.

✔ **Layer 2, Data Link:** This layer is normally divided into two sublayers: Logical Link Control (LLC) and Media Access Control (MAC). Overall, the Data Link layer is responsible for the raw data communication over the physical link (Layer 1). One protocol at the Data Link layer is Ethernet. The Logical Link Control layer is responsible for communication with remote systems, and the Media Access Control layer is responsible for traffic control on the link and the physical addressing of the network interface. At the MAC layer, the MAC address is defined. Every network adapter ever made has a unique MAC address assigned to it (in theory, anyway). Media Access Control protocols determine when the physical link is clear so that the system can use it to send data. Most MAC protocols also perform collision avoidance or collision detection, which occurs when two systems send data on a physical link at the same time.

✔ **Layer 1, Physical:** The physical media and electrical interfaces on the network devices reside on this layer. The physical layer specifications control how the data signals are sent from one system to another, including the wiring and the format of the electrical (or optical) signals.

Wrap it up: Encapsulation

Encapsulation is a term you may hear in any situation in which multiple network protocols are in use. It's an important concept in networking that refers to the process in which low-level protocols are used to transport data provided by higher-level protocols. The information from one protocol is placed (encapsulated) inside information from the encapsulating protocol. Remember that the packets or frames sent by any particular protocol are made of two distinct sections: the header and the data.

Encapsulation is perhaps best understood if you take a top-down look at the process. Suppose that the protocol stack being used is TCP/IP. Suppose also that you want to move some data from one host on the network to another and that you want to use FTP to do so. Your data, which is sent using FTP, needs to make the journey by being carried by the Data Link layer protocol, such as Ethernet. FTP data cannot be placed directly in an Ethernet frame, though, because Ethernet doesn't have the capability to transport the FTP data in an error-free manner and in the proper-size segments. Neither does Ethernet know the address of the receiving node. These jobs belong to the Transport and Network layers, respectively.

When the FTP data is sent, the TCP protocol is used as a transport protocol. FTP data is sent as either a block or stream of data; for the purposes of this example, however, assume that a block format is being used. The FTP data is sent in fixed-length blocks, each with some information in a header. The header on each block is used to contain status and processing information, which is read by the FTP protocol on the receiving system. The FTP block, including the header, is then *segmented* (divided into chunks small enough to be sent by TCP/IP), if necessary, and encapsulated in the TCP protocol.

The encapsulation process just means that another set of headers (TCP, in this case) are appended and the original data and headers become the data of the TCP packet — One set of data is surrounded by the other (see Figure 1–2).

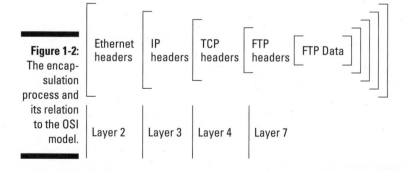

Figure 1-2: The encapsulation process and its relation to the OSI model.

These TCP headers are read by the receiving system's TCP protocol. The next step is the encapsulation of the TCP data by the IP protocol. The IP protocol has other responsibilities, such as addressing, and it appends its own headers to the TCP packet. The TCP packet, including TCP headers, becomes the data in the IP packet. The same process occurs when the IP data is sent over the Data Link protocol, whatever it may be. If it's Ethernet, the IP packet becomes the data in an Ethernet frame and Ethernet headers are appended to the frame.

The decapsulation process is the opposite of the encapsulation process. The Ethernet protocol on the receiving system gets the Ethernet frame created in the encapsulation process. The protocol then reads the Ethernet headers and sends the data portion of the frame untouched to the IP protocol. Remember that the data portion of the Ethernet frame contained the IP packet including IP headers, so the IP protocol can now read those headers. The IP protocol then forwards the data section of the IP packet to the TCP protocol, which then reads the untouched TCP headers and forwards the data to FTP. FTP then reads the FTP headers, and the block of FTP data becomes part of a file on the receiving system.

The encapsulation/decapsulation process makes things easier on the developers of network protocols because each protocol layer can be developed separately. The process becomes a problem, however, for performing content scanning and stateful firewall inspection. These processes rely on being able to see the application data in a network packet, so every time a packet of data passes through this type of system, it must be decapsulated and then reencapsulated and sent on to the receiving system. This process is highly CPU intensive and can slow network traffic significantly.

Although encapsulation and decapsulation may seem like a heavy-duty task that would eat system resources, that's not really the case. The amount of power used on a normal server or workstation sending, encapsulating, and decapsulating typical streams of data isn't significant. The CPU power issue becomes an issue, however, on network hardware, such as firewalls and multilayer routers. Data Link layer protocols are often embedded in hardware, and the higher-level protocols are implemented in software, so at least one step of encapsulation would be required. One way to prevent undue processor utilization from the encapsulation process that has been used by many network hardware vendors is to implement the entire protocol stack used by the encapsulation and decapsulation process in a hardware device called an Application Specific Integrated Circuit (ASIC). Processing the packets in hardware is much faster than processing them in software, so the CPU requirements are removed. Because the ASIC devices can also usually be reprogrammed, the processing code can be updated if required.

DNS: What It Is and What It Does

In essence, DNS is simply a database that links meaningful names (known as host names), such as `www.microsoft.com`, to a specific IP address, such as `192.168.124.1`. Simply linking addresses to names is just the beginning, though, because DNS has many more features in addition to host name to address mapping. We examine the advanced functions of DNS in later chapters, but for now you should focus on the host name to IP mapping features. The key features you need to be aware of are shown in this list:

- Mappings of addresses to names and vice versa (known as records) are stored in a database.
- The DNS database is distributed.
- A DNS database also stores additional records.

Although DNS is a database, most importantly it's a distributed database. Each DNS server contains only a small portion of the host name to IP address mappings (relative to the number of records for the entire Internet). Each DNS server is configured with a special record that tells the DNS server where (the IP address of another DNS server) it will perform a lookup for records it doesn't have in its portion of the DNS database. Because of this arrangement, each DNS server maintains only a small portion of the total DNS host to IP address mappings. The collection of host-name-to-IP-address mappings contained with the DNS database is also known as a *namespace*. The DNS namespace is discussed in Chapter 2, and the way DNS lookups function is explained in Chapter 3. Essentially, when looking for a name in DNS, the DNS client first checks a top-level DNS server database. That server tells the client which DNS server hosts the next part of the DNS name, and the client then queries that server. This lookup-and-handoff process continues until the client finds the DNS server that hosts the DNS record in question, and that server provides the IP address.

In addition to the basic IP-address-to-host-name mapping records stored by the DNS database, records are also maintained by DNS for other purposes. DNS contains a number of record types that facilitate other applications, as we discuss in Chapter 4. The mail exchanger (MX) record, for example, provides mail servers with the information required to forward e-mail messages to the recipient's e-mail server. Another type of record, the service (SVC) record, is used by Microsoft Active Directory to locate network services.

Seeing the DNS Difference

By itself, DNS doesn't appear to do much, and on top of that DNS can seem a bit intimidating because it has number of different features and record types. One key to understanding the importance of DNS is understanding how other processes and applications depend on the services DNS provides. By understanding how DNS provides the underlying services used by various applications, you can get a clearer picture of why DNS exists and how it works.

DNS services are used by many common applications, including

- ✔ World Wide Web (WWW)
- ✔ E-mail
- ✔ Other applications, such as instant messaging

The World Wide Web depends on DNS for user-friendly navigation. You could get to a Web site by entering the IP address of a site in your Web browser, but remembering lots of arbitrary numbers isn't easy for most folks. It's much easier to remember a DNS name for a Web site that reflects its content, such as `www.yahoo.com` or `www.microsoft.com`. It's fair to say that without DNS, the Web wouldn't have become quite the phenomenon that it is now.

E-mail is one of the most popular applications that utilizes DNS. Although the Web simply uses DNS for linking names to IP addresses for Web sites, e-mail servers also require some specialized records above and beyond what is required for basic host name to IP addresses. For example, when an e-mail message is sent from your e-mail client (such as Microsoft Outlook or Netscape Messenger), it can be sent either directly to the target domain (Microsoft.com if the note was sent to `user@microsoft.com`) or to another e-mail server that is providing a relay service. If your e-mail application specifies an outgoing (SMTP) mail server that is not the final destination server for the message, you're making use of the relay process.

As you may know, an e-mail address is made up of two parts:, a recipient and a host. In the address `postmaster@domain.tld`, `postmaster` is the recipient, the user who will receive the message. This is irrelevant to the SMTP process, though, because the mail transfer agent (MTA) is responsible for making sure that the message gets into the mailbox of the recipient.

The host, `domain.tld`, is of much more interest. In this case, `domain.tld` refers not to a host in the traditional sense of an A record but rather to a mail server known as a *mail exchanger (MX)*. This server is responsible for accepting all mail for `domain.tld`, denoted by a special record — an MX record — in DNS.

Beyond the Web and e-mail are many applications that either rely on or can use DNS services. These applications can include databases, multi-tier Web applications built by using middleware or an application server, peer-to-peer sharing programs, instant messaging, and multiplayer games.

In quite a practical sense, any application that uses the Internet to connect two or more hosts to share information, or otherwise communicate, is probably relying on DNS services in one form or another.

Setting Up Your Systems to Use DNS

Many different DNS clients as well as a number of DNS servers exist. This book focuses on the clients and servers for Microsoft Windows 2000, Windows XP, and Linux and also discusses the Microsoft DNS server on Windows 2000 and the Berkeley Internet Name Domain (BIND) on Linux. BIND is the most popular Unix-based DNS server, and in fact many vendor-provided DNS servers are based on BIND code. BIND is also available for Windows, but is rarely used.

Microsoft Windows contains two types of DNS client: an integrated client and a command-line client. They're used for different purposes:

- ✔ **Integrated client:** The integrated DNS client in Windows is used for all applications that don't have custom-written DNS clients. Considering that the integrated DNS client is built into Windows for any application to use and writing a DNS client from scratch is lots of work, most programs use this integrated client, such as Microsoft Internet Explorer and Microsoft Outlook.

- ✔ **Command-line client:** The command-line DNS client in Windows is named `nslookup`. Normally used to troubleshoot DNS problems, it can look up any type of record from any DNS server. If you're having DNS-related problems, you can check your records to ensure that they're correct or to locate the specific problem.

Serving DNS with Windows

Windows server operating systems (Windows .NET Server, Windows 2000, and Windows NT) all support DNS servers in addition to the various client tools. The Microsoft DNS server is integrated into all versions of Windows NT, Windows 2000, and Windows .NET Server. This book focuses specifically on the Windows 2000 implementation, although much of the information carries both forward and backward in different versions. The Windows 2000 and Windows .NET DNS servers are essentially identical, although the Windows NT 4.0 DNS Server is similar but without the integrated Active Directory support.

The Microsoft DNS server has all the functionality of any standard DNS server. It can host the standard records and provide services to any client. A few major differences exist between the Microsoft DNS Server and the most popular Unix DNS server, BIND:

- ✔ **GUI interface:** Microsoft DNS allows you to configure your zones and records through a graphical interface by default rather than have to know the format of specific configuration and zone files.

  ✔ **Records stored in the Registry:** Although BIND records are stored in flat (nonrelational) text files by default, Microsoft DNS records and configuration information is stored in either the system Registry or Active Directory. You can configure Microsoft DNS to store zones in files, and you can configure BIND to use a database for record storage.

  ✔ **Extended record types:** Microsoft DNS on Windows 2000 and later also supports SRV (Service) records in a way to enable Active Directory and the global catalog. These SRV records are used by clients to locate services on the network.

Most versions of Unix also include an integrated client and at least one (and sometimes more) command-line client.

The integrated Unix DNS client is implemented in a slightly different fashion from the integrated Windows client, but that only really matters from a programming perspective. To users, they're effectively the same. The integrated client provides DNS services to Web browsers, e-mail applications, and any other applications that don't have a custom-programmed DNS client.

Unix also contains the `nslookup` command-line DNS client, and it's almost functionally identical to the Windows version. With the implementation of BIND 9 on newer Unix systems, though, `nslookup` is being deprecated in favor of a new DNS client named `dig`. It's a more powerful client in that it provides far more information about the lookup process than simply the final result. With `nslookup`, you can search for a DNS record, but with `dig` you can determine exactly why a certain lookup is failing.

Getting your name on Unix

The BIND DNS server service (operating on a Unix operating system) is the most common DNS server now in use on the Internet. This book focuses primarily on the newest version of BIND, version 9. BIND also provides all the standard DNS features, but it has advantages and disadvantages when compared to the Microsoft DNS Server. BIND running on Unix is understood to be more robust and scalable than Microsoft DNS because of the efficiency of Unix applications and the inherent stability in Unix over Microsoft Windows. Since the release of Microsoft Windows 2000, though, Windows has become a much more stable platform than older Windows versions for critical applications such as DNS, although it doesn't yet have the same for stability as Unix.

In addition, Unix is often, from a performance standpoint, a favorable platform for infrastructure applications such as DNS. Unix was designed with efficiency in mind mostly with no regard for usability because it's primarily a server operating system. Windows, on the other hand, was designed with usability rather than efficiency in mind. For this reason, a Unix system typically runs an equivalent application faster than Windows does on similar hardware. Proprietary Unix systems are, with a few exceptions, often far more scalable than the Intel-based hardware Windows runs on.

The main disadvantage to BIND on Unix is its difficulty of configuration. BIND uses a series of text files, including a configuration file (typically named `/etc/named.conf`), and zone files to store its configuration. When BIND is started, these files are read and the BIND configuration is stored in memory. If these files have syntax errors, either the DNS server doesn't start (if the configuration file has errors) or the zone doesn't load (if the zone file has errors). In addition, sometimes the DNS server starts or the zone loads and you have unexpected results.

Organizing and Subdividing DNS

Although most DNS on the Internet is fairly simple, having only NS records identifying the name servers, a few A records (or only one in many cases), and an MX record, not all domains are that simple. If you're implementing DNS at your site for naming your corporate systems, for example, you may have a huge number of A records and possibly a number of other records. In this case, you should organize your DNS namespace into subdomains.

A *subdomain* is a child domain of another domain you control. For example, if you have the domain name `domain.tld`, you can have as many sub-domains under `domain.tld` as you want, such as `eng.domain.tld`, `acct.domain.tld`, and `corp.ca.domain.tld`. Only two requirements must be met:

- ✔ **The domain tree must not be more than 128 levels deep, including the namespace root.** This situation is unlikely because it defeats the purpose of DNS, which is usability.

- ✔ **Every subdomain on each level must be unique.** Obviously, you can have `eng.ca.domain.tld`, `eng.ny.domain.tld`, and `eng.domain.tld` all coexisting, but you cannot have more than one `eng.domain.tld`.

Through the implementation of subdomains, you can organize your DNS namespace into a structured tree rather than a flat space. This organization eases administration and makes the domain tree more intuitive to users. You may choose to organize your namespace in a variety of ways, such as by geographical location or by business group.

Making DNS Work Harder, Safer, and Better

In addition to all the basic DNS features, DNS implements a number of advanced features meant to both increase the functionality of DNS and increase its security.

DNS security is implemented through a number of methods, including

- ✔ Securing the server
- ✔ Implementing transactional signatures (TSIGs) for secure zone transfers and updates
- ✔ Limiting the amount of information a DNS server divulges to an untrusted party

When it comes to advanced functionality, DNS has an array of features to both increase efficiency and ease administration. This list outlines the key features you should be aware of:

- ✔ **Dynamic DNS:** A method of allowing a DNS client to update a record in a DNS zone. By using dynamic DNS on a network of workstations, for example, the workstations can automatically register in DNS rather than an administrator having to create a record for each one. Dynamic DNS introduces a number of security issues, which we address in Chapter 11.

- ✔ **DNS round robin:** A method of using DNS as a "poor person's load balancer." A traditional network load balancer uses a wide variety of network performance *metrics* to measure the performance of a number of hosts and route incoming requests to the one with the least load. With DNS round robin, DNS clients are routed sequentially to each server on the list, starting over with the first server after the last one is reached. Because this method doesn't take into account any load on the systems, a system could even go down and traffic would still be routed to it. Round robin can be useful in many situations where the cost of a full load-balancing solution cannot be justified.

  The NOTIFY feature in DNS allows slave DNS servers to be automatically notified whenever a zone is updated on the master DNS server. Without NOTIFY, slave servers wait until the cache timeout of the zone expires before updating it from the master server. With NOTIFY, however, whenever a zone is updated on the master server, a NOTIFY message is sent to each slave server listed on the notify list. These servers then perform a zone transfer without waiting for the cache timeout to expire.

- ✔ **DNS zone change notification:** The method by which a slave DNS server transfers zone data from the master DNS server. This way, zone data can be changed on the master server, and it's automatically updated in the caches of each slave instead of having to change the zone data numerous times, as is the case when you have more than one master DNS server. The problem with zone transfers, however, is that they can use lots of bandwidth across network links, especially with large zones or slow links.

- ✔ **Incremental zone transfer:** Allows the updated part of the zone data to be transferred to the slave server rather than to the entire zone. This feature can have a large effect on network bandwidth, especially with large zones. Incremental zone transfer uses a special protocol to function and is limited to most zones on Windows DNS servers and dynamically updated zones on BIND servers.

Chapter 2

DNS Namespaces

*T*he first three chapters in this book explore the concepts relating to how DNS is designed and how it generally functions, and how DNS is maintained on the large (Internet) scale. This information is important because it forms the core knowledge you need in order to successfully implement and maintain DNS services in your home or business. After thoroughly examining these fundamentals, we show you how to begin traversing the more hands-on process of making the needed server and software configuration changes to get DNS services up and running.

As you may or may not know, DNS is (in its most basic form) simply a database that matches names to IP addresses. For example, a Web site such as www.dummies.com is mapped to a particular IP address — 168.215.86.100, in this case. If you don't care about a connection to any networks outside your Local Area Network (LAN), such as the Internet, you can set up a DNS server to serve any names you want. You don't even have to use top-level domains such as .com or .net with a private DNS implementation. If, like most network users, you want to make use of that wacky old Internet or remote hosts on your Wide Area Network (WAN), you need to understand that DNS is a bit more complex.

The structure of domain names using top-level domains such as .com and .net is required only if hosts will be making use of the Internet. Because this is the case, you must understand the manner in which domain names are structured if you will be working with Internet-connected DNS servers or hosts that must reach resources located on the Internet.

The structure used to organize domain names is a *namespace*. The namespace for Internet hosts is arranged in what is known as an inverted hierarchical tree. In more simplified terms, this arrangement, displayed graphically, is a pyramid. At the top of the "tree" (the point of the pyramid) is the root of the namespace. The root, which is absolutely the highest level in the namespace, is used as the starting point for locating subdomains, and, ultimately hosts, within the namespace. For example, in `myhost.myserver.com`, `com` is the namespace and `""` (a null character) is the root.

Take a step back and make sure that you have some of the necessary background before we begin a detailed description of namespaces. At this point, you need to examine domain names themselves before you delve into how they're arranged. After we have described domain names, you can revisit the idea of DNS namespace.

A domain in DNS isn't the same as a domain in Microsoft Windows NT. Although a domain in DNS refers to a group of systems in a segment of the DNS namespace, a Windows domain is a group of systems that share authentication information provided by domain controllers. Even more confusing, in Windows 2000 and later, both DNS domains and Windows domains are used, making it even more difficult to keep them straight.

Playing the Domain Name Game

A *domain name* links a user-friendly name (such as `www.microsoft.com`) to a computer's network address information (IP address `207.46.197.113`, in this case). Because somewhat logical names have more meaning than esoteric numbers for most people (except for extra-nerdy folks), this system adds a great deal of "ease of use" for general users. A fully qualified domain name (FQDN) consists of a number of parts and refers to a domain name specified in absolute terms rather than relative to another domain.

The following example shows a fully qualified domain name. In this case, the host is a Web server (denoted with the `www` label) and the domain is `microsoft.com`:

```
www.microsoft.com
```

A domain name's parts are separated by (not surprisingly) a *separator,* which is a period.

You can see how this domain name, if you look at it from right to left, fits into the tree discussed in the preceding section. The highest level in the tree is the top-level domain, `.com`. As you move to the left, the name becomes more specific: `.microsoft` specifies the child domain within `.com`. Finally, the `www` indicates the specific host within that domain.

If you're being picky, the domain www.microsoft.com isn't a true fully quali-fied domain name. Using the strictest definition (which isn't needed with all DNS server configurations), a fully qualified domain name must have a trail-ing separator (a period), as in this example:

```
www.microsoft.com.
```

This trailing period is used to separate the top-level domain, .com, from the root of the namespace, which is identified by a null (blank) character. This nomenclature is obviously not used on a regular basis, though.

Back Off — You're in My DNS Namespace!

As noted earlier in this chapter, the DNS namespace used on the Internet is a hierarchical inverted tree. Although this term may seem complex, the name-space is quite simple. At the top of the tree, as shown in Figure 2-1, is the root of the namespace. Notice that the root is represented by a null character. Although this null character isn't usually used (such as when you enter a URL into a Web browser), its presence is assumed by any application following the DNS specification.

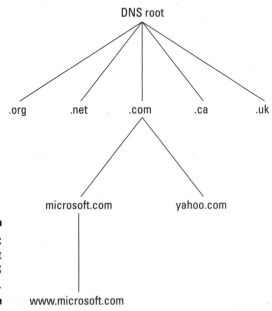

Figure 2-1:
The Internet
DNS
namespace.

The next level below the root always contains the relevant top-level domains (TLDs), including the common TLDs (COM, NET, and GOV, for example) in addition to country TLDs (UK, for example). The term *top-level* domains refers to the domains directly below the root of the namespace. Although the Internet namespace allows only certain TLDs, if you're running a private namespace that will never be publicly connected to the Internet, you can use any TLDs you want. Top-level domains aren't controlled by users but rather by domain registrars. We describe registrars in more detail later in this chapter, in the sidebar "Becoming master of your own domain" and the section "Whose Name Is It, Anyway? (Top-Level Domains)."

Below the top-level domains is the beginning of the actual domain. An example of a domain on this level is `microsoft.com`. The domains at this level can be subdivided (the branches of the inverted tree start to develop), and multiple subdomains can be defined; for example, domains such as `windows.microsoft.com`, `95.windows.microsoft.com`, and `windows.operatingsystems.software.microsoft.com`. These domains are typically referred to, not surprisingly, as subdomains. A tree can have a maximum of 128 levels. In these examples (and counting the null root), 5 levels are in the first two examples, and 6 levels are in `windows.operating systems.software.microsoft.com`. You're unlikely, however, to ever have 127 levels of domains under any parent. The user-friendly nature of domain names begins to fade as more levels are added, because IP addresses (`192.168.1.25`, for example) are almost as memorable as overly long DNS names, such as (and this one is pure fiction) `xlibs.hvacinf.pomeroy.wa.us`.

When designing your namespace (later on) or working with several of the other aspects of DNS configuration, keep in mind the KISS principle: Keep It Simple, Stupid. If you reduce the complexity of your naming conventions (keeping things simple), users spend less time thinking about the DNS name and structure and more time getting to whatever resources they need. After all, the user isn't the one who needs to focus on DNS — that's *your* job!

Every entry in a single level of one branch of the DNS namespace must be unique. For example, all top-level domains must be unique, and all domains under `.com` must be unique. This restriction is effective on only a single level of the hierarchy and only within the current branch. You can have `microsoft.com` and `microsoft.net`, for example, and you can also have `microsoft.com` and `microsoft.windows.com`. You cannot, however, have `microsoft.com` and add another domain named `microsoft` under the `.com` domain.

Within domains and subdomains exist nodes, or hosts. *Hosts* are the lowest level in the hierarchy and define systems such as the Web or FTP server. A host is typically defined in DNS using an A (host) record, which assigns an IP address to the host's name. For example, an A record for `www.microsoft.com` would contain the host name `www` and the IP address of the Web server. Although a domain normally contains hosts, no rule exists against a domain containing both subdomains and hosts, and that situation is quite common. For example, the domain `domain.tld` can contain a host named `www.domain.tld` in addition to a subdomain named `engineering.domain.tld`. The subdomain would also contain hosts such as `cad1.engineering.domain.tld`.

DNS is even more flexible than that, though. A domain entry such as `engineering.domain.tld` can even be both a host and a subdomain. By defining `engineering.domain.tld` as a subdomain and then specifying an A record for @ within the `engineering.domain.tld` zone file (in BIND) or creating a record in the subdomain with the same name as the parent domain (in Windows), `engineering.domain.tld` points to that host. This is common practice on the Internet because users can reach a Web site such as `www.microsoft.com` even if they forget to specify the host and simply type **microsoft.com**. Chapter 10 explains exactly how subdomains work and how they're configured.

Planning Your DNS Namespace

An important part of implementing DNS across your network is planning your DNS namespace. Even if you register an Internet domain name with a domain name registrar, you need to plan how you're going to distribute your hosts within the domain. With only a few hosts, placing them all in the domain you registered is simple; when you have a larger number of hosts, however, carefully planning your namespace for ease of use and ease of administration is often useful. Also, a good plan ensures that as new DNS host name and subdomain requests and requirements arise, you can accommodate them.

The terms *parent* and *child* are often used in discussing DNS namespaces. These terms simply refer to two domains in relation to each other. For example, in the domain `den.lanhosts.tld`, `lanhosts` is the parent of the `den` subdomain, and `den` is the child of `lanhosts`.

Planning a namespace for Internet or corporate applications

When examining basic DNS applications in the business environment (either Internet resources or LAN use), the requirements are fairly simple when it comes to planning a namespace. In almost all cases, you first register a domain with a domain registrar. This is your "home" on the Internet. All your hosts are under this domain name, either directly or in a subdomain. In a simple environment with only a few hosts, you will probably place all your hosts directly under the domain name. For the sake of example, assume that

---

Becoming master of your own domain

To make use of a DNS name on the Internet — for yourself, your company, or your organization — you need to have that name registered. The first step is to determine whether the name you want is still available. The InterNIC (one of the original registrars for the Internet) maintains a Web site that lists an alphabetical and geographical list of authorized registrars at www.internic.com/regist. html. Additionally, many Internet Service Providers (ISPs) either provide domain name registration services themselves or act as an intermediary between you and the registrar (if you're a customer). Most registrations sites have a search feature on their home page. Many registrars even suggest alternative names if the one you came looking for is already taken.

After you find the name you want and it's available, you can begin the registration process. To register a domain, you need to contact one of the many DNS registrars. If you're adventurous and want to have complete control over how your DNS name is registered and managed, you should consider a service such as the one provided by www.dotster.com. Dotster (and other, similar registrars) allow you to register your domain, change DNS records on the dotster name servers, and perform a wide range of parallel tasks, such as e-mail forwarding and URL masking. DNS name registration typically costs between $15 and $50 per year, depending on the features you purchase and the kind of domain name purchased (such as .com, .tv, or .biz). Shop around using the list on the InterNIC Web site, and you should be able to find a good price for your domain. After you have registered the domain and configured it to direct requests to your Internet-accessible server, you're ready to being using the name. Typically, the new domain name registration takes at least 24 to 48 hours to replicate to all the Internet domain name servers, so it isn't something you should expect to work instantly.

---

the domain you registered is domain.tld. Your hosts would be www.domain. tld, mail.domain.tld, and accounting.domain.tld.

The real challenge in planning a namespace comes when you have either a large number of hosts or hosts distributed in multiple locations. That's where the flexibility of DNS becomes obvious. In both cases, you most likely want to plan a DNS namespace with subdomains.

Subdomains are often created based on one or more of these criteria:

- Internal or external system
- Workstation/server
- Geographical location
- Business function
- System function

Planning subdomains is simpler than it might sound. Determining where subdomains are appropriate is usually just a matter of common sense. The first use for subdomains is the separation of internal and external systems. Internal systems, such as workstations, are placed on one subdomain, and external servers are placed on another. This internal/external division isn't commonly used explicitly. Rather than an explicit internal/external split, many networks have a subdomain for workstations, such as `corp.domain.tld` or `ws.domain.tld`, and servers reside in the parent domain.

If you decide to use geographical locations for DNS names, you can use the city name as the subdomain. For example, the Vancouver office subdomain would be `vancouver.domain.tld` or `van.domain.tld`, and the Seattle subdomain would be `seattle.domain.tld` or `sea.domain.tld`. An example of a namespace with geographically derived subdomains is shown in Figure 2-2. It's the simplest method of dividing domains because the separation is the most obvious.

Figure 2-2:
An example of geo-graphically based sub-domains.

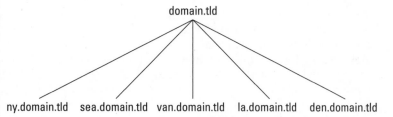

The next DNS namespace-planning method is used when a large number of hosts are in one location. Subdomains are created based on the business purpose of the system function, in this case. The business purpose divides subdomains into the area of the business they serve, including such subdomains as `accounting.domain.tld` or `acct.domain.tld` and `engineering.domain.tld` or `eng.domain.tld`. Dividing subdomains based on their business purpose is most useful in a traditional corporate environment where business unit boundaries are clearly defined.

Segregation based on system function is a little more complex in that it's harder to determine which subdomains you require. Dividing up systems based on system function is most useful in environments such as application development, where systems have a specific function. In this case, different subdomains are used for development systems (`dev.domain.tld`), staging or testing systems (`test.domain.tld`), and production systems (`prod.domain.tld` or just `domain.tld`).

In addition to these divisions being used individually, they can be combined. For example, you can use geographical locations as the highest-level subdomain (where they fit logically), such as `sea.domain.tld` and `van.domain.tld`, and have below that subdomains based on system function. This arrangement results in domains such as `dev.sea.domain.tld` and `prod.van.domain.tld`, as shown in Figure 2-3.

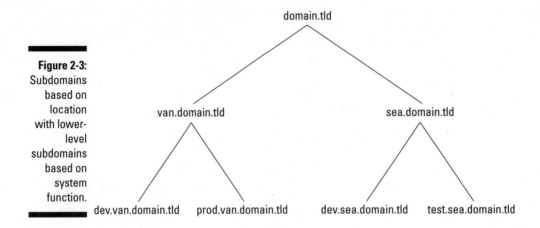

You can take this combination of subdomains as far as you want as long as your DNS tree is no more than 128 levels deep, including the root. The tree also doesn't need to be symmetrical. If you have a large organization in Washington, for example, you may have a business-function-based subdomain named `applications.wash.domain.tld` with system-function-based subdomains, such as `dev.applications.wash.domain.tld`. The accounting group has no need for system-function-based subdomains, so all those hosts would reside in the domain `acct.wash.domain.tld`. If you have a smaller office in New York, it may have all the hosts under the `ny.domain.tld` subdomain. In addition, your main Web site is probably directly in the `domain.tld` domain. Figure 2-4 shows a theoretical namespace incorporating a number of levels of subdomains in the `domain.tld` domain.

Planning a namespace for Microsoft Windows Active Directory

Planning the namespace for an Active Directory (AD) DNS implementation is more complex than planning the namespace for a simple corporate or Internet organization. Rather than consider only ease of administration, you also have to consider the function of Active Directory. For more information about Active Directory, check out the Microsoft Active Directory Web site, at

```
www.microsoft.com/windows2000/technologies/directory/ad/
              default.asp
```

This site contains a wealth of information, including information about configuring, administering, planning, and deploying Active Directory. This is your one-stop shop for up-to-date Active Directory information from Microsoft.

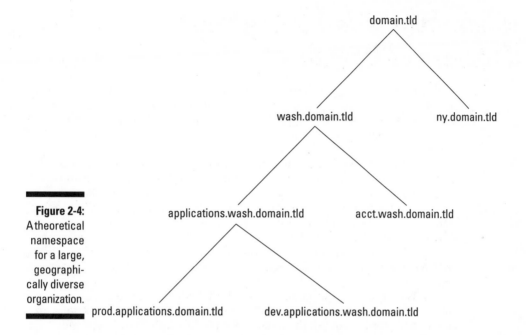

domain.tld

wash.domain.tld   ny.domain.tld

applications.wash.domain.tld   acct.wash.domain.tld

prod.applications.domain.tld   dev.applications.wash.domain.tld

Figure 2-4:
A theoretical
namespace
for a large,
geographi-
cally diverse
organization.

The first design consideration for Active Directory is the optional step of registering a domain with a domain registrar. Registration isn't required for
Active Directory to function, but it does enable connections to network services on your Windows network from the Internet. When you aren't using a
registered Internet domain, you should use the domain suffix `.local` to indicate it. Your domain name under this configuration would be similar to
`mydomain.local`, for example.

The next step in planning your Active Directory DNS namespace is to plan
your Active Directory infrastructure. The structure of the namespace is
designed around the structure of AD, and each AD domain is also a DNS
domain. A simple AD implementation with only one AD domain, therefore,
will have only a single DNS domain. Domains (AD and DNS) should be separated along geographical or other logical boundaries. Also, internal and external systems should be separated into separate DNS domains, and internal
and external DNS hosting should be separated on different servers. The separation of the internal and external resources is primarily a security issue, but
is also a matter of organizing resources into logical — and therefore manageable — groups. Although DNS arrangements are a component of good network security, DNS isn't effective as the sole method of securing a network.
We explain DNS and its related security implications in much greater detail in
Chapter 11.

Whose Name Is It, Anyway?
(Top-Level Domains)

In the Internet namespace is a series of top-level domains (TLDs), such as
`.com`, `.net`, `.org`, `.mil`, `.us`, and `.ca`. An important concept concerning DNS
on the Internet is how the highest level of the Internet hierarchy functions
and who is responsible for it.

The Internet DNS namespace is global, although in essence it's controlled by
a single organization: the Internet Corporation for Assigned Names and
Numbers (ICANN). The nonprofit ICANN organization is responsible for con-
trolling both the IP address space and the DNS namespace on the Internet.
ICANN has a suborganization, the Domain Name Supporting Organization
(DNSO), which is the specific group responsible for the Internet namespace.
Within DNSO are a number of constituency groups, each representing a group
with a stake in the namespace, such as ISPs, businesses, and name registrars.

ICANN is responsible for the maintenance of the list of root name servers, the
first and most important part of the DNS namespace. Root name servers are
responsible for the root of the namespace (the area above the top-level
domains. The root name servers are distributed across the Internet and geographically across the world (theoretically) and are responsible for the first
step in name resolution. The root name servers are maintained individually
by specific organizations. A DNS query sent to a caching DNS server first
queries a root server to determine which server hosts the TLD of the name in
the request.

Thirteen root name servers now exist, as shown in the following list. This list
changes from time to time, although not often:

- `a.root-servers.net`: Network Solutions Inc., Herndon, Virginia
- `b.root-servers.net`: USC-ISI, Marina del Rey, California
- `c.root-servers.net`: PSInet, Herndon, Virginia
- `d.root-servers.net`: University of Maryland, College Park, MD
- `e.root-servers.net`: NASA, Mountain View, California
- `f.root-servers.net`: Internet Software Consortium, Palo Alto, California
- `g.root-servers.net`: Defense Information Systems Agency, Vienna, Virginia
- `h.root-servers.net`: Army Research Library, Aberdeen, MD
- `i.root-servers.net`: NORDUnet, Stockholm, Sweden
- `j.root-servers.net`: Network Solutions, Inc., Herndon, Virginia

Who maintains the IP address allocation?

Because the TLDs are maintained by ICANN, you may be wondering who maintains the allocation of IP addresses. As you may know, each IP address on the Internet must be unique. Some authority must ensure that no IP address is assigned twice. This authority is the Internet Assigned Numbers Authority (IANA), a nonprofit organization responsible for assigning IP address space and maintaining the information for protocols used on the Internet.

IANA, the top-level authority for assigning addresses, delegates that authority to a number of other organizations for specific regions, including Réseaux IP Européens (RIPE) in Europe and the American Registry for Internet Numbers (ARIN) in North America.

Even though these organizations are responsible for assigning IP addresses, you cannot simply ask one for an address and have it assigned. The organizations assign IP addresses in blocks to Internet Service Providers (ISPs). If you need an IP address, you must have it assigned by an ISP. The reason that IP addresses are assigned in blocks to ISPs is to ease the administration of the Internet

backbone. The Internet *backbone,* composed of the main links that carry Internet traffic from major ISP to major ISP, contains several routers known as *core* routers. Although not all Internet traffic passes through these core routers, they're responsible for maintaining the routing infrastructure of the Internet and ensuring that all traffic gets to its destination, using the routing protocol named Border Gateway Protocol, or BGP. All routers connected to the Internet use BGP to communicate with other Internet routers.

The reason that IP addresses are assigned to ISPs in blocks? Rather than have a route to reach each IP address on the Internet, the core routers have only a few routes (relative to the total number of IP addresses). Using *aggregation,* the core routers will have a route to an entire block of IP addresses that reside at one ISP. If the core router receives a request for an address in one of these blocks, the requestor is forwarded to the ISP's router rather than directly to the address. The ISP's router can then route the data to its final destination. This hierarchical layout is similar to the one used by the root DNS servers on the Internet.

✔ `k.root-servers.net`: Reseaux IP Europeens, London, UK

✔ `l.root-servers.net`: ICANN, Marina del Rey, California

✔ `m.root-servers.net`: WIDE Tokyo, Japan

As you can see, the root name servers aren't as geographically dispersed as they could be. There's no specific reason that the majority of root servers are in the United States, but a number of factors may be responsible, such as the development of the Internet in the United States and the control of U.S.-based ICANN in the DNS namespace.

Below the root of the namespace are the top-level domains. The TLDs are controlled by a variety of different registrars who are responsible for the registration of DNS names under their respective TLD. Two broad types of TLDs exist: generic, or gTLD, and country code, or ccTLD. In addition, gTLDs contain a subgroup: restricted gTLDs.

Here's a list of TLDs:

gTLDs

- ✔ `.biz`: Businesses
- ✔ `.com`: Commercial enterprises
- ✔ `.info`: Unrestricted
- ✔ `.name`: Individuals (for example, John Smith would register `smith.name` or `johnsmith.name`)
- ✔ `.net`: ISPs, telecommunications companies (telcos), and other network providers
- ✔ `.org`: Nonprofit organizations

Restricted gTLDs

- ✔ `.edu`: Educational institutions
- ✔ `.gov`: U.S. government agencies
- ✔ `.int`: Specifically for organizations under special international treaties
- ✔ `.mil`: U.S. military

ccTLDs

- ✔ `.au`: Australia
- ✔ `.ca`: Canada
- ✔ `.de`: Germany
- ✔ `.jp`: Japan
- ✔ `.nz`: New Zealand
- ✔ `.tw`: Taiwan

The gTLDs originally started with only `.com`, `.net`, and `.org`. They were (originally) intended for commercial ventures for `.com`, ISPs, and other network providers for `.net`, and nonprofit organizations for `.org`. These limitations didn't really work out, though, and now `.com`, `.net`, and `.org` are free-for-alls that anyone can register. The `.biz`, `.info`, and `.name` gTLDs are new and are supposedly more restricted than the originals, but, even so, they have proven fairly open. In fact, `.biz` was intended for business only; `.name`, for individuals only; and `.name`, for anyone. The gTLDs are controlled by a group of domain registrars accredited by ICANN. You can find the list of ICANN-accredited gTLD registrars at

`www.icann.org/registrars/accredited-list.html`

The gTLDs are hosted by a number of servers similar to the root servers except that they use the form `a.gtld-servers.net`.

The restricted gTLDs, unlike the regular gTLDs, aren't open. In fact, you must be able to prove that you're a member of the U.S. military or a government agency, an accredited educational institution, or an organization with a recognized international treaty in order to register a domain name in these TLDs. The restricted gTLDs are controlled by four organizations:

- ✔ `.edu`: VeriSign/Network Solutions
- ✔ `.gov`: U.S. General Services Administration (GSA) at `www.nic.gov`
- ✔ `.mil`: U.S. Department of Defense Network Information Center and the (DISA) at `www.nic.mil`
- ✔ `.int`: Internet Assigned Numbers Authority (IANA), a part of ICANN

These TLDs each use their own DNS servers, unlike the other gTLDs, which use centralized name servers.

The regular gTLDs use centralized name servers to offload the root name servers.

The ccTLDs are different from the gTLDs. Based not on the type of registrant, ccTLDs are based on the geographical location of the registrants. These ccTLDs are based on the ISO 3166-1 list of countries and two-letter codes (known as alpha-2 codes) and are managed by an organization within each country, the Canadian Internet Registration Authority (CIRA) in Canada, for example. Requirements for registering a domain in a ccTLD vary between countries. For example, in Canada, you must have a Canadian mailing address, although you can register a domain in other ccTLDs with no proof required that you're a resident, such as the `.cx` TLD for Christmas Island. The `.cx` ccTLD is intentionally registered to nonresidents as a method of economic development for Christmas Island. The DNS servers for the ccTLDs are the responsibility of the organization operating the ccTLD.

Chapter 3

The DNS Request Process

*T*he process of successfully making a DNS request is important to understand if you're going to be doing any work with DNS. If you understand the process, you can be better prepared to understand the administration of a DNS server and how to troubleshoot DNS problems.

As you may know, DNS is one of the fundamental technologies that allows the Internet to operate in a useful manner. In Figure 3-1, you can see an example of how DNS is most commonly used by Internet users, to view a Web site.

Virtually every Internet user (except for that rare ultra-geek) browses to Web sites using friendly DNS names, such as www.microsoft.com, rather than the alternative, numeric IP addresses. In addition, users send e-mail to other users using the traditional user@domain.tld notation rather than user@ipaddress, which would be both cumbersome and occasionally unsuccessful.

Making the Connection

We briefly discuss the TCP/IP protocol suite in Chapter 1. The TCP/IP suite is made up of a set of individual networking protocols. These protocols — in particular, IP — are used on the Internet for a dizzying array of services from e-mail to browsing the World Wide Web. The protocols of the TCP/IP suite support these networking functions by providing a range of services at the various layers of the Open Systems Interconnect (OSI) model (refer to the section in Chapter 1 that introduces TCP/IP). Like all other layered protocols of the OSI model, this structure isolates the applications themselves (such as

the World Wide Web and e-mail) from the physical wire or fiber-optic cable on which they're carried. Because TCP/IP provides abstraction from the hardware and physical link, any application protocol that supports TCP/IP functions over any physical network that also supports TCP/IP.

Your Internet connection may be a Digital Subscriber Line (DSL) or a cable modem, and your connection at work may be a leased line, such as a T1 or T3 connection. Although all these types are vastly different physical connections with different low-level protocols, the one thing they have in common is their support for TCP/IP with the appropriate network hardware. Although the TCP/IP suite has a number of protocols, one of the most important is a Layer 3 protocol: IP.

The term *Internet* is used as a proper name to refer to the current global network of computers everyone now uses, but the term really refers to any network of geographically or organizationally separate hosts. You may also have heard the term *intranet,* which refers to a similar network, but with geographically or organizationally consolidated hosts, such as those within a company.

Layer 3: I see IP

As we state in the preceding section, the IP protocol runs on Layer 3 of the OSI model. Without getting into too much technical detail, Layer 3 (the network layer) is essentially the point at which the hardware protocols, such as MAC for Ethernet, are abstracted from the software protocols, such as the TCP/IP stack or the IPX/SPX stack commonly used with Novell Netware. You can think of the network layer as the boundary between network hardware and software.

The importance of IP is that it's the lowest-level protocol that every node on the Internet shares. For this reason, IP is where addressing must happen. Each node on the Internet has a unique *IP address,* which is simply a unique identifier that allows one node to reach another node. Think of a postal mail analogy: If you want to send a letter to someone, you need only the person's address. Similarly, if you want to send an IP packet of data to someone on the Internet, you need only the IP address.

A great deal of jargon is associated with networking — in particular, the terms hosts, routers, and nodes. A *host* is a system that doesn't route packets — it simply sends and receives them. A *router* is a system that routes packets toward their destination. A *node* refers to either a router or a host.

Getting from A to B

Let's take a quick look at how IP manages to move traffic around a network. When you send a snail-mail letter to someone, the letter isn't delivered directly from your house to the other person's house. The letter is routed through a series of post offices until it reaches its destination. The behavior of IP is exactly the same. You can think of the Internet as a mesh, or web. Some nodes are connected to other nodes, but not every node is connected to every other node. Theoretically, however, a path from one node to any other node always exists through a combination of *routers,* the hardware used to route traffic over the Internet. Each trip a packet of data takes from one router to the next is called a *hop,* and there's a maximum of 30 hops from one node to another. This limitation in the IP protocol protects packets from getting caught in *routing loops,* where the destination is never reached and the packet is simply passed back and forth forever.

You can see in detail the process of data moving from one IP host to another by using the `tracert` command in Microsoft Windows, as shown in Figure 3-2, or by using the `tracepath` or `traceroute` commands in Unix/Linux, if they're installed. These commands show each hop taken to reach a destination host as long as each of the routers along the path supports the ICMP messages used for the trace. Although these utilities used to be a useful tool for network troubleshooting, many ISPs disable the required ICMP messages because they can be used for some denial-of-service (DoS) attacks.

Figure 3-2:
Using the
`tracert`
command to
view the
path an IP
packet
takes to the
destination
host.

```
C:\WINNT\System32\cmd.exe                                           _ □ ✕

C:\>tracert www.google.com

Tracing route to www.google.com [216.239.33.101]
over a maximum of 30 hops:

  1    <10 ms     10 ms    <10 ms   localhost.domain.tld [192.168.100.1]
  2     50 ms     30 ms     30 ms   24.78.60.1
  3     50 ms     30 ms     30 ms   rd1bb-ge0-6.vc.shawcable.net [24.69.254.130]
  4     20 ms     20 ms     20 ms   rc1bb-pos15-0.vc.shawcable.net [66.163.69.70]
  5     30 ms     30 ms     30 ms   rc2wt-pos2-2.wa.shawcable.net [66.163.76.58]
  6     50 ms     60 ms     50 ms   rc1sj-pos1-0.cl.shawcable.net [66.163.76.46]
  7     50 ms     50 ms     60 ms   eqixsj-google-gige.google.com [206.223.116.21]
  8     50 ms     50 ms     60 ms   core2-0-2-0.pao.net.google.com [216.239.48.213]

  9     50 ms     61 ms     50 ms   core1-1-1-0.pao.net.google.com [216.239.48.173]

 10     50 ms     50 ms     60 ms   exni2-1-2.net.google.com [216.239.47.75]
 11     50 ms     50 ms     60 ms   exbi2-1-1.net.google.com [216.239.47.6]
 12     80 ms     50 ms     50 ms   www.google.com [216.239.33.101]

Trace complete.

C:\>_
```

Dealing with Decimals

This section introduces a common sticking point for new administrators of IP devices and a limitation of IP addressing. An IP address is made up of four octets of binary data, usually converted to decimal. An example is the IP address `192.168.100.5`. It refers to the binary address `11000000 10101000 01100100 00000101`. These binary addresses are required because Internet routers are, at heart, simply computers, and all computers work with binary data. The conversion to decimal is done simply for ease of notation.

The term *octet* refers to a collection of eight binary digits. Although they're in decimal, each part of a decimal-notated address, such as `192.168.100.5`, is referred to as an octet.

Most people have a telephone directory in which they record the phone numbers of their friends and family members because remembering all those numbers all the time seems impossible. How many 10-digit phone numbers are in your phone directory? You're obviously not likely to remember them all (although a few people do), so imagine trying to memorize all the 12-digit IP addresses of the Web sites you visit often and the people with whom you exchange e-mail.

Looking at an IP address as a collection of four octets of binary data (32 bits total), you get a theoretical number of unique addresses, or address spaces, of 2^{32} addresses. Many of these addresses aren't used on the Internet because they're reserved for special purposes; even so, the number of available addresses is staggering. Surprisingly enough, though, the end is in sight. What will happen when the Internet eventually runs out of usable addresses? The answer is IPv6, a replacement for the current IP specification, IPv4. With the eventual adoption of IPv6 (IP version 6), the address space will grow to 128 bits, providing an absurdly large number of host addresses (2^{128}).

A Cure for Growing Pains: IPv6

The current version of the IP protocol, used by zillions of Internet users daily, is Version 4. This version of IP, which has been in place for quite some time, has proven to be the addressing protocol of choice because it's more widely used than any other. IP doesn't change often, and the configuration of the address space and the number of IP addresses available has remained unchanged for basically the entire life span of IP. As we explain in the preceding section, "Dealing with Decimals," the term *address space* refers to the number of IP addresses available in the IP address system. With IPv4, the addresses are composed of 32 binary bits divided into groups of 8 called octets (00000000 00000000 00000000 00000000). Normally, an IP address is converted from binary to decimal (000.000.000.000) for representational purposes. Thirty-two binary bits gives IPv4 an address space of 2^{32} (4.2 billion) addresses. Granted, some of them are reserved for special purposes, although billions of addresses are still available for use.

You would think that with billions of addresses, the world would have plenty to go around, right? Because of the way IP addresses are allocated, though, it's not true. IP addresses are allocated in blocks rather than individually in order to ease routing administration on the Internet. This block arrangement essentially takes addresses out of circulation and, in combination with the explosion of the Internet, limits the way addresses can be assigned. Even if addresses are available globally in the address space, if they're not in the correct block, they cannot be assigned to you.

Three classes of IP address allocation blocks exist:

- ✔ Class C contains 254 usable addresses.
- ✔ Class B contains 65,534 addresses.
- ✔ Class A contains roughly 16 million usable addresses.

Although only about 32 class A blocks are available to be allocated, it's still a large portion of the IPv4 address space.

In addition to assigning IP addresses in blocks, the assigned addresses have traditionally been used up quickly. The traditional method of creating a Web site was to assign an IP address to each site, even if more than one site was on a server. Although this system may seem wasteful, in the early days of the Internet, other arrangements weren't always practical because the software available for Web hosting at the time wasn't sophisticated. In any event, old habits had persisted. Most modern Web servers have the capability to use one IP address for the Web server and have each site referenced by a host header. Essentially, the Web browser passes to the server the DNS name specified by the client in a field in the HTTP protocol called the *host header*. The host header is then used by the Web server to direct the request to the correct Web site. This arrangement removes the one-IP-address-per-site requirement.

Now that you know why a shortage of IP addresses exists, you can move on to read about what is being done to mitigate the shortage. IPv6 is one of the solutions, but it's a long-term solution that cannot be implemented rapidly. First, you should understand what is being done in the short term to carry the Internet over until IPv6 can be implemented. Note that many of these solutions are coming at the ISP level because it's becoming more difficult for ISPs to request more addresses to be allocated and they're being forced to limit their use of addresses. One leading short-term solution is to make use of the Network Address Translation (NAT) protocol. In the traditional configuration, a company wanting to connect its entire network to the Internet through an ISP would tell the ISP, and the ISP would assign an IP address for each system needing an address. NAT allows the ISP to assign only a single address to be used by a single gateway device. All internal systems then use private addresses that don't need to be assigned by a central registrar because they cannot be used on the Internet.

As we just mentioned, a more permanent solution is planned, although it hasn't yet seen widespread implementation. For several years, a standard known as IP version 6 (IPv6) has existed. It implements a number of features not found in IPv4, such as quality-of-service (QoS) prioritizing for traffic to enable multimedia applications. More important than the new features is the expansion of the address space. Although the IPv4 address space is 32 bits, the IPv6 address space is 128 bits, which expands the total number of available addresses from 2^{32} to 2^{128}, or from 4.2 billion to $3.4x10^{38}$. The number of addresses in IPv6 is an incredibly high number — 2^{96} times as many as IPv4. The implementation of IPv6 would eradicate the problem of the diminishing address space.

An IPv6 address contains 128 binary bits; when an address is being written out, however, a hexadecimal notation is used:

```
3F40:00CA:0000:0000:B192:59F1:A3B5:DC09
```

Each part of the address separated by colons represents two bytes, or 16 bits of the total address represented in hexadecimal. The bytes of the address are 3F, 40, 00, CA, and so on. For ease of notation, leading zeroes and groups of zeroes can be left off, although only the first group of zeroes can be left out if there's more than one. The preceding address would then look like this:

```
3F40:CA::B192:59F1:A3B5:DC09
```

If any group of zeroes appears later in the address, they're represented by :0: rather than being dropped altogether, like the first group; for example:

```
3ffe:8271:0000:0000:0001:0000:0000:0001
```

becomes

```
3ffe:8271::0001:0:0:0001
```

The implementation of IPv6 has one major problem: the sheer size of the undertaking. As we note earlier in this chapter, in the section "Dealing with Decimals," millions of hosts are now using the IPv4 standard. Not all those hosts can be moved simultaneously to the IPv6 standard. Moreover, you have to consider the issue of configuring all the network equipment, such as routers and switches, to support IPv6. These issues aren't insurmountable, though, and IPv6 even has a built-in solution: It can communicate to IPv4 hosts through a special type of address prefix. By appending the 32-bit address of an IPv4 host to a special IPv6 prefix, the IPv6 system can address that host. No similar method is available for an IPv4 host to talk to an IPv6 host, however.

The implementation of IPv6 is under way on a small scale. Many modern operating systems, such as the various versions of Unix, have IPv6 support, and Windows XP includes an incomplete IPv6 implementation that isn't meant for full production use. Many network hardware vendors also provide IPv6 support, which makes possible the creation of an IPv6 network. A few of these networks are in place. One of the oldest IPv6 networks in existence is 6bone (www.6bone.net), which is similar to the original Internet test network: Mbone. The 6bone network was originally set up as a testing facility for people writing IPv6 software, although anyone can connect to 6bone. Its connections can be made either through rare IPv6 links or the encapsulation of IPv6 in IPv4 packets. The encapsulated packets are then decapsulated on the 6bone end and appear as proper IPv6 traffic.

The 6bone network isn't the only IPv6 network under development. The U.S. Department of Energy has undertaken the development of its own network: The Energy Sciences Network (ESnet) is a large IPv6 network designed to interconnect scientific and government organizations. (Note the similarities to the origins of the IPv4 Internet, when ARPAnet — refer to the section in Chapter 1 that gives a brief history of the Internet — was used to connect educational and government facilities.)

No matter how the implementation of IPv6 occurs, it will take a long time. The scale of the project is incredibly large and growing every day as the Internet is adopted by more and more users. In addition, the IPv6 transition isn't a directed project; rather, it relies on the involved parties, such as the major carriers and ISPs, to make the required changes on their systems, which they do on their own schedules. It may be several years until you see IPv6 running in concert with IPv4 and many more years until IPv6 makes IPv4 obsolete.

Getting Down to Business

DNS resembles a global telephone directory, except that rather than look up the phone number and dial it, as you do with your "landline" phone or cell phone, you simply type in your "phone" (your Web browser) the name of the party you're trying to contact and the party is contacted automatically. DNS is useful because it's much easier to remember a name like www.dummies.com than an address like 192.168.100.5.

Although DNS seems like a big phone book full of names and IP addresses, it's much more complex than that. It's laid out in a hierarchical manner, for two reasons: It removes the requirement to have either one large directory that everyone uses or to have every directory contain every DNS name and IP address in existence. Instead, a large number of DNS servers exist; they're distributed and then queried only for the addresses they contain. If a DNS server houses the zone for a certain domain, it's known as *authoritative* for that domain.

The best way to understand how a DNS request is processed is to follow along step-by-step. In this example, assume that the DNS name is www. microsoft.com and that the recursive DNS server's cache is empty:

1. You type a DNS name, such as **www.microsoft.com**, in your Web browser or any other DNS-enabled software.

2. The DNS client, which is usually part of the operating system, is called. The DNS client is contained in a dynamic loaded library (DLL) in Windows. In Unix, however, the process works a little differently: The application passes the DNS name to the DNS client and waits for a response, including the corresponding IP address or an error.

3. The DNS client then takes over. It makes the DNS request to the DNS server that's configured in your network settings. The DNS servers are set in the network properties in Windows or in the resolv.conf file in Unix. The DNS client doesn't do any resolution itself; it only passes the request from the application to the DNS server. The DNS client's job is to accept the request from the application in a format the application understands, convert the request to a proper DNS request that the server understands, and then convert the response again and return it to the application.

4. The DNS server configured in the client's network settings receives the request. This DNS server must be a *recursive* DNS server, which means that it can process requests for domains for which it isn't authoritative. Some DNS servers have recursion disabled and cannot process requests unless they're for the requested domain.

5. The recursive DNS server begins the resolution process. It first looks at the DNS name in the request in reverse order. In this case, the DNS name is www.microsoft.com. — with the trailing period. The first thing the DNS server notices is the trailing period, indicating the root of the DNS namespace. Because the recursive DNS server already has addresses for the root DNS servers in a root hint file, it doesn't need to look up that address (it can't because no DNS server is above the root in the hierarchy).

6. The recursive DNS server picks a root server from its root hint file and requests the address for the server hosting the next component of the DNS name — in this case, .com. The root server returns a list of name servers that are authoritative for .com, and the recursive DNS server caches those servers as authoritative for .com so that it doesn't need to make the request again until the TTL expires.

7. The recursive server then chooses an authoritative server for `.com` from the list returned by the root server and sends a request for the name server authoritative for the `.microsoft.com` domain.

8. The `.com` authoritative server returns a list of authoritative servers, and the recursive DNS server caches that list in association with `.microsoft.com`.

9. Now that the recursive server has resolved the entire domain name, all that's left is to resolve the IP address of the host. It chooses an authoritative server from the list for `.microsoft.com` and sends a request for the host (A) record associated with `www.microsoft.com`. The authoritative server for `.microsoft.com` returns all the A records for `www` (if there's more than one) to the recursive DNS server. Round robin DNS then occurs (see Chapter 12). The authoritative server returns the A records in order of the lowest metric first, or, if the metrics are equal, it rotates the order in which it returns the records with each request. The recursive server caches the list of A records associated with `www.microsoft.com`.

10. The recursive DNS server returns the list of A records to the DNS client. The client decides which IP address to use. According to the DNS standards, the client is supposed to use the first address in the list (if there's more than one). By default, however, Windows 2000 and newer DNS clients place priority on IP addresses on the local subnet, although this behavior can be disabled.

11. When the DNS client has decided which address to return to the application, it formats the IP address data in the correct format and returns it to the application through the appropriate communication channel.

12. The application can now use the IP address to open a *socket* to the remote host and begin the network communication.

Although this process seems arduous, it's fast (relative to a human timeframe — in computer time, it's slow). A huge advantage also exists in this massively distributed architecture: Although the root servers must be incredibly powerful and the servers that are authoritative for the top-level domains must be fairly powerful — especially for the busier TLDs, such as `.com` — the lower-level name servers don't need to be powerful. At a company doing Web hosting, for example, the root servers may be authoritative for 1,000 domains, but they can have one moderately powered system hosting all 1,000 domains or 10 slow machines hosting 100 domains each, and it makes no difference to users or any other DNS server.

Taking a Close Look with NSLOOKUP

You can follow the resolution process in the preceding section manually, by using the NSLOOKUP command. For the sake of example, follow along with the process described in this section. We show you in detail how each step in the DNS resolution process works.

First, use NSLOOKUP to locate the servers that are authoritative for the .com domain using one of the root servers. The root servers are contained in the root hint file on every recursive DNS server and are also listed in Chapter 2. They're fairly easy to remember because they're named a-m.rootservers .net. Figure 3-3 shows the process in NSLOOKUP. Use the server command to change the server to one of the root servers and then type **com** to look up the servers that are authoritative for .com.

Next, you must find the servers that are authoritative for microsoft.com, as shown in Figure 3-4. You must first change the server to one of the authoritative servers for .com and then type **microsoft.com** to find the list of servers.

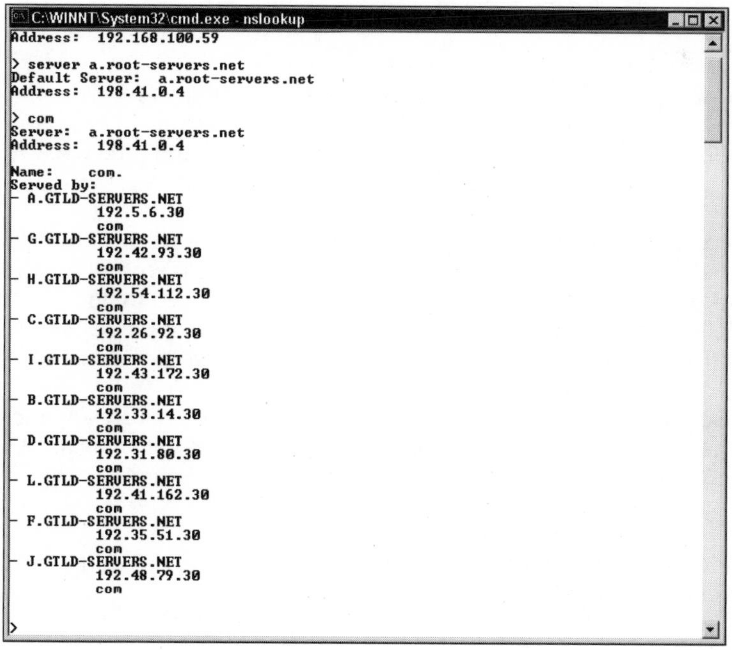

Figure 3-3: Using NSLOOKUP to locate authoritative servers.

```
C:\WINNT\System32\cmd.exe - nslookup
Address:  192.168.100.59

> server a.root-servers.net
Default Server:  a.root-servers.net
Address:  198.41.0.4

> com
Server:  a.root-servers.net
Address:  198.41.0.4

Name:    com.
Served by:
- A.GTLD-SERVERS.NET
            192.5.6.30
            com
- G.GTLD-SERVERS.NET
            192.42.93.30
            com
- H.GTLD-SERVERS.NET
            192.54.112.30
            com
- C.GTLD-SERVERS.NET
            192.26.92.30
            com
- I.GTLD-SERVERS.NET
            192.43.172.30
            com
- B.GTLD-SERVERS.NET
            192.33.14.30
            com
- D.GTLD-SERVERS.NET
            192.31.80.30
            com
- L.GTLD-SERVERS.NET
            192.41.162.30
            com
- F.GTLD-SERVERS.NET
            192.35.51.30
            com
- J.GTLD-SERVERS.NET
            192.48.79.30
            com
>
```

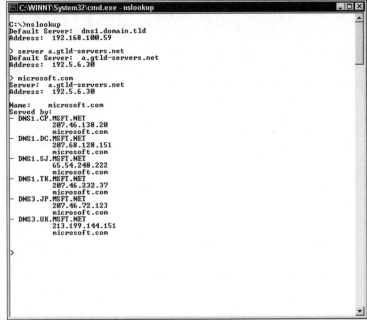

Figure 3-4:
Using
NSLOOKUP
to find *more*
authoritative
servers.

Now that you know the servers that are authoritative for microsoft.com, you can look up the www host. Use the server command again to change to one of the authoritative microsoft.com servers and type **www** to retrieve the A record, as shown in Figure 3-5.

A problem seems to have occurred in that last paragraph, though: When you're looking up www.microsoft.com, no data is returned by the authoritative server. The reason is simple: NSLOOKUP is used to find A records by default, and www.microsoft.com doesn't have an A record on the authoritative server. There's a good reason for that, as we explain next.

Use the command set type=any in NSLOOKUP to retrieve any record for the www.microsoft.com host and type **www.microsoft.com** again. As you can see, www.microsoft.com is a CNAME record to www.microsoft.akadns. net, as shown in Figure 3-6.

Having gone through all this work, you need to go back and do it all again, as shown in Figure 3-7, Figure 3-8, and Figure 3-9:

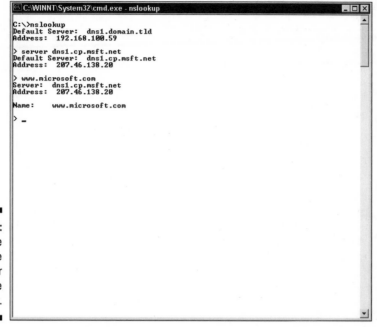

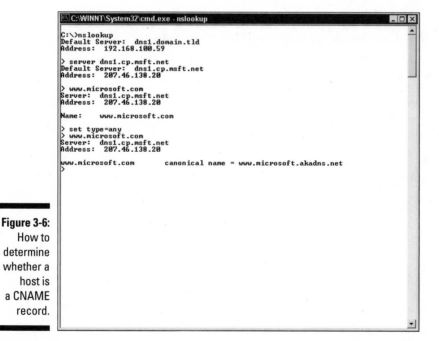

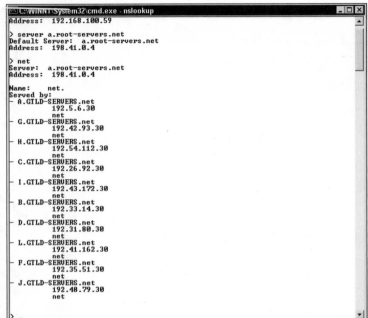

Figure 3-7:
Finding authoritative servers for the .net top-level domain.

1. **Find the servers that are authoritative for the** net **TLD.**

2. **Find the servers that are authoritative for** akadns.net.

3. **Find the servers that are authoritative for the subdomain** microsoft.akadns.net.

Figure 3-9 shows another problem, though. Again, an apparent dead end has been reached. When you're trying to find the authoritative servers for microsoft.akadns.net, no data is returned.

Using the same set type=any command, as shown in Figure 3-10, you can attempt to see what is happening.

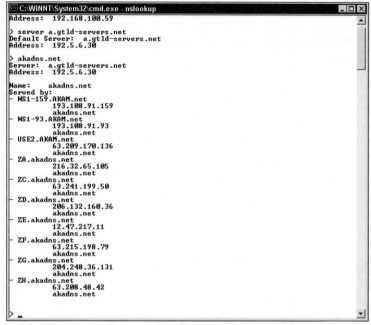

```
C:\WINNT\System32\cmd.exe - nslookup
Address:  192.168.100.59

> server a.gtld-servers.net
Default Server:  a.gtld-servers.net
Address:  192.5.6.30

> akadns.net
Server:  a.gtld-servers.net
Address:  192.5.6.30

Name:    akadns.net
Served by:
- NS1-159.AKAM.net
           193.108.91.159
           akadns.net
- NS1-93.AKAM.net
           193.108.91.93
           akadns.net
- USE2.AKAM.net
           63.209.170.136
           akadns.net
- ZA.akadns.net
           216.32.65.105
           akadns.net
- ZC.akadns.net
           63.241.199.50
           akadns.net
- ZD.akadns.net
           206.132.160.36
           akadns.net
- ZE.akadns.net
           12.47.217.11
           akadns.net
- ZF.akadns.net
           63.215.198.79
           akadns.net
- ZG.akadns.net
           204.248.36.131
           akadns.net
- ZH.akadns.net
           63.208.48.42
           akadns.net
> _
```

Figure 3-8:
Finding
authoritative
servers for
akadns.
net.

As you can see in the figure, a number of NS records are returned for
`microsoft.akadns.net`, including the server that `NSLOOKUP` is querying.
The presence of these NS records indicates that the subdomain `microsoft.`
`akadns.net` hasn't been delegated, as we describe in Chapter 10. Rather
than be hosted on yet another DNS server, is the subdomain is hosted on the
current DNS server. You can then look up the host `www.microsoft.akadns.`
`net` without switching servers again. First, use the command `set type=a` to
change the record type back to A (`set type=a`), and then type **www.microsoft.**
akadns.net, as shown in Figure 3-11. Finally, you see a list of A records associated with `www.microsoft.akadns.net` and, therefore, `www.microsoft.com`,
which is a CNAME to `www.microsoft.akadns.net`.

All this work is automated by using recursive DNS servers. You can see the
main advantage of DNS: It automates an arduous process into something
transparent to users. Now that you understand how DNS resolution works,
you can move on to configuring DNS. This information also gives you a great
level of insight in troubleshooting DNS because you understand what is happening in the background.

Figure 3-9:
More of the same. . . .

Figure 3-10:
Using the
set
type=any
command to
attempt to
see what is
happening
with a
subdomain.

```
C:\WINNT\System32\cmd.exe - nslookup
Address:   193.108.91.159

Name:      microsoft.akadns.net

> set type=any
> microsoft.akadns.net
Server:  ns1-159.akam.net
Address:  193.108.91.159

microsoft.akadns.net      nameserver = ze.akadns.net
microsoft.akadns.net      nameserver = use2.akam.net
microsoft.akadns.net      nameserver = zd.akadns.net
microsoft.akadns.net      nameserver = zg.akadns.net
microsoft.akadns.net
        primary name server = ns1-159.akam.net
        responsible mail addr = hostmaster.akamai.com
        serial  = 50
        refresh = 50 (50 secs)
        retry   = 50 (50 secs)
        expire  = 50 (50 secs)
        default TTL = 50 (50 secs)
microsoft.akadns.net      nameserver = zh.akadns.net
microsoft.akadns.net      nameserver = zc.akadns.net
microsoft.akadns.net      nameserver = za.akadns.net
microsoft.akadns.net      nameserver = ns1-159.akam.net
microsoft.akadns.net      nameserver = zf.akadns.net
ze.akadns.net    internet address = 12.47.217.11
za.akadns.net    internet address = 216.32.65.105
zc.akadns.net    internet address = 63.241.199.50
zg.akadns.net    internet address = 204.248.36.131
zd.akadns.net    internet address = 206.132.160.36
zh.akadns.net    internet address = 63.208.48.42
ns1-159.akam.net         internet address = 193.108.91.159
use2.akam.net    internet address = 63.209.170.136
zf.akadns.net    internet address = 63.215.198.79
> set type=a
> www.microsoft.akadns.net
Server:  ns1-159.akam.net
Address:  193.108.91.159

Name:    www.microsoft.akadns.net
Addresses:  207.46.134.155, 207.46.134.190, 207.46.197.113, 207.46.230.220
        207.46.230.219, 207.46.230.218
>
```

Figure 3-11:
Finally, an
answer.

Chapter 4

Facilitating Other Applications with DNS

. . . .

. . . .

Although DNS is known mostly for enabling the World Wide Web because that is where it's most obviously used, it also plays a critical role in other network communications processes. DNS is used to facilitate many other applications also, from databases to multi-tier applications to instant messaging. although these applications are all vastly different, they all use DNS in one way or another. One popular function that depends on DNS is e-mail. It's reported to be the most widely used Internet application, and it could not function as it does now without the services of DNS.

Getting into E-Mail

Every time you send an e-mail to user@domain.tld, DNS is used. Because DNS was built with e-mail in mind (among other things), it has e-mail functionality built right in. E-mail uses a special type of DNS record known as a *mail exchanger (MX)* record to facilitate the exchange of e-mail. First, however, we describe the Simple Mail Transport Protocol (SMTP).

SMTP is the protocol used to move mail around the Internet, so it's the Internet equivalent of your friendly neighborhood postal worker. You may have also heard of a protocol named POP3 and its role in the use of e-mail. Unlike SMTP, POP3 is used only for the retrieval of mail from a mail server and is a minor part of the e-mail process. SMTP, on the other hand, handles all mail duties for e-mail on the Internet until the message reaches its destination server.

When you use a mail client such as Outlook or Eudora in Windows, you define both an outgoing and incoming mail server. The outgoing server is known as an SMTP relay because it's responsible for relaying messages from the client to the recipient server. This setting in Outlook also uses DNS, but not in the same way that DNS is used for mail routing, as you can see in Figure 4-1. It shows an example of the outgoing mail server setting.

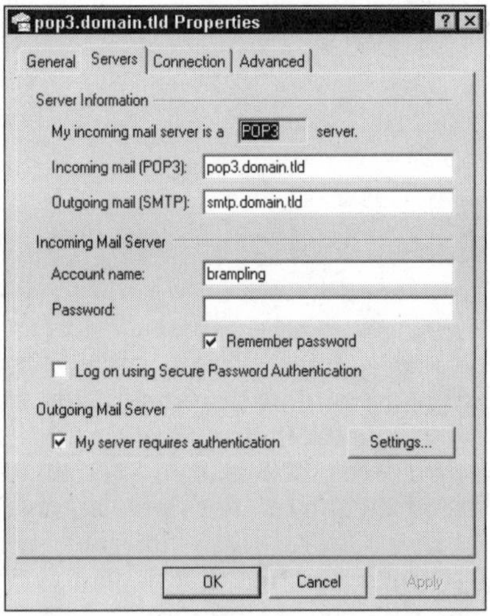

Figure 4-1:
The server configuration in a mail client.

You can see how DNS is used to deliver mail to the SMTP relay server. The host name of the relay server is specified, and the mail client uses DNS to retrieve the A record for that host. The SMTP message is then delivered to the SMTP relay server at the IP address in the A record.

In Unix, *mail user agents* (MUAs), such as mutt and pine, don't use an outgoing SMTP server like other mail clients, such as Netscape Mail. Rather, they use *injection* to place the outgoing messages directly in the outgoing mail queue of a local *mail transport agent* (MTA), such as sendmail or qmail. Although the process for getting the mail into the queue is different, the way the mail is handled after it's in the queue is the same.

After the message has been delivered to the SMTP server, the mail-routing process begins, which is where the DNS mail-enabling features come into play. First, here's some background. For each domain serving e-mail to users, such as user@domain.tld, is a server known as a mail exchanger. It's responsible for receiving all e-mail destined for that domain. A mail exchanger can be responsible for any number of domains as long as it's capable of handling the load. You can also have more than one mail exchanger for a domain, which we explain later in this chapter, in the section "Using Multiple MX Records."

The key in the SMTP process is the SMTP relay server's getting the message to the correct mail exchanger. When a relay server receives a message from a client, is the message is placed in an outgoing mail queue. When the message is processed, the SMTP relay server disregards the user portion (user@domain.tld) and simply looks at the domain portion. The domain portion is used to determine the mail exchanger for that domain. The SMTP relay server does a DNS lookup on the domain, but doesn't look up the A record. Rather, the server does a lookup for the mail exchanger (MX) record for that domain. (We mention MX records in Chapter 9.)

Understanding MX Records

An *MX,* or mail exchanger, record is a fairly simple form of DNS record. Each domain — microsoft.com, for example — has at least one MX record if it will be used to receive e-mail. The MX record consists of a name (typically the domain name or @), a metric value (BIND) or priority value (Microsoft Windows), though when there's one MX record, the priority is an arbitrary value, and a value (the IP address of the mail exchanger). To create an MX record in Windows DNS, first open the DNS snap-in by clicking the Start button and choosing Programs➪Administrative Tools.

We describe this process in detail in Chapter 9. Rather than give you a walk-through on how to configure your server, however, we mention the process here to give you an idea of how mail is facilitated by DNS. See Chapter 9 for the details on adding records and zones to your DNS server.

Locate the zone in which to create the MX record, right-click, and choose New Mail Exchanger. The New Resource Record dialog box is displayed, as shown in Figure 4-2.

The MX record requires a few values. The first is the name value for the domain. To use the current domain, leave this box blank. For example, this MX record is being created in the domain sample.tld. The MX record is associated with sample.tld if you leave the box blank, and mail to user@sample.tld goes to the host you specify. You can also specify other hosts or domains for the MX record if you want to deliver mail for user@host.sample.tld, for example. In most cases, you simply create the MX record for the default domain.

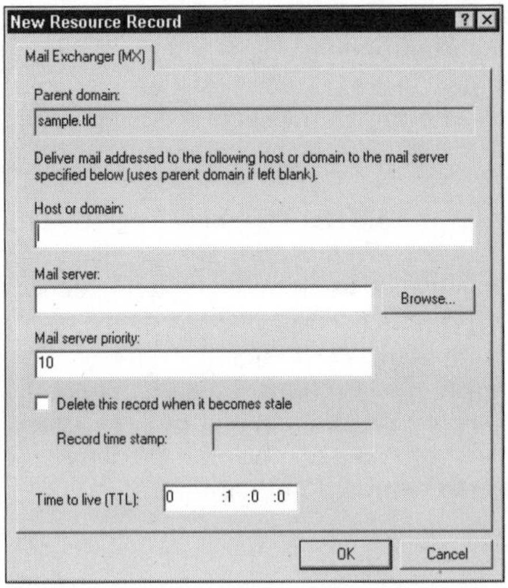

Figure 4-2:
Creating a
new MX
record in
Windows.

You must now specify in the Mail server box the mail exchanger host, which can be either an IP address or a DNS host name of the mail server configured to receive mail for this domain. (In the following section, "Configuring Mail Servers as Mail Exchangers," we tell you how to configure mail servers as mail exchangers.) The other important value is the priority. This value is set to 10 by default. If you have only one MX record, you can leave it as the default. We address the use of multiple MX records in the following section. The last two values in the dialog box are the check box labeled Delete this record when it becomes stale, which should be checked only if you're scavenging (which is unlikely), and the TTL value. The TTL value is taken from the parent zone by default. Click OK to create the record. Figure 4-3 shows the new MX record in the zone.

In BIND too, creating an MX record is simple. All you need to do is add a record to the zone file in which the MX record will reside. The MX record has the same values as the Windows version: a name, a priority, and a name or address for the mail exchanger. An MX record in BIND looks like this:

```
sample.tld.              IN    MX    10  mail.sample.tld.
```

Assuming that this MX record is in the sample.tld zone file, though, you can do the same thing with less verbosity:

```
@                        IN    MX    10  mail
```

The @ sign indicates the current origin, typically the name of the zone (sample.tld.) unless it has been changed using an $ORIGIN statement; mail without the trailing period indicates that the parent domain name should be appended. Both methods are functionally identical.

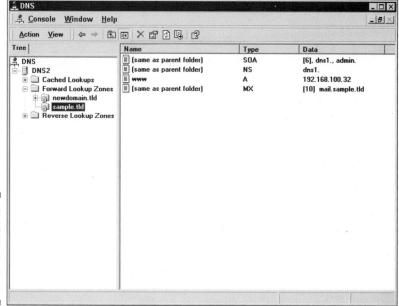

Figure 4-3:
The MX record has been created in the zone.

Using Multiple MX Records

You can have more than one mail exchanger for a domain. You would want to have multiple mail exchangers for two reasons: to balance a high load of incoming mail across multiple servers and to provide a backup mail server in case one of the mail servers goes "belly up." Each scenario using multiple MX records is implemented slightly differently.

The details of how to configure multiple mail servers to receive mail for the same domain, for either load balancing or backup, are complex and not described in this book. Consult the documentation for your mail server if you want to implement one of these configurations.

For load balancing, you can create multiple MX records with the same priority values. Figure 4-4 shows an example in Windows DNS of a configuration with three mail servers with equal priorities. The mail traffic will be split between these three servers.

In BIND, the procedure is the same. You add multiple MX records to your zone file like this:

```
@                      IN    MX    10   mail
@                      IN    MX    10   mail2
@                      IN    MX    10   mail3
```

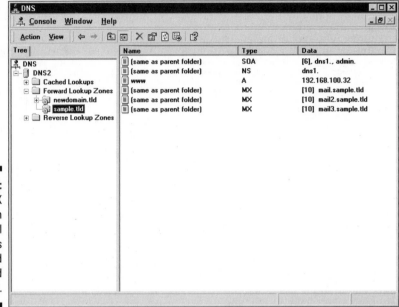

Figure 4-4:
Multiple MX
records with
equal
priorities
are used
for load
balancing.

The procedure for establishing a backup mail server is similar except that you set the priority of the MX records to different values.

The DNS record with the *lowest* numerical priority value has the *highest* priority to a client. Likewise, a record with a higher numerical priority value has a lower priority to a client. Simply put, lower values equal higher-priority records. A record with a priority of 10 is always used before a record with a priority of 20.

Figure 4-5 shows a Windows DNS implementation of the required MX records for a backup mail server. Note that the main mail exchanger has a priority of 10 and the backup has a priority of 20. The main mail exchanger is always used before the backup.

In BIND, the MX records are created in the zone file as follows:

```
@                              IN    MX    10   mail
@                              IN    MX    20   backupmail
```

The lower-priority-value record is used before the higher-priority record.

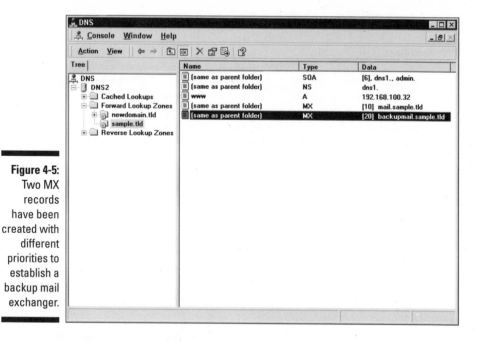

Figure 4-5:
Two MX
records
have been
created with
different
priorities to
establish a
backup mail
exchanger.

Configuring Mail Servers As Mail Exchangers

When an MX record is used, all mail to a domain is "dumped" on the server
with the MX record for that domain. Every SMTP server in existence forwards
mail with the format user@domain.tld to the MX record value for domain.
tld. The key is to configure the mail server so that it knows it's supposed to
receive mail for that domain.

Microsoft Exchange 2000

Microsoft Exchange 2000 is integrated into Microsoft Active Directory (AD).
Rather than store Exchange accounts in Exchange, as in Version 5.5 and earlier, Exchange integrates into Active Directory and assigns mailboxes to existing Active Directory accounts.

In Microsoft Exchange 2000, SMTP mail is sent and received by using an
SMTP connector. By default, Exchange is automatically configured to accept

mail for the default domain in which it's installed. Exchange allows the intre-
pid mail administrator to configure multiple e-mail addresses for any user
who has an account in Active Directory with a mailbox on the Exchange
server. For example, an Exchange server on the foo.com domain may accept
inbound e-mail for usr@foo.com, user@foosales.com, and user@superfoo.
com, for example. Another handy feature is the ability to import existing
users from a Windows domain and to create mailboxes (in a single import)
for every account. Mailboxes can also be created for both nondomain users
and domain users, which is handy if the server is providing ISP-like services,
such as Web (HTTP) or POP mail access.

qmail

qmail, a common Unix-/Linux-based message-transfer agent (MTA), can be
configured to accept mail for any domains you want. To configure qmail to
accept mail for a domain, that domain must be listed in the file /var/qmail/
control/rcpthosts. This file simply contains a list of the domains for which
qmail will accept mail in the format domain.tld. The content of a sample
rcpthosts file looks something like this:

```
sample.tld
newdomain.tld
domain.tld
acct.domain.tld
```

qmail also uses two other files that control how mail is delivered after it's
received by the SMTP component: /var/qmail/control/locals and
/var/qmail/control/virtualdomains. These files have nothing to do with
DNS — only with the qmail delivery process. Although rcpthosts controls
for which domains mail is accepted by the SMTP component, the locals and
virtualdomains files control how qmail delivers the messages after they're
in the system.

Multi-Tier Applications and DNS

Multi-tier applications — a hot topic these days — are being implemented in
many mid- to large-size networks. A *multi-tier* application simply refers to any
application that runs on distributed systems. For example, applications that
use an application server and a Web server in the front end comprise a two-
tiered system; more often, however, *multi-tier* refers to systems that make use
of three or more components. A common example of a three-tier system is a
database server in the back end (housing the data), an application server or
middleware server in the middle (processing user requests), and a Web
server on the front end (providing an interface for the end user).

Middleware is one of those buzzwords that everyone seems to be using but nobody seems to be able to clearly explain. In most cases, *middleware* simply refers to an application responsible for ensuring that the data from the database is accessible to the user through a Web-based interface. In many cases, the middleware application is built by using a Java (a programming language) engine with a series of extensions to make developing the application easier. When a middleware application, such as BEA WebLogic, is used, often no processing is done by the Web server itself — the middleware does it all. The Web server is in place only to provide a gateway from the user's Web browser to the middleware.

When a multi-tier application is used, the separate tiers almost always need to communicate with each other over a network connection — a connection typically based on TCP/IP. A connection can be made by an IP address, but for the sake of administrative ease, the connection between the tiers is usually done by using DNS names. Just like when you browse the Internet for fun or work, using the DNS name is much easier than remembering the IP address; for example, the name `application.domain.tld` is easier to remember than the IP address `192.168.100.43`.

In addition, the use of DNS can allow for the tiers of the application to be switched from one system to another by changing the DNS record, not the IP address configured directly in the application. The benefit is relatively clear: You move the application without having to modify its operating parameters, which in some cases can involve recoding part of the application. In this case, using DNS may save lots of time and money. If the application is configured to use the Web server `web1.domain.tld`, for example, and you want to swap the `web1.domain.tld` system for a new, more powerful Web server, you can simply configure the new Web server in parallel with the old Web server, but with a different IP address. After the new server is in place and tested, you can change the IP address for `web1.domain.tld` to the address of the new Web server. And, after the TTL expires on the DNS record, the new Web server is used.

You can use the same technique for the application tier if it doesn't use dynamic data, but it doesn't work well for the database tier because the data in the new database server becomes stale while you're changing the DNS record. The process for changing a server that did have *dynamic* data (data that changed with application activity) is different. You have to make the change in a way which ensures that the data remains "factory fresh."

Wait — there's more! DNS can even be used to easily add load balancing within a more complex multi-tier application. DNS can be configured in such a way that you can make use of a cluster of more than one server in each tier. In a multi-tier application in which the data on the Web and on application servers is static (as is the case with many multi-tier systems), a DNS round robin can be used at each level. Users can be load-balanced to different Web servers by using DNS round robin on the front end, and the Web servers can be load-balanced to a group of application servers by using the same technique. The application servers can even be load-balanced to a cluster of database servers. This arrangement works as long as the database cluster was already configured to share data across the members of the cluster. When you get this deep into a major multi-tier application, though, the DNS configuration takes a great deal of planning and design to ensure that everything works properly. You don't want your major enterprise resource planning (ERP) application failing because of an oversight in the DNS configuration.

Microsoft Active Directory and DNS

Microsoft Active Directory (AD) uses DNS as a critical part of its operation. DNS is used in place of the Windows Internet Naming System (WINS) that was so widely used in "pre-Active Directory" days. WINS was used in older versions of Windows as the main protocol for name resolution in the versions of Windows in which NetBIOS names were depended on for communication between systems. With a more rigorous adoption of the TCP/IP protocol stack by Windows, DNS was the obvious choice for maintaining the host name information used by Active Directory.

Active Directory uses a number of advanced DNS features to function, including dynamic updates (see Chapter 12). As systems are added and removed from the network, their DNS information is dynamically updated. This process is completely automated, saving the system administrator from having to manually add any systems. In addition to keeping a record of systems on the network, Active Directory uses DNS to maintain on the network a list of services, such as printers, Active Directory servers, and global catalogs. Active Directory does this by using a service (SRV) record, which is a special type of DNS record. (We briefly discuss these records in Chapter 9.) SRV records give a client system everything it needs to locate an appropriate service or services, determine where on the network the services are located, and choose the best one.

SRV records are also automatically added to the DNS database by the Active Directory server as services come online — saving the administrator from having to manually maintain a service list or even configure services on the workstations. Theoretically, a user who needs to print can simply indicate to the system that she wants to print, and then an appropriate printer or list of printers is provided. This feature is generally quite useful because large networks may have hundreds or thousands of hosts and each one may have numerous available services. Active Directory centralizes the process of accessing and locating the available services.

Part II
Working with DNS Clients

In this part . . .

DNS clients are everywhere. They're built into operating systems, Web browsers, e-mail clients, database clients, and more.

In the chapters in this part, you will learn about the DNS clients you have on your system, including several kinds of clients you probably don't know exist. You will also find out how each of these clients works and how you can use them to *do* something. In addition to allowing you to perform useful tasks, such as find Web sites and send e-mail, your knowledge of DNS clients will become a great benefit to you if you ever have to troubleshoot a DNS-related problem.

Chapter 5

Configuring a DNS Client

● ●

In This Chapter

▶ Determining your DNS client settings

▶ Configuring a Windows DNS client

▶ Configuring a Unix DNS client

● ●

A computer that uses the services of another device on the network is known as a *client*. Almost all network-connected computers (including such items as desktops or laptops, network printers, routers, and switches) are clients. Strangely enough, even servers are clients. A computer is rarely so specialized that it's a server and nothing else. For example, the administrator responsible for a server may log on to that server and download a software patch or update. The server then becomes a client making use of other network resources — in this case, another server that houses the necessary files. This chapter looks at computers that are domain name server clients.

Computers that must have a means of resolving DNS names need to have their DNS client components configured. The DNS client is responsible for retrieving from a DNS server the associated IP address for any DNS name you enter (in a Web browser, for example). Because the DNS server is used to perform this name translation, you must specify the IP address (or addresses) of the DNS server (or servers).

This chapter describes the methods for configuring DNS clients in both the Windows and Linux environments. Although the purpose of each client is the same and they do essentially the same tasks, the configuration steps are as different as night and day.

Making the Server Connection

You need to have a few things handy before you delve into the DNS configuration of your computer. First and foremost, you need to have the IP addresses for the DNS servers available to you. Your Internet Service Provider (ISP) or system administrator provides them, or you have them yourself if you have your own DNS servers. With most operating systems, you can have as many

DNS servers configured on the client system as you want. Windows 2000, Windows XP, Linux, and many other operating systems can accept any number of DNS server IP addresses. Some earlier systems, such as Windows 95, can accept only two or three simultaneous DNS server entries.

If possible, you should always use more than one DNS server for your client configuration (or configurations). As the old saying goes, two is better than one. Having two or more servers in your client configuration reduces the possibility of an outage because the only specified server is down. Even if you have only one DNS server on your network, you can specify, for example, a DNS server from your ISP to be second on your list so that it's used only if your server is unavailable. In most cases, each server specified in the client configuration is contacted in order (the first server in the list is contacted first). Each successive server is tried if the preceding one cannot be contacted.

If only one DNS server is available and you want to make use of added *redundancy* (having more than one server defined in case one goes down), you can add publicly available DNS servers to your configuration. Sometimes, finding these servers is a matter of looking through search engines for a public DNS server. For example, the Open Root Server Confederation provides several public-access DNS servers. You can find the list of servers at `support. open-rsc.org/.servers/`.

You should now have a list of DNS server IP addresses. It's the first piece of required information. The next bits of information aren't normally mandatory, but configuring them makes life much easier for users. The DNS suffix is a good configuration setting to use because it allows you to specify hosts in your local domain without fully qualifying them, but search domains are needed only in some cases. If more than one domain are is under your control, you may have a number of search domains to specify.

When a computer is in a DNS domain itself, it normally has a DNS suffix. This suffix is the DNS name of the system, not including the host name. In the `host.domain.tld` example, `domain.tld` is the DNS suffix. In many cases, the computer doesn't know what its DNS suffix is because it must be entered by the user and isn't required in order for DNS to function. The only situations in which this statement isn't true is in a Windows 2000 or Windows XP domain using Active Directory with DNS. In these cases, the DNS suffix is automatically assigned.

Suppose that you're doing something basic with DNS, such as pinging another computer. You can use the `ping` command; `ping deadhost. domain.tld`, for example. If the computer from which you're running the command is a member of the `domain.tld` domain, this command may be more than is needed. You would expect, because both hosts are on the same domain, that you wouldn't need to type the entire host and domain name (also known as the Fully Qualified Domain Name, or FQDN) for the target computer. By specifying a DNS suffix in you client configuration (`domain.tld`, in this case), you can then use the command `ping deadhost` and omit the DNS suffix. The DNS suffix specified in the DNS client configuration is automatically appended to any host names you type. For example, if you configure your computer with the DNS suffix `domain.tld`, typing **ping deadhost** causes the system to attempt to ping `deadhost.domain.tld`.

The next piece of configuration information you need to supply to your client is a list of search domains. Search domains function in a manner similar to the DNS suffix. The DNS suffix is typically used first when you attempt to resolve an unqualified host name. You can also provide a list of search domains used as alternatives to the DNS suffix if the suffix doesn't resolve the host name. Suppose that you have a system with a DNS suffix of `domain.tld` and search domains of `foo.com` and `bar.net`. You then type **ping deadhost**. The computer first attempts to ping `deadhost.domain.tld`. If this name cannot be resolved, it then attempts to ping `deadhost.foo.com`. If that doesn't resolve, the process fails and returns an error.

You should now have all the information you need in order to configure the DNS clients, including the DNS server IP addresses, the DNS suffix, and the search domains. The following sections show you how to configure Windows and Linux DNS clients.

Getting Your Client a Windows Seat

You can configure Windows DNS clients in a number of ways. If your computer is using the Dynamic Host Configuration Protocol (DHCP) to automatically obtain its IP address, it most likely retrieves its DNS client configuration from the same DHCP server. If this is the case, you're in luck and the client doesn't require any additional configuration. If the DHCP server isn't assigning a DNS server (or you want to override the DHCP setting), read on.

DNS clients are configured either during the installation of Windows or after it has been installed. The configuration during installation is similar to that of an installed system, and we describe here only the configuration for an installed system. The process differs slightly depending on which version of Windows you're using.

Windows sherbert: It's mulitflavored!

You can override many settings listed in this section by setting group policies in a Windows 2000 Server or Windows .NET Server Active Directory. If your network has Active Directory in place, check with your systems administrators before changing these settings, or else you may be wasting your time. Changes made to settings configured through a group policy have no effect.

Setting your DNS network configuration

To set your client configuration on a Windows system, follow these steps:

1. **Right-click the My Network Places icon on the desktop and choose Properties from the pop-up menu.**

   The Network and Dial-up Connections window opens, as shown in Figure 5-1.

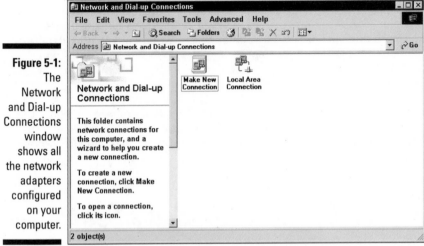

Figure 5-1: The Network and Dial-up Connections window shows all the network adapters configured on your computer.

2. **Locate the network adapter for which you will configure the DNS settings.**

   Although you most likely have only one network adapter, you can have more than one, as shown in the figure.

3. **Right-click the network adapter and choose Properties.**

   This step opens the Properties dialog box for that adapter, as shown in Figure 5-2. The dialog box is used to set the configuration options for all protocols and services associated with that interface.

   Because DNS requires the TCP/IP protocol in order to function, you configure DNS through the Properties dialog box for TCP/IP:

4. **Select the Internet Protocol (TCP/IP) from the list of installed protocols and click the Properties button.**

   The Properties dialog box for the TCP/IP protocol appears, as shown in Figure 5-3.

   As you can see, you can set the primary and secondary DNS servers in the TCP/IP Properties dialog box.

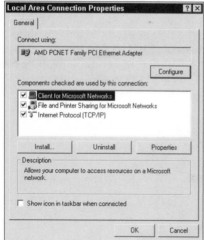

Figure 5-2:
Setting the con-figuration options for the adapter and the services and protocols associated with the interface.

5. **Simply type the IP address of each server in the appropriate boxes.**

   When you click OK to close the Properties dialog box and click OK again to close the network adapter properties dialog box, the changes are saved.

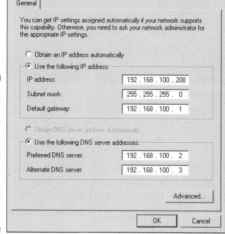

Figure 5-3:
You use the TCP/IP Properties dialog box to set con-figuration options for the protocol.

Configuring the DNS server addresses isn't the only setting available, though. As discussed earlier in this chapter, in the section "Making the Server Connection," you may need to set a DNS suffix or search domains, depending on the configuration of your network, which you do from the Advanced TCP/IP Settings dialog box. In the TCP/IP Properties dialog box, click the Advanced button. Click to select the DNS tab in the Advanced TCP/IP Settings dialog box, as shown in Figure 5-4.

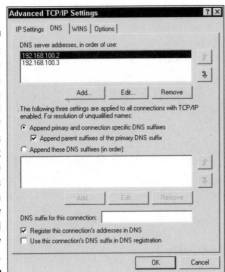

Figure 5-4: You use the DNS tab of the Advanced TCP/IP Settings dialog box to configure DNS options other than the primary and secondary servers.

This tab contains a large amount of information. At the top of the window is the list of DNS servers to be used. The primary and secondary servers specified in the basic TCP/IP Properties dialog box appear in this box. You can add as many DNS servers as you want to this list by clicking the Add button, specifying the DNS server IP address to add, and clicking Add. You can also select a DNS server from the list and click Remove to delete the server from the list or click Edit to change its address.

Finally, you can select a server from the list and press the up- and down-arrow buttons to change the order in which it's used. DNS servers are accessed in order from the top of the list down. You want your main DNS servers (those at your site) first on the list and your backup DNS servers, such as those at your ISP, lower on the list.

The next option you can select involves DNS suffixes. Recall that DNS suffixes are automatically added to unqualified names typed in applications. For example, if the suffix is mydomain.com, any request for a host (such as running the ping command) will have the suffix added if another suffix isn't specified by the user or applications. The default setting, as shown in Figure 5-4, is Append primary and connection specific DNS suffixes. This setting causes the primary DNS suffix to be appended first, followed by the connection-specific DNS suffix. The primary DNS suffix isn't specified in the Network Settings dialog box — it's specified in a different location and is discussed in the following section, "Configuring your primary DNS suffix."

The primary DNS suffix, which is global to the computer, applies to all connections unless specified otherwise.

The connection-specific DNS suffix is specified in the DNS suffix for this connection box. Although the primary DNS suffix applies to all connections, the connection-specific suffix applies to only this particular adapter.

When the Append primary and connection-specific DNS suffixes option is selected, another of the options available becomes enabled. The Append parent suffixes of the primary DNS suffix option makes the subject of DNS suffixes even more confusing. If your domain is host.sales.domain.tld, for example, the domain suffix is sales.domain.tld. If you type **ping remotehost**, your computer attempts to ping remotehost.sales.domain.tld if the previously discussed option (Append primary and connection specific DNS suffixes) is selected. When the Append parent suffixes of the primary DNS suffix option is selected, the computer also attempts to ping remotehost.domain.tld. This option uses the specified primary DNS suffix to resolve DNS names as well as each level of the parent DNS suffix, removing one subdomain at a time.. The example shows one level (sales.domain.tld), but it works for any number of parent domain suffixes. If your primary domain suffix is sales.west.domain.tld, for example, west.domain.tld and domain.tld also are used to resolve names if this option is selected. If the option isn't selected, only the primary DNS suffix is used.

Although using the primary and connection-specific DNS suffixes may be enough in most cases, you may want to provide a list of other suffixes to be used to resolve DNS names. You can select the Append these DNS suffixes (in order) option in the Advanced TCP/IP Settings dialog box to enable it.

When the option labeled Append these DNS suffixes (in order) is selected, the primary and connection-specific DNS suffixes aren't used. You must specify explicitly all suffixes you want to use in the list, including the primary and connection-specific suffixes, if required.

To add suffixes to the list, follow these steps:

1. **Click the Add button.**

2. **In the Domain suffix box, enter the DNS suffix (**domain.com**, for example).**

3. **Click the Add button in the TCP/IP Domain Suffix dialog box window.**

You can use these steps to add as many domain suffixes as you want. If you have gone a bit overboard and need to remove some entries, have no fear: It's a fairly painless process. To remove a domain, select the offending suffix from the list and click the Remove button to ditch the entry. You can also use the Edit button to (can you guess?) edit any existing entries. You can also select a list entry and click the up- and down-arrow buttons to the right of the list to change the list order. Suffixes are used in the order, from top to bottom, in which they appear on the list. For example, if domain.tld is followed by microsoft.com on the list, when you type the command **ping remotehost**, the computer attempts to ping remotehost.domain.tld. If that doesn't resolve anything, it attempts to ping remotehost.microsoft.com.

You must plan carefully which domains to put on this list. If too many domain suffixes are on the list, you end up accidentally resolving computers in the wrong domains. To avoid unnecessary problems, use the Append primary and connection specific DNS suffixes option rather than the Append these DNS suffixes (in order) option.

Notice two other options on the DNS tab of the Advanced TCP/IP Settings dialog box:

- ✔ Register this connection's address in DNS.
- ✔ Use this connection's DNS suffix in DNS registration.

These options control the Windows-based dynamic DNS behavior. By default, all newer Windows-based systems register their IP addresses in the DNS server. This functionality works only if the DNS server is a Windows-based dynamic DNS server (Windows 2000 Server or Windows .NET Server) or a specially configured Unix or third-party DNS server.

The automatic registration feature was introduced in Windows 2000 Server and Active Directory. Active Directory closely integrates DNS as a catalog of computers. The automatic registration allows simpler communications from one computer to another because they're all registered in DNS and can be contacted by name rather than by IP address. If you're familiar with Windows Internet Naming Service (WINS), the traditional way of resolving computer names in older versions of Windows, you know that this service performs well across networks. The new solution using DNS functions well across multiple networks. Like WINS, the new automatic DNS registration (also called Dynamic DNS) allows hosts to notify the DNS server when they become available and when they're removing themselves from the network. This strategy ensures that the DNS table carries entries for the active hosts and that the records correctly reflect the addressing information associated with any given host automatically.

This option should be enabled if your system is in a Windows 2000– or Windows .NET Server–based domain using dynamic DNS. If your environment doesn't have dynamic DNS servers or you don't have a need for dynamic DNS updates, disable this option.

The other dynamic DNS option is Use this connection's DNS suffix in DNS registration. When this option is selected in addition to the Register this connection's address in DNS option, the connection-specific DNS suffix and the primary suffix are used to register in DNS. This option causes the computer to be registered in the DNS server twice — once with the computer name and primary suffix and once with the computer name and connection-specific suffix.

Configuring your primary DNS suffix

We discuss a primary DNS suffix frequently in this chapter. This suffix isn't set in the TCP/IP configuration with other DNS settings. Right-click the My Computer icon on the desktop and choose Properties from the pop-up menu. Click the Network Identification tab in the System Properties dialog box, as shown in Figure 5-5.

The full computer name, including computer name and the domain name, are shown on the Network Identification tab. The domain name shown there is the primary domain name for this computer. By default, this domain name is gleaned from the domain membership of the computer. Not all environments have domain controllers, however, and you can manually configure the primary DNS suffix for the system if it belongs to either a domain or a workgroup. If your computer participates in a network, such as a company LAN that more often than not makes use of centralized authentication, you can save yourself from many headaches by not altering this setting.

Figure 5-5:
You use the Network Identification tab in the System Properties dialog box to view and edit the computer name and primary domain.

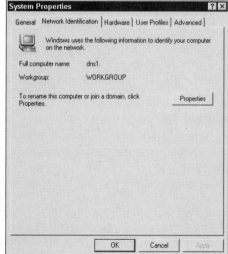

In the Network Identification tab of the System Properties dialog box, click the Change button. Figure 5-6 shows the Identification Changes dialog box. Use it to change the computer's name or domain or workgroup membership; the current goal is to set the primary DNS suffix.

To view the primary DNS suffix setting, click the More button in the Identification Changes dialog box. The DNS Suffix and NetBIOS Computer Name dialog box is displayed, as shown in Figure 5-7. To specify or change the primary DNS suffix, simply type the suffix in the box and click OK. If the computer is a domain member, the automatically assigned primary DNS suffix is shown in the box. You can change it.

Figure 5-6:
The Iden-
tification
Changes
dialog box
is used to
set the
computer
name and
domain or
workgroup
member-
ship.

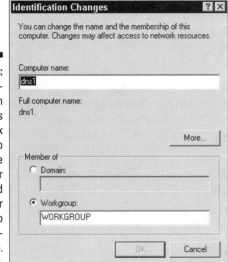

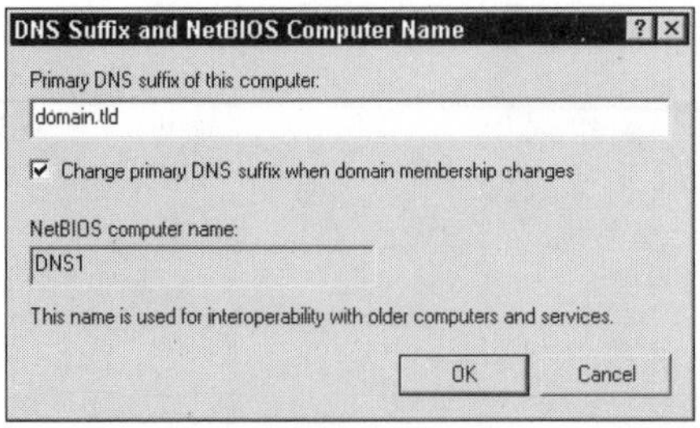

Figure 5-7:
You can
change the
primary
DNS suffix
for the
computer
from the
DNS Suffix
and
NetBIOS
Computer
Name
dialog box.

One other important option is in the DNS Suffix and NetBIOS Computer Name dialog box. The Change primary DNS suffix when domain membership changes option controls what happens when the computer is added to a domain or moved to another domain. When the option is selected, the primary DNS suffix changes to the appropriate suffix for the new domain after a change in domain membership. When the option isn't selected, the primary DNS suffix stays the same when domain membership changes.

Working with older versions of Windows

Configuring DNS on older Windows systems — such as Windows 95, Windows 98, and Windows NT — is much simpler than in Windows 2000 and later, basically because the earlier Windows operating systems didn't support a great deal of DNS functions. These operating systems were created before dynamic DNS was commonplace, and fewer configuration options were available.

To begin configuring DNS, right-click Network Neighborhood on the desktop and choose Properties. This step opens the Network dialog box. Click the Protocols tab in this dialog box. From the list of protocols, select TCP/IP and click Properties, as shown in Figure 5-8.

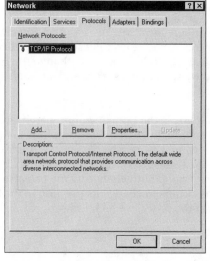

Figure 5-8:
The
Protocols
tab of the
Network
dialog box
is used
to add,
remove,
and
configure
protocols.

In the TCP/IP Properties dialog box, click the DNS tab, as shown in Figure 5-9. You make all DNS configuration changes there. The first two options are Host Name and Domain. The Host Name option is where you configure the host name used with DNS. By default, it's set to the same value as the computer's NetBIOS name. You can change it to any value, though. The Domain setting is used to configure the primary DNS suffix for the system. This suffix is appended to all unqualified names. If your domain is set to `domain.tld`, for example, typing **ping remotehost** causes the computer to ping `remotehost.domain.tld`.

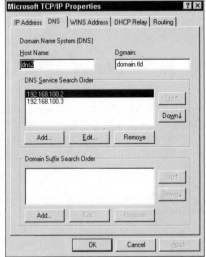

Figure 5-9:
The DNS tab in the TCP/IP Properties dialog box is used to set all DNS settings.

The DNS Service Search Order setting is used to specify DNS servers for the connection. These tools are relatively intuitive. You can add any number of servers by clicking the Add button. Remove existing servers by clicking Remove or change them by clicking Edit. You can also change the order in which the servers are accessed by selecting a server and clicking Up or Down to move it up or down in the list.

The last DNS setting in the dialog box is the Domain Suffix Search Order. You can specify as many as six DNS suffixes to search. These suffixes are used in order when an unqualified name cannot be resolved using the primary DNS suffix. Click the Add button to add a suffix to the list. Select a suffix from the list and click Remove to remove it or click Edit to change it. You can also select a suffix and use the Up and Down buttons to change its position in the list. Suffixes are used for resolution in the order in which they appear on the list.

Penguins Like DNS Too (Linux)

As you may or may not know, a wide variety of different Unix and Unix-type operating systems exist, including Linux, Sun Solaris, HP-UX, IBM AIX, and FreeBSD. By far, the most talked about (in the media, anyway) is the operating system with the penguin mascot: Linux.

The term *Unix-like operating system* refers to an operating system that functionally resembles Unix but isn't based on the original BSD or AT&T UNIX source code. Linux is commonly referred to as Unix-like because it was written completely from scratch and used no original Unix code.

The problem with all these different Unix operating systems is that one of the most visible differences between them lies in their configuration procedures. although most Unix systems have their DNS client settings in the same place, some vary.

Even Linux itself has more than one way to configure the DNS client settings. A number of tools are available, such as `netconf` and `linuxconf`, that provide graphical interfaces to network settings. These tools are sometimes unreliable, for a number of reasons. One common problem with the multiple methods of configuring network settings in Linux is that the same configuration option is set in more than one location, causing one to take precedence. If you make a change to the setting that doesn't take precedence, nothing happens.

The safest way to configure the DNS client settings in Linux is by using the old-fashioned method of editing the configuration file directly. All DNS client settings are stored in a file named `resolv.conf` that is commonly stored in the `/etc/` directory of the Linux installation. This is almost always the case in Linux. You can edit this file using any text editor you prefer — for example, vi or pico.

The text editor vi is installed on almost all versions of Unix, although it's somewhat difficult to use. After you have initially figured out how to use vi, it's much easier. A more simple text editor pico, isn't installed on most systems. You may want to use pico if it's installed.

Open the `resolv.conf` file in your text editor. Figure 5-10 shows a sample `resolv.conf` file. Although this file can contain a variety of configuration information, only a few important settings are shown in the sample file. Here are the three settings (discussed at the beginning of this chapter, in the section "Making the Server Connection"):

- ✔ The DNS servers
- ✔ The domain for the computer
- ✔ The DNS suffix search order

The first line in the `resolv.conf` file typically contains the domain or search keyword. The domain keyword is used to specify the domain suffix for the computer, as shown in the sample `resolv.conf` file. This domain is appended to unqualified domain names automatically. The search keyword is used to specify domains appended to unqualified names except that rather than specify only one domain, you can specify as many as six with a maximum of 256 total characters. The search domains are appended in the order in which they're listed.

Only the domain or search keywords can be used, not both. If both are specified, the last one listed takes precedence.

The `resolv.conf` file should also contain a list of DNS servers. These are specified using the name server keyword followed by the IP address of the server, as shown in the example shown in Figure 5-10. You can specify a number of servers, which are used in the order they're specified. The first server listed is used first, and if it cannot be contacted, the next server in the list is used. A limit exists on the number of servers that can be specified (three, by default).

You can change the maximum number of DNS servers that can be specified only in the source code to the resolver library.

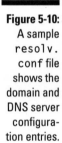

Figure 5-10:
A sample
`resolv.`
`conf` file
shows the
domain and
DNS server
configura-
tion entries.

Chapter 6

Using the DNS Clients on Your System

*F*or most users, the greatest thing about DNS is that it's almost transparent. That is, even though most users perform many daily activities that use DNS, such as browsing the Internet and connecting to network servers, they don't have to concern themselves with what's going on behind the scenes. Anything you can make transparent to users is a big advantage to both them and any network technicians who are supporting them. Although a user may be able to remain blissfully unaware of the processes of a DNS client, the typical network administrator is probably allowed to tinker with the details and the available troubleshooting tools.

Although DNS is almost always used as a transparent part of the Internet infrastructure, you can interact with it explicitly by using command-line and graphical DNS client tools. In many cases, making use of a command-line DNS client for troubleshooting is most practical. In this chapter, we describe the DNS clients on both Windows and Unix operating systems and the configuration details of each one. We also examine a powerful (and, fortunately, easy-to-use) command-line tool, NSLOOKUP. Although the activities of the DNS client are unnoticed by users, the folks in charge of maintaining network hosts need to interact with the DNS servers.

Discovering the Two Types of DNS Clients

Clients versus resolvers: An important differentiation to make when discussing the client side of DNS is that between *clients* and *resolvers*. Clients include any application with which the end user interacts. This includes both integrated clients in applications such as Microsoft Internet Explorer and command-line clients, such as NSLOOKUP. Resolvers, however, work in the background and never interact with users directly. Resolvers provide the back-end infrastructure that DNS clients use to perform DNS tasks. Two types of DNS clients exist, and each type has an important use:

✔ **Integrated clients:** Used all the time by everyone who accesses the Internet, integrated clients allow Internet users to transparently access Web sites and e-mail servers (identified by IP addresses) by knowing only their DNS names. This transparency means that the end user does not need to know DNS exists.

You may or may not realize it, but every computer contains a number of integrated transparent DNS clients. On Windows systems, you can find DNS clients integrated in applications such as Internet Explorer and Microsoft Outlook. In Unix and Linux, you also find integrated DNS clients in Web browsers and mail applications, among others. Most integrated clients are subcomponents of applications that make wide use of network services. This client integration is designed to, in addition to other tasks, speed the DNS resolution process.

✔ **Command-line clients:** Command-line DNS clients serve an important purpose, and most computer users don't even know that these clients exist on almost every system. The most common use for a command-line DNS client is troubleshooting. You can determine exactly how e-mail is routed, for example, by using a command-line DNS client. Command-line DNS clients make it possible to access any DNS database record from any computer. Microsoft Windows includes a command-line DNS client named NSLOOKUP, and Unix usually includes the NSLOOKUP and DIG command-line DNS clients. In addition, other command-line DNS clients you can purchase or download provide additional functionality that you may find useful if you perform lots of DNS troubleshooting.

Looking at Resolvers and What They Do for DNS

Windows and Unix/Linux are similar in that they both use a resolver for DNS. A *resolver,* typically a DLL in Windows and a kernel module in Unix/Linux, is the most basic set of routines used by DNS clients.

The resolver is responsible for performing the DNS resolution process (we describe the DNS request-and-response process in detail in Chapter 3):

1. Receive the request for a name resolution from an application (typically through a procedure call).

2. Format the request in the correct manner for the server to process.

3. Send the request to the name server, which is responsible for doing the majority of the work and returning the response. The name server returns the response to the resolver.

4. Format the response from the name server in a way that's appropriate for the application, and return the formatted response to the application.

Many resolvers have more features than the basic resolver features. The Windows resolver, for example, caches DNS results so that a new request doesn't need to be sent for the same information. *Caching* occurs when DNS results are stored in memory temporarily so that if the same DNS name is requested more than once, the request is served from memory rather than through another name server request. Many resolvers have the caching feature, although it can cause a problem. If an IP address is cached by the resolver and that address changes before the cached information expires, you cannot reach the server. In this case, you need to either wait until the cached information expires or clear the cache.

In older versions of Windows, you can clear the DNS resolver cache by restarting the DNS client service. If you're using Windows 2000 or later, such as Windows XP or Windows .NET Server, you can use the `ipconfig \/flushdns` command (from a command prompt) to empty the DNS resolver cache.

Working with the Windows resolver

Windows 2000 and later (including Windows XP and Windows .NET Server) use the Windows 2000-style resolver by default. The Windows 2000 resolver runs the DNS Client service. This resolver is responsible for a number of tasks:

- ✔ **The caching of DNS responses regardless of a successful or unsuccessful event.** The caching of both successful and unsuccessful queries allows DNS requests from applications to be answered quickly regardless of whether an IP address is returned. The resolver also maintains this cache, removing names and addresses if they change or become invalid.

- ✔ **Tracking network adapter DNS names (including plug-and-play adapters).**

> ✔ **Updating the cache whenever changes are made to the** HOSTS **file.**
>
> ✔ **Managing unresponsive DNS servers.** When DNS servers are unresponsive, the resolver automatically stops querying them for a time, instead using only the functioning servers.

The HOSTS file contains a list of DNS names and IP addresses stored locally on the computer. These names and addresses override those on a DNS server and can also be used when no entry exists for a specific name on a DNS server.

One of the more complex tasks the Windows 2000 resolver performs is to prioritize IP addresses in a query response. Whenever a DNS server contains more than one IP address for a DNS name (known as round robin DNS and described in Chapter 12), the normal behavior is for the DNS server to send all addresses in a list with the address of its choice first in the list. By default, most systems use the first address on the list. The Windows 2000 resolver, however, attempts to request all IP addresses associated with the name in a priority sequence. The server then returns any address that is local to the system (on a connected subnet) first and then defaults to the first address in the list if none is local. This behavior causes round robin behavior to fail, but is in place so that Microsoft-based systems always access local systems before they access remote systems. You can disable this behavior in the Registry.

One more thing the resolver does is time-out in case of a network failure. If no responses are received from any DNS servers, the resolver assumes that a network connection failure has occurred and stops all communications for a length of time — 30 seconds, by default. This behavior is in place so that the resolver doesn't flood a failed network with requests. You can disable this behavior.

Changing the behavior of the Windows resolver

You can change the Windows resolver behavior in a number of ways. Here's the most drastic method of disabling the DNS Client service:

1. In Windows 2000, Windows XP, or Windows .NET Server, open the Services snap-in by choosing Programs➪Administrative Tools from the Start menu.

2. Select the DNS Client service, as shown in Figure 6-1.

Starting and stopping a service is simple. As you can see in the figure, the DNS Client service is started, which is the default. You can click Stop the Service, and the service stops.

After the DNS Client service is stopped, the system reverts to the Windows NT-style resolver. This basic resolver doesn't do any caching or request manipulation. It simply accepts requests from applications, forwards them to DNS servers, and returns the results to the application.

When you stop the service, as you may already know, it restarts the next time you start Windows. You must set the Startup Type to Manual or Disabled in order for the service not to start automatically. There's a difference between the Manual and Disabled options, however. When the startup type is set to Manual, the service starts if an application requests the service. When the Disabled option is set, the service never starts.

To set the startup type:

1. **Right-click the DNS Client service and choose Properties.**

   The service Properties dialog box opens, as shown in Figure 6-2.

2. **Set the startup type to Manual or Disabled from the drop-down box.**

3. **Click OK to save the changes.**

In addition to stopping the new style resolver, you can change certain resolver properties through the Windows Registry. For more information about this complex task, check Microsoft TechNet, at www.microsoft.com/technet.

Finding the Integrated DNS Clients in Windows

Windows contains a number of integrated DNS clients in addition to a command-line DNS client, NSLOOKUP, which is covered in the next section. Integrated clients are in applications such as Internet Explorer and Outlook and serve to resolve DNS names to IP addresses for the application.

The integrated DNS client you're likely to use most often is built into Internet Explorer. Internet Explorer has an integrated DNS client that uses the Windows resolver. The DNS Client service is used, as described in the preceding section, unless it's not running, and then the basic resolver is used.

Figure 6-3 shows an example of the Internet Explorer DNS client. We typed the Web address www.google.com on the Address bar, and Internet Explorer automatically resolved the name to an IP address and retrieved the Web page. If the page has links to off-site content, Internet Explorer may resolve a number of DNS names.

Outlook is another example of an application with an integrated DNS client. Although Outlook doesn't process any e-mail itself, it must still send and retrieve e-mail to and from the mail servers. When you're configuring your e-mail accounts, you can simply enter the DNS names of the outgoing and incoming mail servers, and Outlook resolves those names to addresses every time you send or receive e-mail.

Figure 6-3:
Internet
Explorer
has an
integrated
DNS client.

If the DNS Client service is started (as it is by default), the responses to Outlook's request for the IP address are served from the resolver cache rather than from the DNS servers as long as the cached entry is valid. For example, if the cached entry is valid for one hour and you check your e-mail once per minute, only one request to the DNS server is made each hour; the other 59 requests are served from the cache. Without caching, the DNS server would have to answer 60 requests for the same information every hour.

Using the Command-Line Client (NSLOOKUP) in Windows

NSLOOKUP is used in Windows from the command line. The simplest way to begin using NSLOOKUP is to open a command-line window. From Windows 2000 and later, click the Start button and choose Programs⇨ Accessories⇨Command Prompt. The command prompt window is shown in Figure 6-4.

Before you begin using NSLOOKUP, you should have DNS servers configured, as discussed in Chapter 4.

Figure 6-4:
Using the
Windows
command
prompt to
access
NSLOOKUP.

NSLOOKUP has two modes: batch and interactive. Batch mode is the simplest to use, and we cover it first, in the following section. Typically, the NSLOOKUP batch mode is used to find A records. *A records* are the primary DNS records for a domain name. They're used to associate server IP addresses with DNS names. They're not used for special purposes, such as e-mail. When you access a Web site, such as www.google.com, you're accessing the IP address listed in the A record for that DNS name. We describe record types in detail in Chapter 9.

Using NSLOOKUP in batch mode

To use NSLOOKUP in batch mode, simply type **NSLOOKUP** *domainname* at the command prompt, where *domainname* is the DNS name you want to look up (see Figure 6-5 for an example). NSLOOKUP is being used to retrieve the A record for the domain name www.google.com. The record is retrieved from the DNS server configured in the computer's network settings and returned.

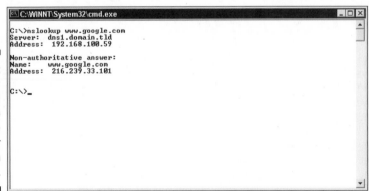

Figure 6-5:
NSLOOKUP
is being
used to
retrieve the
A record for
a domain
name.

Try it yourself. Use NSLOOKUP to find the IP address for a Web site, and then type that IP address on the Address bar of Internet Explorer and press Enter. The Web site should load as though you had typed the DNS name of the site.

This technique is the most basic way to use NSLOOKUP in batch mode. You can do much more with NSLOOKUP in batch mode, but doing more complex work in interactive mode of NSLOOKUP is much easier.

In batch mode, nslookup uses the same commands as in interactive mode (explained in the next section). You can see a list of the nslookup commands by first starting nslookup in interactive mode: Type **nslookup** at the command prompt. From the nslookup prompt (>), press ? and press Enter.

To use these commands, simply specify them as options on the command line in the format nslookup *<options> <domain> <server>*. The *<server>* option specifies the DNS server that will be queried. If omitted, the DNS servers configured on the system are used in their specified order. To see the MX records for a domain, for example, you use the command **nslookup -type=mx dummies. com**. It queries the default DNS server for the MX records for dummies.com.

Not all the interactive mode nslookup commands can be used in batch mode. The set command, for example, is invalid because it is used to set the parameters with which nslookup runs in interactive mode.

Using NSLOOKUP in interactive mode

To start NSLOOKUP in interactive mode, type **NSLOOKUP** at the command prompt. NSLOOKUP starts, as shown in Figure 6-6.

Figure 6-6:
NSLOOKUP
is now
running in
interactive
mode.

The basic prompt in NSLOOKUP interactive mode is >. All commands are typed at this prompt. By default, NSLOOKUP is configured to search for A (host) records. As in the earlier batch mode example in the preceding section, you can retrieve the A record for a DNS name. Type the DNS name for which to retrieve the record at the NSLOOKUP prompt and press Enter. The record is retrieved, as shown in Figure 6-7.

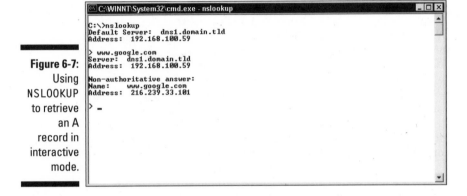

Figure 6-7: Using NSLOOKUP to retrieve an A record in interactive mode.

The advantage to using NSLOOKUP in interactive mode is that you can change its behavior by changing parameters. These settings are *modal:* They stay set as long as NSLOOKUP is running or until they're changed again. One of the most basic configuration changes you can make in NSLOOKUP is to the DNS server that is queried. You can change your DNS server to something different by typing **SERVER <*servername*>** and pressing Enter at the NSLOOKUP prompt, as shown in Figure 6-8. DNS requests are now sent to this server rather than to the default. This technique is useful for determining whether different DNS servers are maintaining different addresses for a domain or whether to use another server if the default server is unavailable.

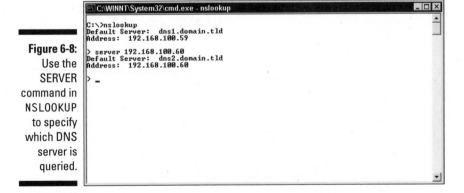

Figure 6-8: Use the SERVER command in NSLOOKUP to specify which DNS server is queried.

The only record type you have retrieved in this section has been an A record. What if you want to retrieve another type of record, such as an MX (mail exchanger) record to find the name and IP address of the server providing e-mail services for a given domain? Use the SET TYPE command to specify which record type to retrieve. Type **SET TYPE=<*record type*>** and press Enter at the NSLOOKUP prompt. The record type can be any of the standard DNS records, such as A or MX, or it can be ANY, which retrieves any record. After you set the record type to retrieve, you can enter a domain name at the NSLOOKUP prompt and the specified record type is retrieved, as shown in Figure 6-9.

Figure 6-9:
Use the
SET TYPE
command
to set the
record type
to retrieve
to the MX.

```
C:\WINNT\System32\cmd.exe - nslookup                              _ □ ×

C:\>nslookup
Default Server:  dns1.domain.tld
Address:  192.168.100.59

> set type=mx
> google.com
Server:  dns1.domain.tld
Address:  192.168.100.59

Non-authoritative answer:
google.com       MX preference = 20, mail exchanger = smtp2.google.com
google.com       MX preference = 40, mail exchanger = smtp3.google.com
google.com       MX preference = 10, mail exchanger = smtp1.google.com

google.com       nameserver = ns1.google.com
google.com       nameserver = ns2.google.com
google.com       nameserver = ns4.google.com
smtp1.google.com         internet address = 216.239.33.25
smtp2.google.com         internet address = 216.239.37.25
smtp3.google.com         internet address = 216.239.33.26
> _
```

The SERVER and SET TYPE commands are the most commonly used in NSLOOKUP; however, you can use many more. To see a list of all NSLOOKUP commands, type ? and press Enter at the NSLOOKUP prompt. Figure 6-10 shows the NSLOOKUP help information. Most of these commands are rarely used.

One command in NSLOOKUP looks promising: the LS command. By typing **LS <*domain*>**, you can retrieve a list of all records in the domain. This feature must be useful because you can see all the hosts in a domain if you don't know the exact host you're looking for. Alas, it's too good to be true. Almost every DNS server in existence is configured *not* to allow you to list all records in the domain. The problem with the LS command is that it can lead to security problems.

If a malicious user wants to attack your domain, he first needs to know which hosts to attack. Without knowing which systems are on your network, he cannot attack any of them. The LS command in NSLOOKUP provides with an excellent way to see which computers are on the network. For that reason, most servers don't allow a listing of records.

```
C:\WINNT\System32\cmd.exe - nslookup                                    _ □ ×
> ?
Commands:    (identifiers are shown in uppercase, [] means optional)
NAME            - print info about the host/domain NAME using default server
NAME1 NAME2     - as above, but use NAME2 as server
help or ?       - print info on common commands
set OPTION      - set an option
    all                 - print options, current server and host
    [no]debug           - print debugging information
    [no]d2              - print exhaustive debugging information
    [no]defname         - append domain name to each query
    [no]recurse         - ask for recursive answer to query
    [no]search          - use domain search list
    [no]vc              - always use a virtual circuit
    domain=NAME         - set default domain name to NAME
    srchlist=N1[/N2/.../N6] - set domain to N1 and search list to N1,N2, etc.
    root=NAME           - set root server to NAME
    retry=X             - set number of retries to X
    timeout=X           - set initial time-out interval to X seconds
    type=X              - set query type (ex. A,ANY,CNAME,MX,NS,PTR,SOA,SRV)
    querytype=X         - same as type
    class=X             - set query class (ex. IN (Internet), ANY)
    [no]msxfr           - use MS fast zone transfer
    ixfrver=X           - current version to use in IXFR transfer request
server NAME     - set default server to NAME, using current default server
lserver NAME    - set default server to NAME, using initial server
finger [USER]   - finger the optional NAME at the current default host
root            - set current default server to the root
ls [opt] DOMAIN [> FILE] - list addresses in DOMAIN (optional: output to FILE)
    -a              - list canonical names and aliases
    -d              - list all records
    -t TYPE         - list records of the given type (e.g. A,CNAME,MX,NS,PTR etc.)
view FILE           - sort an 'ls' output file and view it with pg
exit            - exit the program
> _
```

Figure 6-10:
Typing a
question
mark (?)
at the
NSLOOKUP
prompt
displays
the list of
available
commands.

This type of security vulnerability is known as an *information leak* vulnerability because information about your private network is leaked to the outside world.

To exit from NSLOOKUP, type **EXIT** and press Enter at the NSLOOKUP prompt.

Finding the DNS Clients in Unix/Linux

Most versions of Unix/Linux include a resolver integrated into the TCP/IP protocols. This resolver is available for use by any piece of software. Integration between applications and the resolver in Unix/Linux works somewhat differently from how it works in Windows, though: Rather than interact with the resolver through procedure calls, the resolver is usually compiled into the applications that require it.

Figure 6-11 shows Netscape running under Linux. As you can see, the Web browser has resolved the DNS name www.google.com. This example shows an integrated DNS client.

Unix/Linux also has command-line-based DNS clients. Most Unix/Linux systems have a DNS client named NSLOOKUP, similar to NSLOOKUP in Windows. You can use NSLOOKUP, which is fairly flexible, to find any type of DNS record.

The second most common DNS client in Unix/Linux is DIG. With the introduction of BIND Version 9 (see Chapter 8), NSLOOKUP is obsolete. It still works, but it's no longer the preferred client. DIG, which has been around for a while, has been introduced as a replacement. DIG is replacing NSLOOKUP because NSLOOKUP lacks sufficient support for IPv6 and NSLOOKUP fails if reverse name resolution fails.

DIG is similar to NSLOOKUP and can retrieve any DNS information. One advantage to DIG is that it requests only the information you specify; NSLOOKUP has a habit of requesting spurious information.

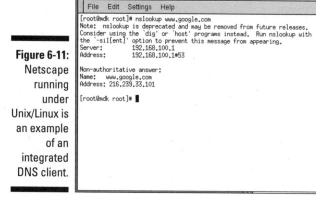

Figure 6-11:
Netscape
running
under
Unix/Linux is
an example
of an
integrated
DNS client.

Using Command-Line Clients with Unix/Linux

Almost all versions of Unix/Linux contain NSLOOKUP out of the box. NSLOOKUP is the most widely included DNS client on all systems. Your Unix/Linux system may or may not include DIG. If your system doesn't include DIG, it can be downloaded as a package or as source code and is also included in BIND 9. Like their Windows-compatible counterparts, these resolvers are designed to provide interactive access to DNS information.

Using NSLOOKUP

NSLOOKUP should be available on almost all systems. In Linux, it's most commonly located in /usr/bin.

On some Unix/Linux systems, you may need to have root privileges to use NSLOOKUP, and it may be in the /usr/sbin directory.

Even though NSLOOKUP is being phased out in favor of DIG on many systems, it's still widely used. NSLOOKUP under Unix/Linux is similar to the Windows version in that it has two modes: interactive and non-interactive (batch).

Using NSLOOKUP in Unix/Linux in batch mode

The simplest way to use NSLOOKUP is in batch mode to retrieve an A record from a DNS server: Type **NSLOOKUP <*DNS name*>** at the command prompt, as shown in Figure 6-12.

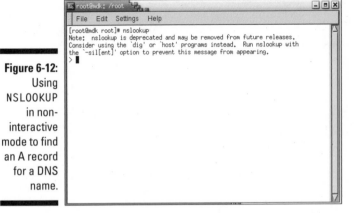

Figure 6-12: Using NSLOOKUP in non-interactive mode to find an A record for a DNS name.

Using NSLOOKUP in Unix/Linux in interactive mode

To get full use of NSLOOKUP, run it in interactive mode. To start NSLOOKUP in interactive mode, type **NSLOOKUP** at the command prompt. Figure 6-13 shows NSLOOKUP running in interactive mode.

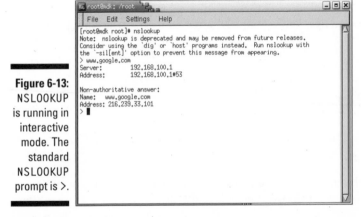

Figure 6-13: NSLOOKUP is running in interactive mode. The standard NSLOOKUP prompt is >.

From the main NSLOOKUP prompt, you can type a DNS name and press Enter to retrieve the A record for that name. Figure 6-14 shows an example of retrieving an A record. By default, NSLOOKUP retrieves an A record from the first configured DNS server.

Figure 6-14:
Using
NSLOOKUP in
interactive
mode to
retrieve an
A record
from the
primary
DNS server.

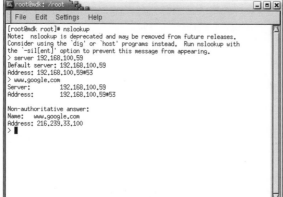

NSLOOKUP has many more functions than simply retrieving A records from the default DNS server, though. NSLOOKUP has many settings you can use to retrieve almost any information from a DNS server. In some versions of NSLOOKUP under Unix/Linux, you can type **?** and press Enter to see a complete listing of available options. Some versions of NSLOOKUP don't implement the help feature, though, and you can type **man nslookup** from the command prompt to view the NSLOOKUP man page.

You're most likely to use two major commands in NSLOOKUP:

✔ SERVER: Specifies which DNS server is queried by NSLOOKUP. By default, the DNS servers configured in your resolv.conf file are used in order. Using the SERVER command, you can set a different server to be used, which is useful if none of the servers in the resolv.conf file is available or if you want to check a record on another server. You may need to check a record on another server if you suspect that your DNS servers aren't updating properly. Using the SERVER command is simple: Type **SERVER <*servername*>**, where *servername* is the name or IP address of the DNS server you want to use. Figure 6-15 shows the DNS server being changed and a record being retrieved from the new server.

✔ SET TYPE: Specifies which DNS records are retrieved from the server. By default, NSLOOKUP retrieves A records from a DNS server. Often, you need to retrieve a record other than an A record, such as a mail exchanger (MX) record for e-mail or a pointer (PTR) record for reverse DNS lookups. To change the type of record that's retrieved, type **SET TYPE=<*recordtype*>**; recordtype can be any type of record, such as A,

PTR, MX, or a special type, ANY, which retrieves any record from the server. Figure 6-16 shows the record type being changed to MX and the MX record for a domain being retrieved.

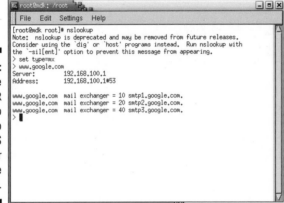

Figure 6-15: Use the SERVER command to change to which DNS server requests are sent.

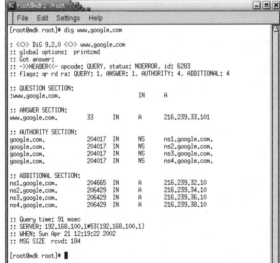

Figure 6-16: Use the SET TYPE command to configure which record type is retrieved from the DNS server.

Using DIG

DIG is another command-line DNS client that traditionally hasn't been included with most Unix/Linux systems. In the newer versions of BIND, however, many newer Linux distributions are including DIG and deprecating

NSLOOKUP. DIG is different from NSLOOKUP in that it has only a non-interactive mode, but, as with NSLOOKUP, you can use it to retrieve any information from the database of a DNS server.

The most basic use of DIG is to retrieve an A record. From the command prompt, simply type **DIG *<domainname>***, where *domainname* is the DNS name for which you want to retrieve information. Figure 6-17 shows DIG used to retrieve an A record. One of the main differences between DIG and NSLOOKUP is the amount of information displayed with the query results. NSLOOKUP shows only the information requested, but DIG shows all information returned from the DNS server.

Figure 6-17: DIG retrieves an A record when no command-line options are specified.

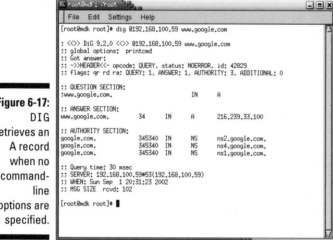

```
root@mdk : /root
 File  Edit  Settings  Help
[root@mdk root]# dig @192.168.100.59 www.google.com

; <<>> DiG 9.2.0 <<>> @192.168.100.59 www.google.com
;; global options:  printcmd
;; Got answer:
;; ->>HEADER<<- opcode: QUERY, status: NOERROR, id: 42829
;; flags: qr rd ra; QUERY: 1, ANSWER: 1, AUTHORITY: 3, ADDITIONAL: 0

;; QUESTION SECTION:
;www.google.com.                 IN      A

;; ANSWER SECTION:
www.google.com.         34      IN      A       216.239.33.100

;; AUTHORITY SECTION:
google.com.             345340  IN      NS      ns2.google.com.
google.com.             345340  IN      NS      ns4.google.com.
google.com.             345340  IN      NS      ns1.google.com.

;; Query time: 30 msec
;; SERVER: 192.168.100.59#53(192.168.100.59)
;; WHEN: Sun Sep  1 20:31:23 2002
;; MSG SIZE  rcvd: 102

[root@mdk root]# 
```

If you look at the results from DIG, you can see the transcript of the DNS request. In the Question section, the request for the A record is passed to the DNS server. which was for the A record for www.google.com. The Answer section contains the explicit answer to the request. This answer is the actual A record. The next section, Authority, has a list of the DNS server names that are authoritative for the DNS name in the request. Finally, the Additional section shows the IP addresses for the authoritative DNS servers. A few more pieces of information are in the DIG results, including the amount of time the query took, the DNS server that responded, a timestamp, the response message size, and the message header, including status message and flags.

DIG is also capable of requesting information from a DNS server that isn't the default server for the computer. To request the information from a different server, type **DIG @*<dnsserver>* *<domainname>***, where *dnsserver* is the server you want to use and *domainname* is the DNS name for which you want to retrieve the information. Figure 6-18 shows DIG being used to query a DNS server that isn't in the resolv.conf file for the system.

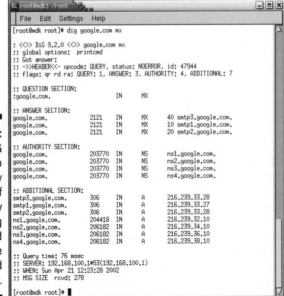

```
root@mdk: /root
 File  Edit  Settings  Help
[root@mdk root]# dig google.com mx

; <<>> DiG 9.2.0 <<>> google.com mx
;; global options:  printcmd
;; Got answer:
;; ->>HEADER<<- opcode: QUERY, status: NOERROR, id: 47944
;; flags: qr rd ra; QUERY: 1, ANSWER: 3, AUTHORITY: 4, ADDITIONAL: 7

;; QUESTION SECTION:
;google.com.                    IN      MX

;; ANSWER SECTION:
google.com.             2121    IN      MX      40 smtp3.google.com.
google.com.             2121    IN      MX      10 smtp1.google.com.
google.com.             2121    IN      MX      20 smtp2.google.com.

;; AUTHORITY SECTION:
google.com.             203770  IN      NS      ns1.google.com.
google.com.             203770  IN      NS      ns2.google.com.
google.com.             203770  IN      NS      ns3.google.com.
google.com.             203770  IN      NS      ns4.google.com.

;; ADDITIONAL SECTION:
smtp3.google.com.       306     IN      A       216.239.33.28
smtp1.google.com.       306     IN      A       216.239.33.27
smtp2.google.com.       306     IN      A       216.239.33.28
ns1.google.com.         204418  IN      A       216.239.32.10
ns2.google.com.         206182  IN      A       216.239.34.10
ns3.google.com.         206182  IN      A       216.239.36.10
ns4.google.com.         206182  IN      A       216.239.38.10

;; Query time: 76 msec
;; SERVER: 192.168.100.1#53(192.168.100.1)
;; WHEN: Sun Apr 21 12:23:28 2002
;; MSG SIZE  rcvd: 278

[root@mdk root]#
```

Figure 6-18:
Use DIG to query any DNS server using the @ command-line option.

Again, as with NSLOOKUP (refer to the preceding section), you can use DIG to retrieve any record type from a DNS server. You type **DIG <*domainname*> <*recordtype*>**, where recordtype is any of the available records, such as A, MX, or PTR. Figure 6-19 shows DIG being used to retrieve an MX record.

```
root@mdk: /root
 File  Edit  Settings  Help
[root@mdk root]# dig google.com mx

; <<>> DiG 9.2.0 <<>> google.com mx
;; global options:  printcmd
;; Got answer:
;; ->>HEADER<<- opcode: QUERY, status: NOERROR, id: 47944
;; flags: qr rd ra; QUERY: 1, ANSWER: 3, AUTHORITY: 4, ADDITIONAL: 7

;; QUESTION SECTION:
;google.com.                    IN      MX

;; ANSWER SECTION:
google.com.             2121    IN      MX      40 smtp3.google.com.
google.com.             2121    IN      MX      10 smtp1.google.com.
google.com.             2121    IN      MX      20 smtp2.google.com.

;; AUTHORITY SECTION:
google.com.             203770  IN      NS      ns1.google.com.
google.com.             203770  IN      NS      ns2.google.com.
google.com.             203770  IN      NS      ns3.google.com.
google.com.             203770  IN      NS      ns4.google.com.

;; ADDITIONAL SECTION:
smtp3.google.com.       306     IN      A       216.239.33.28
smtp1.google.com.       306     IN      A       216.239.33.27
smtp2.google.com.       306     IN      A       216.239.33.28
ns1.google.com.         204418  IN      A       216.239.32.10
ns2.google.com.         206182  IN      A       216.239.34.10
ns3.google.com.         206182  IN      A       216.239.36.10
ns4.google.com.         206182  IN      A       216.239.38.10

;; Query time: 76 msec
;; SERVER: 192.168.100.1#53(192.168.100.1)
;; WHEN: Sun Apr 21 12:23:28 2002
;; MSG SIZE  rcvd: 278

[root@mdk root]#
```

Figure 6-19:
Use the DIG command to retrieve any type of record by specifying the record type on the command line.

WHOIS

Every domain registered on the Internet is registered to a person or organization. You have to have a way to see exactly who has registered a name: Use WHOIS. The WHOIS utility is a DNS-related client, although it isn't used to retrieve DNS records in the traditional sense. NSLOOKUP and DIG are used to query a DNS server and retrieve records from its database. WHOIS, on the other hand, is used to query a WHOIS server for information about a specific domain name.

WHOIS is used to determine who has registered a domain name, such as domain.com. The issue with WHOIS is that you need to query the correct server to get the information you need. For example, you can query the VeriSign/Network Solutions WHOIS servers for .com, .net, and .org domains, but you must use a different server for other domains, such as .ca or .uk.

WHOIS in Windows

Windows doesn't include a WHOIS client by default. Some Windows WHOIS clients are available, but they're not common. Rather than use an actual WHOIS client, many people use Web-based WHOIS services. The most common is on the VeriSign/Network Solutions Web site, at www.netsol.com/cgi-bin/whois/whois, as shown in Figure 6-20.

Figure 6-20: The Network Solutions/ VeriSign online WHOIS tool.

Using the WHOIS tool is simple: Enter in the box the domain for which you want to look up information in the box and click the Go button. Figure 6-21 shows the WHOIS results from the Web tool. As you can see, all the information about the domain is shown. The information includes administrative and technical contacts, the registrar for the domain under zone contact, and the DNS servers associated with the domain. In addition, you see the dates for when the domain was registered and when it's up for renewal.

WHOIS in Unix

Most versions of Unix have a WHOIS utility. If your version of Unix or Linux doesn't include WHOIS or it wasn't installed during the installation process, you can install it by locating the appropriate package or locating a source code version (see www.linux.it/~md/software/) and compiling. Many of these versions have different feature sets, but the one most often included with Linux is an enhanced version with a full feature set. You can see a list of all options for the WHOIS client by typing **WHOIS** at the shell prompt, as shown in Figure 6-22. A list of all the WHOIS options are displayed.

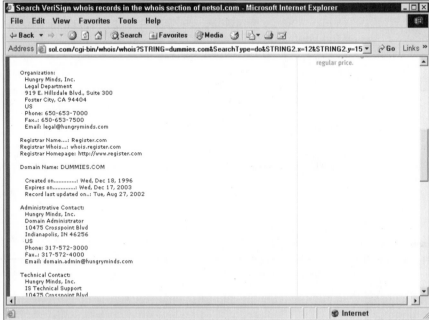

Figure 6-21: The results of a WHOIS query show who has registered a domain.

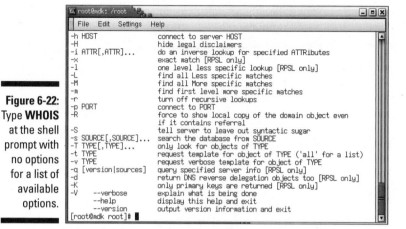

Figure 6-22:
Type **WHOIS**
at the shell
prompt with
no options
for a list of
available
options.

Although many options are available for WHOIS, it's simple to use. The
enhanced WHOIS included with newer versions of Linux determines which
WHOIS server to use automatically. Using WHOIS under Linux is simple: Type
WHOIS <*domain*>. The results are displayed, as shown in Figure 6-23.

The Linux WHOIS client output is the same as what's displayed when you use
the Web-based WHOIS tool because they're querying the same database.

Figure 6-23:
The output
of the
WHOIS
client.

Part III
Working with DNS Servers

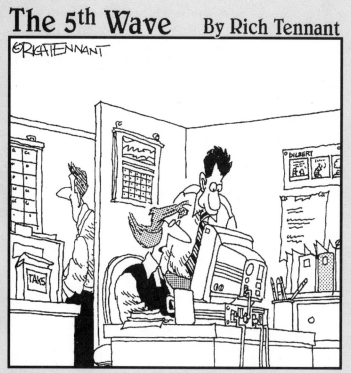

The 5th Wave   By Rich Tennant

"OK, I've got this DNS thing down. Like here, my report on inventory management will include a video clip from www.rottingmeat.com."

In this part . . .

If you're working on a relatively large network or at an Internet Service Provider, you may already have DNS servers in place. In that case, Part III is not for you. This part of the book covers the installation and configuration of the two major DNS servers now in use: the Microsoft Windows DNS Server and BIND on Unix systems.

For a number of reasons, you may want to run your own DNS server. The advantages are obvious in a corporate setting because you can control the system and monitor its performance. In fact, some people even run their own DNS servers at home on their DSL or cable broadband connections because they can get better performance than they can when using their ISP's heavily loaded servers.

Chapter 7

Installing a Microsoft DNS Server

· ·

· ·

*T*his chapter takes you on a tour through the process of installing and configuring a DNS server on Microsoft Windows server operating systems. The DNS server component is packaged with virtually all server operating systems produced by Microsoft. Because these server operating systems are widely used, you may, if you're given the task of configuring DNS, need to work with a Microsoft DNS server at some point. One plus to this situation is that the process for configuring a DNS server is easier on a Windows platform than it is on Unix operating systems. (We describe the Unix DNS servers in Chapter 8.) Keep in mind that many DNS servers are run on Unix because of its reputation for stability and scalability. Regardless, many DNS servers are running on Windows operating systems because of its ease of use. Also, DNS servers providing services to Microsoft clients in a LAN environment are often better served with a Microsoft DNS server.

Providing DNS Services with Windows 2000 or Windows .NET Server

Installing the DNS Server service is fairly simple. You can decide to install it at one of two points: during the initial installation of the operating system or, in the most common scenario, after Windows has been installed. Follow these steps to install the service after the operating system installation has occurred (you must have administrator-level access to the system to perform this procedure):

1. **Double-click the Add/Remove Programs icon in the Control Panel to open the Add/Remove Programs dialog box, as shown in Figure 7-1.**

   You use this dialog box to add programs to, and remove them from, the system.

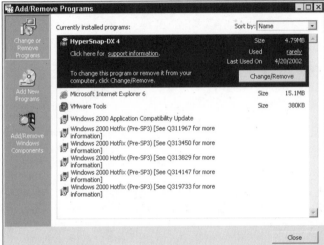

Figure 7-1:
Using the Add/Remove Programs dialog box to install programs and remove them from the system.

2. **Click the Add/Remove Windows Components icon to open the Windows Components Wizard. Scroll down the list and select Networking Services, as shown in Figure 7-2, but don't click to select the check box.**

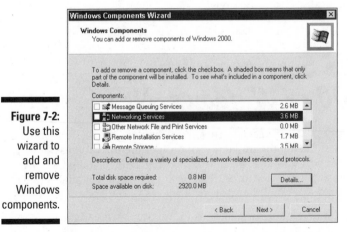

Figure 7-2:
Use this wizard to add and remove Windows components.

3. **In the Windows Components Wizard, select Network Services (without selecting the check box) and click the Details button to open the Networking Services dialog box.**

4. **Select the Domain Name System (DNS) check box, as shown in Figure 7-3, and then click OK.**

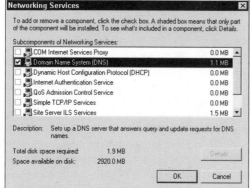

Figure 7-3:
Select
Domain
Name
System
(DNS) and
click OK.

5. **Click Next in the Windows Components Wizard to begin the installation of DNS.**

   You're prompted for your Windows CD. The installation proceeds, and you see a notification dialog box when it's complete.

6. **Click Finish to close that dialog box and click Close to close the Add/Remove Programs dialog box.**

After you complete the preceding steps, it's time to reapply any service packs that have been applied to the system. If Service Pack 2 has been installed on your system, for example, you should reinstall it to apply any service pack updates to the DNS Server service. This issue isn't critical with newer operating systems (the .NET Server family). If one of the earlier versions of Windows is in use, this step can be quite important because the service packs update only the services that are installed when the service pack is executed.

Making DNS Come Alive with Active Directory

A full discussion of the integration of Active Directory (AD) and DNS is beyond the scope of this book; however, you should be sure that you understand a few important concepts. A number of advanced Active Directory and Windows 2000 Server books cover this subject, in addition to related technical white-papers at the Microsoft server home page:

```
www.microsoft.com/windows2000/server/
```

Also, Active Directory integrates automatically with DNS, and no manual configuration is required. Active Directory cannot be used, in fact, unless a DNS server is installed. It's worthwhile, therefore, to follow along with our overview of how DNS plays a role in Active Directory.

In the past (Windows NT 4.0 and earlier versions), computers on the same local network could talk to each other using computer names following the NetBIOS (Network Basic Input Output System) protocol. Other computers could be contacted by using the \\computername syntax. NetBIOS could not be used reliably to support a network with multiple segments, so for larger networks another solution was needed. If the network spanned multiple network segments, a number of Windows Internet Naming Service (WINS) servers had to be implemented to share the computer names across the networks. Network hosts would make queries to the WINS server to find the IP address of a host, thus allowing communications across multiple network segments (across a router). However, WINS has a notoriously bad reputation among system administrators, having earned the reputation of being only sporadically reliable and poorly suited to handling large numbers of client systems (poor scalability).

With the introduction of Windows 2000 Server, the traditional domain controller model from Windows NT 4.0 and earlier was eliminated in favor of Active Directory. The *Active Directory* directory service maintains a database of all users, computers, and groups on the network. Domain controllers in the Windows NT model were replaced with Active Directory servers in the Windows 2000 model, and reliance on the NetBIOS protocol was all but eliminated, although it's still supported.

Because NetBIOS has been phased out for the most part, WINS is no longer useful as a naming service for computers on the local network. Instead, the Windows DNS service is used in its place. The Windows DNS service in Windows 2000, and in all the subsequent operating systems, uses a dynamic DNS server. A workstation, therefore, can automatically register its name and IP address in the DNS database just as Windows NT 4.0-based systems registered their NetBIOS names in WINS. Windows 2000 and newer systems are automatically configured to dynamically register in DNS, so as soon as the system is connected to the network, it can be accessed using its name.

In addition to maintaining the database of computer names, the DNS service maintains a list of available services, such as domain controllers and global resource catalogs. These services are maintained in DNS using service locator (SRV) records. (We discuss these and other record types in Chapter 9.) Keep in mind that these records are used by clients looking for a particular service. The client looks in the DNS database for a service and is pointed to the appropriate server by the SRV record.

The Microsoft dynamic DNS service provides the complete naming infrastructure for an Active Directory-based network. You should note, however, that other dynamic DNS servers, such as BIND 9 running on Unix, have been used successfully in Active Directory. The Microsoft TechNet article "Configuring Berkeley Internet Name Domain (BIND) to Support Active Directory" outlines this process. You can find the article at

```
www.microsoft.com/technet/treeview/default.asp?url=/
            technet/prodtechnol/iis/deploy/depovg/CfgBIND.asp
```

(See Chapter 8 for more information about DNS on Unix.)

Installing a DNS Server on Windows NT 4.0

DNS on Windows NT 4.0 is used only for pure DNS services and must be manually updated. It doesn't integrate into the domain controller infrastructure and doesn't support dynamic updates.

Installing the DNS service on Windows NT is similar to the process on Windows 2000. You must be logged in to the system as a user with administrative privileges.

To install the service:

1. **Right-click Network Neighborhood on the desktop and choose Properties from the context menu that appears.**

2. **Click the Services tab, as shown in Figure 7-4.**

3. **Click the Add button to open the Select Network Service dialog box.**

   You use this dialog box to add new services to the system.

4. **Select Microsoft DNS Server, as shown in Figure 7-5, and click OK.**

   You need to provide the Windows NT distribution media.

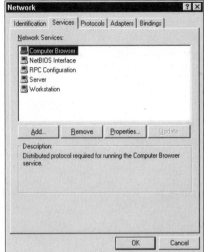

Figure 7-4:
Adding,
removing,
and con-
figuring
network
services on
the system.

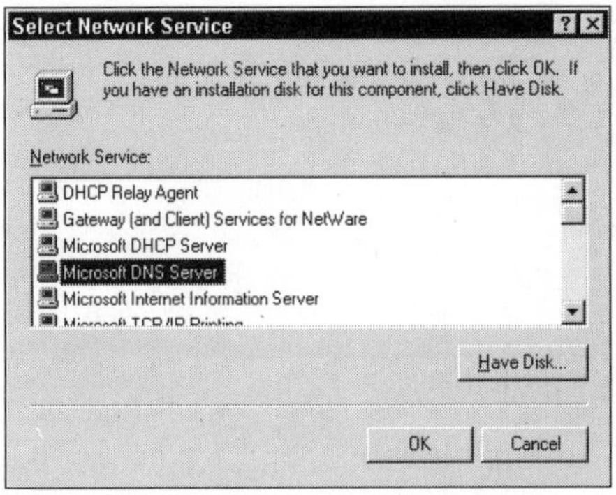

Figure 7-5:
Selecting the
Microsoft
DNS Server
service.

5. **Insert the CD, make sure that the path shown in the dialog box points to the correct location (*x*:\I386, where *x*: is your CD-ROM drive), and click Continue.**

   An entry for the Microsoft DNS Server service appears on the Network Services list, as shown in Figure 7-6.

6. **Click the Close button to close the Network dialog box.**

   The configuration changes will be are applied, and you're prompted to reboot the system. After the system has rebooted, the DNS Server service will be is functional.

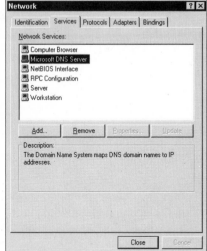

Figure 7-6:
After the
DNS Server
service
has been
installed, it
appears on
the list of
network
services.

Be sure to reapply any service packs that have been applied to the system. If your system has Service Pack 6a installed, for example, you should reinstall it to apply any service pack updates to the DNS Server service.

Getting Under the Hood: DNS Service Configuration

The procedure for configuring the DNS Server service varies between the different Windows operating systems. In Windows 2000, the DNS Microsoft Management Console (MMC) snap-in is used, and in Windows NT 4.0, the DNS Manager utility is used.

Working with Windows 2000 and Windows .NET Server

In Windows 2000 Server and Windows .NET Server, you configure DNS through the DNS MMC snap-in. Open the DNS snap-in, as shown in Figure 7-7, by choosing Programs⇨Administrative Tools from the Start menu.

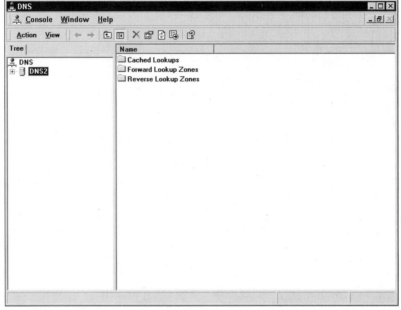

Configuring the server using the Configure DNS Server Wizard

The first thing you notice is that the server is listed in the tree in the left pane of the DNS snap-in. Click the plus icon next to the server name to expand that portion of the tree. The right pane indicates that you need to configure the server:

1. **Choose Action⇨Configure the server.**

   This step launches the Configure DNS Server Wizard. Click Next to proceed past the introductory dialog box.

   You can run the Configure DNS Server Wizard only once to do the initial DNS server setup.

   The first step in the Configure DNS Server Wizard is shown in Figure 7-8.

2. **You can choose to create a new zone, which becomes the first zone on the server.**

   If you choose not to create a new zone, the Configure DNS Server Wizard skips to the last step. You can then click Finish to complete the wizard. For more information about zones, see the section in Chapter 9 about understanding DNS zones.

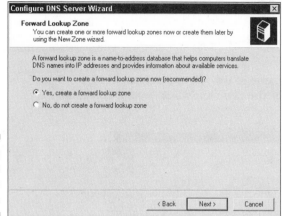

Figure 7-8:
Creating the
first zone on
the server.

3. **If you choose to configure a zone through the Configure DNS Server Wizard, select Yes, create a forward lookup zone and click Next.**

    Now you have to decide whether the zone is a primary or secondary zone, as shown in Figure 7-9. Note that the Active Directory-integrated option is available only if Active Directory is installed.

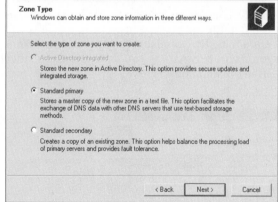

Figure 7-9:
If you
decide to
add a zone,
you must
choose
whether it's
primary or
secondary.

In newer versions of the BIND DNS server, a primary zone is referred to as a *master,* and a secondary zone is referred to as a *slave.* The terms are interchangeable. (We describe primary and secondary, or master and slave, zones in Chapter 3.)

Essentially, a primary zone contains the zone records in a file on the DNS server, and a secondary zone retrieves the records from a primary server through the zone-transfer process.

4. **Choose Standard primary and click Next.**

5. **Specify the name of the zone, as shown in Figure 7-10. Specify the DNS name for the zone and click Next to continue.**

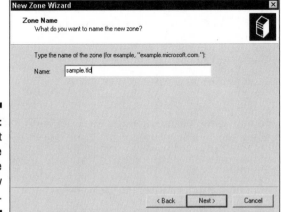

Figure 7-10:
You must specify the zone name for the new zone.

You have to specify a file for the new zone, as shown in Figure 7-11. The zone data is stored in the file you specify. The filename is automatically generated by appending the extension .dns to the zone name. Although you can change this file to anything you want, the automatically generated name is often the most descriptive.

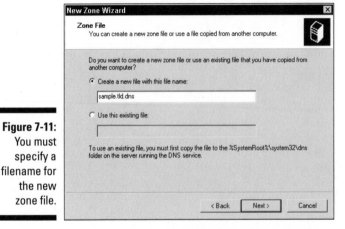

Figure 7-11:
You must specify a filename for the new zone file.

You can also use an existing zone file. By specifying an existing zone file, new records don't need to be created for the zone. The existing zone file must be in the `%systemroot%\system32\dns` directory — `%systemroot%` is typically `c:\WINNT` on Windows 2000 or `c:\WINDOWS` on Windows .NET Server.

6. **For purposes of this example, accept the default zone filename or specify your own zone filename and click Next to continue.**

   Figure 7-12 shows the next step in the Configure DNS Server Wizard. The wizard gives you a chance to create a reverse lookup zone, as we explain in detail in Chapter 9. In essence, reverse lookup zones are used to allow clients to look up an IP address using a DNS client, such as `NSLOOKUP`, and retrieve the associated DNS name. A reverse lookup zone is created for an entire IP subnet, and individual addresses are specified as records in the zone.

7. **Select Yes, create a reverse lookup zone and click Next.**

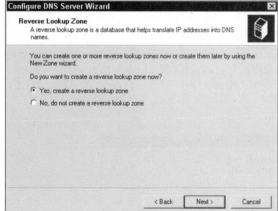

Figure 7-12:
Choose whether to create a reverse lookup zone.

The next step in creating the reverse zone is to select whether it's a primary or secondary zone, exactly like the process of creating a forward zone, as discussed earlier in this chapter (refer to Figure 7-9).

8. **Select a primary zone and click Next.**

   Now you need to specify either the IP subnet for the reverse lookup zone or the zone name. Specifying the subnet is the simplest way to create a reverse lookup zone because you don't need to determine the correct zone name, which can be tricky.

9. **Specify the IP subnet, as shown in Figure 7-13, and click Next.**

   As you type the address, the zone name is determined automatically and shown in the Reverse lookup zone name box.

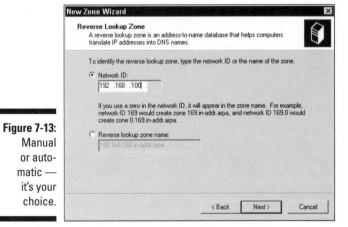

Figure 7-13:
Manual
or auto-
matic —
it's your
choice.

You must specify the name of the zone file or specify an existing zone file, also an identical process as with a forward lookup zone (refer to Figure 7-11).

10. Accept the default zone name and click Next to continue.

Review the configuration changes to be made, as shown in Figure 7-14. If the configuration is correct, click Finish to end the wizard and apply the changes. If you choose not to create a new zone in the Configure DNS Server Wizard, it skips directly to this point.

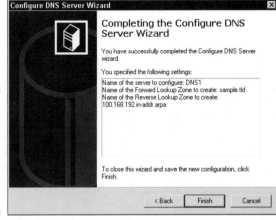

Figure 7-14:
The final
step —
reviewing
the con-
figuration
changes.

Getting into zones

Although you can add a forward and a reverse zone through the Configure DNS Server Wizard, you should add new zones manually as well. You have two containers in the DNS snap-in under your DNS server. These containers are Forward Lookup Zones and Reverse Lookup Zones. Click the Forward Lookup Zones container and the existing zones are shown in the right pane. Click the Action menu and select New Zone.

When you click New Zone, the New Zone Wizard is launched. The process for creating a new zone through the New Zone Wizard is identical to the process for creating a zone through the Configure DNS Server Wizard.

Adding to your record collection

Now that you have added some zones either manually or through the Configure DNS Server Wizard, you can begin to work with records. Click the zone you created using the Configure DNS Server Wizard, as shown in Figure 7-15.

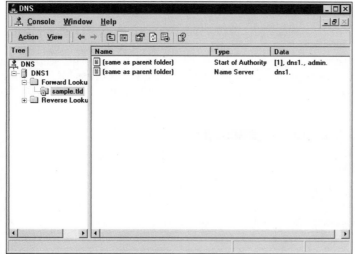

Figure 7-15:
The zone you created is shown in the DNS snap-in.

After you have selected the zone in the left pane, the zone records are shown in the right pane, as you can also see in Figure 7-15. The zone created by the Configure DNS Server Wizard contains a start of authority (SOA) record and a name server (NS) record. (For details about records, see Chapter 9.) You almost certainly need to add records to the zone. Right-click an empty area in the right pane when a zone is selected to open the Action menu, as shown in Figure 7-16.

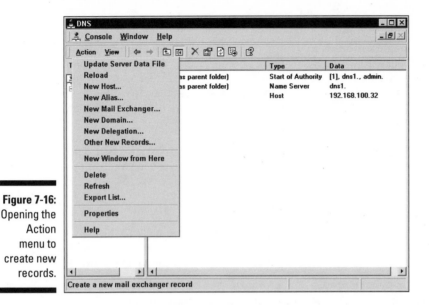

Figure 7-16:
Opening the
Action
menu to
create new
records.

You can create new records by using this Action menu. For example, choosing New Host creates an A record, and choosing New Mail Exchanger creates an MX record. Choose New Host to create an A record. This step opens the New Host dialog box. Specify the host name and IP address for the new record, as shown in Figure 7-17, and click the Add Host button to create the record.

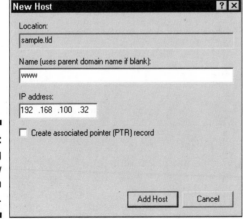

Figure 7-17:
Creating
a new
A record in
a zone.

Selecting the Create associated pointer (PTR) record option in the New Host dialog box automatically creates the correct record in the reverse lookup zone.

Creating other record types, such as MX records, using the New Mail Exchanger command works in a similar manner to the process we just described for an A record. To create a record that isn't listed on the Action menu, however, you must choose Other New Records. This step opens the Resource Record Type dialog box, as shown in Figure 7-18.

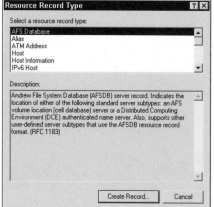

Figure 7-18:
Creating
in a zone a
record that
cannot be
created
from the
Action
menu.

After you select the record type from the list and click the Create Record button, the Record dialog box opens (again, similar to the preceding example, in which you create an A record). You can then complete the record details and click the OK button to add the record.

Adding subdomains

Here's a quick overview on subdomains. (Keep in mind that we describe subdomains in much greater detail in Chapter 10.) In the domain name www.eng.sample.tld, for example, eng is a subdomain of the sample.tld domain. To create a subdomain, select the parent domain in the left pane of the DNS snap-in and choose New Domain from the Action menu. Specify the name of the subdomain and click OK. The subdomain appears under the parent domain in the left pane, and you can add records be added to the subdomain as though it were a regular zone.

Configuring the DNS Server properties

Like any good service, DNS Server has plenty of configuration parameters of its own. To get your hands dirty working with these options, select the target

DNS server in the left pane of the DNS MMC snap-in and choose Properties from the Action menu. This step open the DNS server Properties dialog box, as shown in Figure 7-19. By default, the Interface tab is shown.

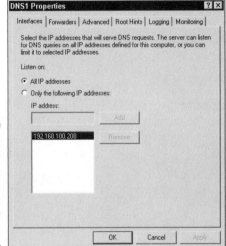

Figure 7-19: Configuring the network interfaces on which the server responds.

Getting connected with interfaces

You have two options on the Interfaces tab: The DNS server can respond to clients on all IP addresses (the default behavior) or just to clients connecting to a specific IP address. This option is useful if you have a multi-homed server (connected to more than one network) and you want clients on only one network to have DNS services from this server. To enable this behavior, select the Only the following IP addresses option and specify the IP addresses on which the server should respond by typing the address and clicking Add. You can remove addresses from the list by selecting the address to remove and clicking the Remove button.

Moving forward

Figure 7-20 shows the Forwarders tab in the Properties dialog box. Forwarders are a somewhat complex subject. Whenever a client makes a request for a DNS entry that isn't hosted by the local DNS server, the recursion process is normally used by the local server to locate the DNS entry on the correct remote DNS server. Recursion (refer to Chapter 3) works like this: The local DNS server first contacts a root DNS server followed by a top-level server (.com or .net, for example) and, finally, the correct authoritative server for the domain name.

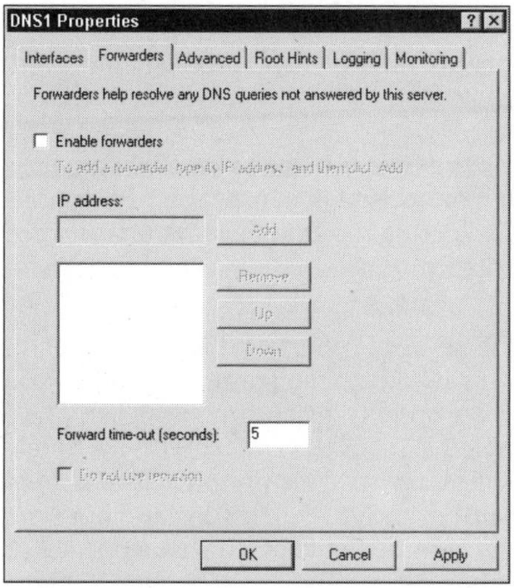

Figure 7-20:
Use this
dialog box if
you want to
use another
DNS server
rather than
recursion.

In some cases, you may not want your local DNS server to perform recursion, or you may want it to perform recursion only as a last resort. That may be the case if you have a slow Internet connection or want to restrict DNS queries across a firewall. In this case, you can configure a forwarder in the DNS server properties dialog box.

To enable a forwarder, follow these steps:

1. **Select the Enable forwarders check box.**

2. **Type the IP address of the remote DNS server in the IP address box.**

3. **Click the Add button.**

You can add a number of DNS servers to the list and change their order by clicking the up- and down-arrow buttons. You should have the closest (on your LAN or LAN segment) or fastest DNS servers at the top of the list.

After you have enabled one or more forwarders, any DNS requests not hosted by the local DNS server are sent to the DNS servers on the list of forwarders. This process is performed in sequence: Requests are sent to the first server on the list, and if a response isn't received, the next server is tried. If the forwarders don't provide a response, the local DNS server uses recursion to provide a response. Two advantages occur when the local DNS server doesn't use recursion (in the case of a forwarder providing a meaningful response to the request):

✔ Only one connection is made from the local DNS server to the forwarder.

✔ The forwarder performs the multiple DNS requests involved in the recursion process.

This process, which reduces the time it takes to resolve names, is quite noticeable if a slow Internet connection is in use. You can disable recursion when using a forwarder by selecting the Don't use recursion check box.

Beyond the basics

The Advanced tab in the DNS server Properties dialog box is shown in Figure 7-21. From this tab, you set advanced parameters on the DNS server. You can set a number of server options, as shown in the list. The Disable recursion option, when enabled, causes the DNS server not to return any DNS entries that aren't hosted by the server. This option is useful if you want to configure a server for only authoritative DNS hosting and not for regular client queries. This configuration is common at ISPs that have one set of servers for fulfilling client requests and one set of servers for hosting DNS zones.

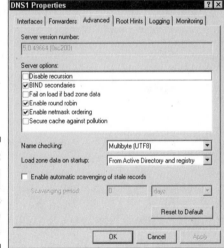

Figure 7-21:
Configuring
advanced
parameters
for the
server.

Another advanced option is BIND secondary servers. DNS records are exchanged from primary to secondary DNS servers through a zone transfer. When you enable the BIND secondaries option, zone transfers take place through the traditional method, and all DNS server applications are supported. If you're using only Windows DNS servers and BIND versions later than 4.9.4, you can deselect this option, and zone transfers then take place through fast zone transfers. *Fast zone transfers* use compression for increased speed. If you choose to deselect this option, you must ensure that you don't need to transfer zones to servers that don't support fast zone transfers.

Fail on load if bad zone data, a fairly simple option, is turned off by default. If it's enabled and a zone file contains invalid data, however, the DNS service doesn't start. The default option allows the DNS service to load even if invalid data is in a zone file. In most cases, the default is preferable. If you aren't a practiced master or mistress of troubleshooting DNS services, enabling this option could lead to quite a frustrating episode if a bad zone transfer file ever occurs.

The Enable round robin option enables DNS round robin load balancing. (We describe this topic in detail in Chapter 12.) The Enable netmask ordering option enables the feature in the Windows DNS server that returns DNS replies based on local subnet priority on a computer connected to more than one subnet. The translation: In a system that has multiple IP addresses mapped to a single host name on the DNS server, the preferred response is the IP that resides on the same subnet as the requestor if a match occurs. If no common subnet between the client and the target computer exists, the first DNS name-to-IP mapping in the list is used instead. Both these features are enabled by default.

The final option in the Server options list is Secure cache against pollution, which is disabled by default. This option provides extra security to the DNS server's cache. If the option is selected and a record is provided by a DNS server for a domain that wasn't requested, that reply isn't cached. For example, if a request is made for the record `www.sample.tld` and the reply contains both `www.sample.tld` and `www.poison.tld`, the `www.poison.tld` record isn't cached because it wasn't requested. (We tell you more about DNS security, including details about cache poisoning, in Chapter 11.)

Three more configuration settings are on the Advanced tab. The Name checking setting controls which zone and record names are allowed on the server. The three settings are

- **Strict RFC:** Allows only those names strictly defined by the DNS RFC (Request for Comment)
- **Non RFC:** Allows more names, including nonstandard characters
- **Multibyte:** Allows the use of the Unicode encoding standard in DNS names

Unicode character encoding is used in DNS names to allow foreign character sets (non-English) to use DNS.

The Load zone data on startup option tells the DNS server where to look for zone data. By default, both the system Registry and Active Directory are checked for zone data. The other options are From registry (it checks only the system Registry) and From file (it loads zone data from a BIND 4 `named.boot` file. This feature is useful if you're transferring zones and configuration information from a Unix system running BIND 4.

The last option on the Advanced tab is Enable automatic scavenging of stale records. *Scavenging* is the process of removing old records (leftover from a host that's no longer present) from zones. Scavenging typically applies to only dynamically added records, not manually added records, although you can configure manually added records for scavenging. Scavenging is disabled at the server level and enabled at the zone level by default. (We tell you about scavenging in more detail in Chapter 12.)

I'll give you a hint

Root hints are used for recursion. Whenever a DNS request is made for a zone not contained on the local server, the server uses the root hints as the first step to locating the zone. Look at the Root Hints tab in the DNS server Properties dialog box, as shown in Figure 7-22. Root hints change only occasionally. You can add, edit, and remove root hints by clicking the appropriate buttons. Typically, root hints don't need to be changed.

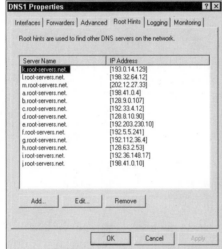

Figure 7-22:
Root hints
are used
for the
recursion
process.

What's goin' on? (Logging)

When you select any of the logging options on the Logging tab in the Properties dialog box, as shown in Figure 7-23, the associated action is logged to a file each time it occurs. The log file location is shown at the bottom of the tab. Logging on to the DNS server is useful for repairing configuration problems, finding security problems, and tracing other traffic.

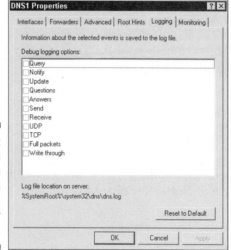

Figure 7-23:
Log certain
actions on
the DNS
server to a
file for
review.

I'll be watching you

On the Monitoring tab in the server Properties dialog box, you can perform
tests on the DNS server. To perform a test, select a test type (simple or recursive) and click the Test Now button. Test results are shown in the window at
the bottom of the tab, as shown in Figure 7-24. You can also schedule a test to
run at certain intervals.

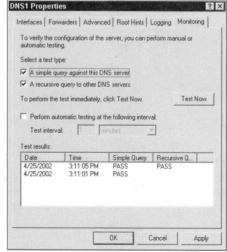

Figure 7-24:
You're in
charge —
use this tab
to run tests
on the DNS
server.

The more often you schedule a test to run, the greater the unnecessary load that is placed on the server. You don't need to run any scheduled tests more than every hour or every few hours, unless you're troubleshooting a specific problem. In that case, you should schedule the tests to run every few minutes at first. If you can't isolate the problem, let the tests run longer and less often to get a better view of what's happening.

Taking control: Configuring zone properties

You can make a number of configuration changes to a zone. Most of the time, you can leave the majority of them set to their default values, although you may need to play "mad scientist" and get creative every once in a while. From the DNS MMC snap-in, select a zone in the left pane and choose Properties from the Action menu. The zone Properties dialog box opens, as shown in Figure 7-25.

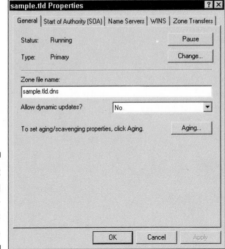

Figure 7-25:
Configuring
zone-
specific
settings.

Generally speaking

From the General tab, you can change the zone from primary to secondary and vice versa by clicking the Change button and changing the zone filename. You can also choose whether to allow dynamic DNS updates, which by default aren't allowed in new zones. *Note:* If you're running Active Directory, zones created during the Active Directory setup process have dynamic updates enabled.

Also on the General tab is the Aging button. Click it to configure the aging properties for the zone, which are used for the scavenging of old records. (See Chapter 12 for more details on scavenging.) Don't change the aging settings until you thoroughly understand their function.

No problems with authority

In BIND under Unix, the Start of Authority, or SOA, record is contained in the beginning of every zone file. In Windows, however, the SOA record for the zone is configured using the Start of Authority (SOA) tab in the zone Properties dialog box, as shown in Figure 7-26. The SOA record and its settings are discussed in detail in Chapter 9.

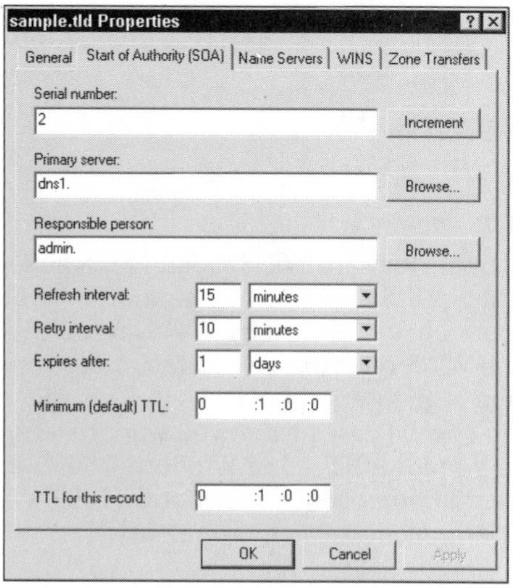

Figure 7-26: Configuring the SOA record for the zone.

Notice that you can set all the SOA values in addition to the zone TTL (time-to-live) from the SOA tab in the zone Properties dialog box.

Name that server

On the Name Servers tab in the zone Properties dialog box, as shown in Figure 7-27, you add name server (NS) records to the zone. The NS records tell other DNS servers and clients which name servers are authoritative for a given domain. The authoritative name servers are the primary and secondary name servers for the zone. You can add, edit, and remove name server records for the zone by clicking the appropriate buttons. Name server records have only one setting and IP address.

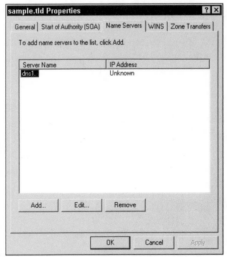

Figure 7-27:
Working
with name
server (NS)
records for
the zone.

Everybody WINS (they used to, anyway)

On the WINS tab, you can enable forward WINS lookup for a zone. When the WINS lookup option is enabled, DNS requests that cannot be fulfilled by the local server or through recursion are fulfilled by WINS instead. When WINS lookups are enabled, special WINS records are created in the zone. You never use this feature if the system is an Internet DNS server. The only time you use this feature, in fact, is in special cases when you want to integrate WINS and DNS (for example, on a Windows NT 4.0 or Windows 2000 Server hybrid network). WINS is rarely used in homogeneous Windows 2000, Windows XP, or Windows .NET Server operating system environments.

From here to there: Zone transfers

On the Zone Transfers tab, as shown in Figure 7-28, you control zone transfer security. In this case, the issue is one of information because this control is used to prevent unauthorized users or rogue servers from getting a list of all your hosts and their IP addresses. Getting this information can be useful if the miscreant plans to try to invade your network. (We describe this security feature and others at length in Chapter 11.) By default, zone transfers are enabled to all servers, which, as you may guess, isn't necessarily the best idea. You can also choose to allow zone transfers to only the DNS servers with name server records in the zone or to a manually specified list of servers. Limiting zone transfers is an important network security step.

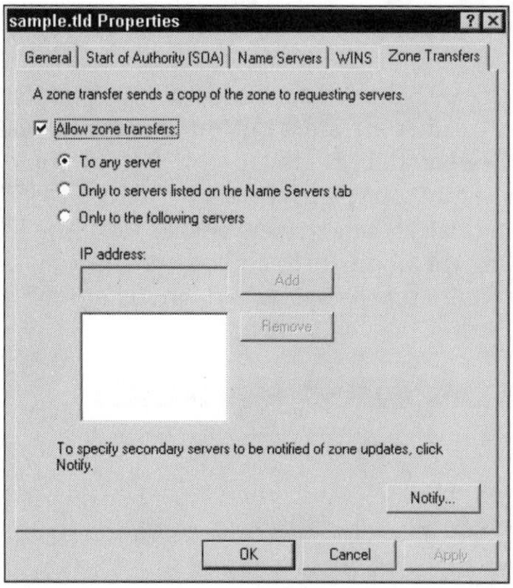

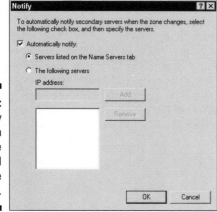

Figure 7-28:
Specify
which
servers are
allowed to
perform
zone
transfers on
the zone.

Also on the Zone Transfers tab is the Notify button. Clicking it opens the Notify dialog box, as shown in Figure 7-29. You use this dialog box to specify which DNS servers are notified when zone information changes. It's sort of the DNS equivalent of a contact list. When you move from one residence to another, you typically use a "notify list" to notify certain people and institutions of your address change. This list ensures that all the included people are on the same page. The purpose of the Notify function is to instruct secondary servers to perform a zone transfer whenever the zone is changed on the primary server. By default, all servers listed as name servers for the zone (those with NS records) are notified. You can also choose to send notify commands to manually specified servers.

Figure 7-29:
Specify
which
servers are
notified
of zone
changes.

Working with Windows NT 4.0

In Windows NT 4.0 Server, the DNS Server service is configured using the DNS Manager utility. To find it, click the Start button, choose Programs⇨ Administrative Tools and click the DNS Manager icon. Before you can configure the DNS server, however, you must first add the server to the DNS Manager because it isn't done automatically. Choose New Server from the DNS menu in the DNS Manager utility, enter the name or IP address of the local computer, and click OK. The server appears on the list, as shown in Figure 7-30.

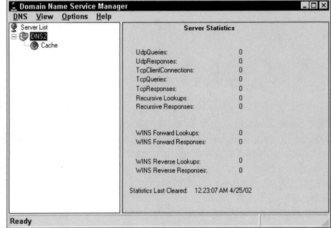

Figure 7-30: The local DNS server has been added to the DNS Manager list.

Working with NT 4.0 zones

After the DNS server is first created, it has no zones configured. The first step in making the DNS server truly useful is to add a zone or two. Select the DNS server in the left pane and choose New Zone from the DNS menu. The first step in the New Zone dialog box is shown in Figure 7-31. You must decide whether the new zone is a primary or secondary zone and, if it's a secondary zone, specify the zone name and the primary DNS server. If this DNS server is the only one on your network, it likely hosts a primary zone for your local network or Windows domain. If a DNS server is in operation and you're unsure of its role, you're safest in making the server a secondary DNS server. Or, you can consult someone to find out whether the other server is a primary one, although it may be more fun to guess. (Just kidding!)

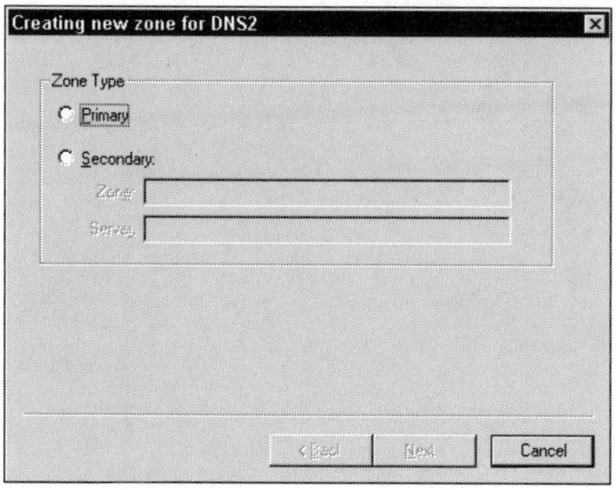

Figure 7-31:
Choose
whether to
make a
new zone
primary or
secondary.

In the figure, a primary zone is being created so that records can be added manually later. Select Primary and click Next. In the next window that appears, you provide the zone name and a zone file. If you type the zone name in the Zone Name box, the zone filename automatically is created when you complete this step and switch to the Zone File field, as shown in Figure 7-32. You probably should stick with the default zone filename (because it can simplify troubleshooting and later configuration attempts). If you're using a different naming convention, however, you can enter a different filename. Click Next to continue.

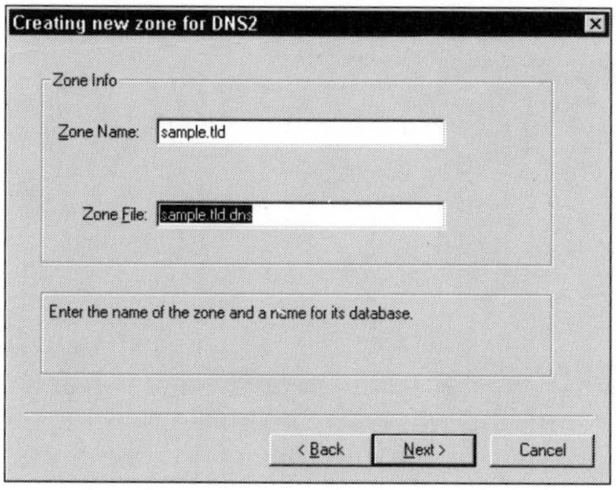

Figure 7-32:
When you
specify a
zone name,
the zone
filename is
generated
automa-
tically.

You're then notified that all information has been provided for the new zone. Click the Finish button to add the zone. The zone appears in the DNS Manager, as shown in Figure 7-33. When the zone is selected, its records are shown in the right pane.

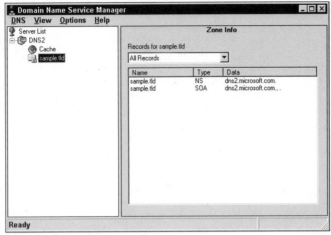

Figure 7-33:
The new
zone
appears
in the left
pane of
the DNS
Manager
with its
records in
the right
pane.

Adding records

You can add records to the new zone in two ways. To add a simple A record for a host, ensure that the correct zone is selected in the left pane and choose New Host from the DNS menu. This step launches the New Host dialog box, as shown in Figure 7-34. Specify the host name and IP address as shown and click the Add Host button. You can also select the Create Associated PTR Record to automatically add the reverse lookup zone entry for the host.

Figure 7-34:
Adding a
simple
A record to
the zone.

The new A record appears in the right pane of the DNS Manager. To add a record other than an A record, though, you can choose New Record from the DNS menu to open the New Resource Record dialog box, as shown in Figure 7-35. Select the record type from the list and enter the record details. Click OK to add the record.

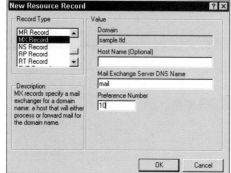

Figure 7-35:
Adding a
new record
to the zone.

Getting into the details: Adding a subdomain

We describe subdomains in detail in Chapter 10, but because the topic is closely related to the topic of DNS configurations, we introduce the subject here. Subdomains exist within the bounds of existing domains. For example, in the domain name www.eng.sample.tld, eng is a subdomain of the sample.tld domain. To create a subdomain, select the parent zone in the left pane and choose New Domain from the DNS menu. Enter the subdomain name in the New Domain dialog box and click OK. The subdomain appears under the parent domain, and records can be added as described in the preceding section.

Configuring the DNS server properties

The Windows NT 4.0 DNS Server service has far fewer available configuration options than the subsequent replacement operating system, Windows 2000 Server. To access the Windows NT 4.0 DNS settings, select the DNS server in the left pane of the DNS Manager and choose Properties from the DNS menu.

When you select the DNS server in the left pane of the DNS Manager when you open the utility, the server statistics may not appear in the right pane. Double-click the server name to connect to the server, and the server statistics appear, indicating that you're connected to the DNS server.

Making use of interfaces

When you first open the Properties dialog box for the DNS server, the Interfaces tab is displayed, as shown in Figure 7-36. Use this tab to configure to which IP addresses (configured on the server network cards) the server

DNS service will respond. If no addresses are specified, the server responds on all IP addresses configured on the server. This setting is most often used when a server is multi-homed (connected to more than one network) and you want only users on specific networks, such as the internal network, to be able to use the DNS server.

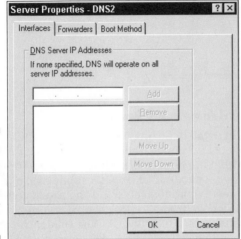

Figure 7-36:
Configuring
on which IP
addresses
the server
responds.

Finding the host that time forgot: Forwarders

On the Forwarders tab in the Server Properties dialog box, as shown in Figure 7-37, you configure DNS servers as forwarders for the local server. A forwarder is beneficial in a number of cases. For example, when a forwarder is configured on a DNS server and a client requests a DNS record that isn't hosted on the server, the DNS server doesn't use recursion to retrieve the record but rather requests the record from the forwarder (another DNS server). The forwarder performs the work of retrieving the record and returns it to the local DNS server, which returns it to the client. We talk about recursion in Chapter 3, in the section about getting down to business.

You realize the benefit of a forwarder when the local DNS server has a slow connection to the Internet. Rather than the multiple DNS queries required for recursion traveling over the slow connection, only one query is made to the forwarder, which ideally has a fast Internet connection.

Figure 7-37:
Setting DNS
forwarders
for the
server.

You can enable forwarders by selecting the Use Forwarder check box. You can add forwarders to the list by specifying the IP address and clicking the Add button. When you need to, remove forwarders from the list by selecting the forwarder and clicking the Remove button. You can change the order of the forwarders by selecting a forwarder and clicking the Move Up and Move Down buttons. The closest or fastest server should be at the top of the list.

The other option on the Forwarders tab is Operate as Slave Server. By default, this check box isn't selected. If the forwarder doesn't provide an appropriate response to the query, the local DNS server reverts to recursion. When the check box is selected and the forwarder fails, recursion isn't attempted and no response is provided to the client.

Getting started

The Boot Method tab displays the current boot method of the DNS server. The DNS server typically boots using the zone information in the system Registry. Although it's rare, you can configure the server to boot from a BIND-style configuration file; if the server is configured in this manner, it's displayed on the Boot Method tab.

Configuring zone properties

To configure the properties for a specific zone, select the zone in the left pane and choose Properties from the DNS menu. The zone Properties dialog box opens to the General tab, as shown in Figure 7-38.

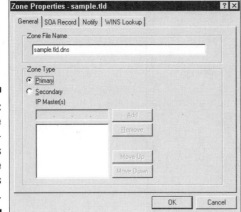

Figure 7-38:
Setting zone
configura-
tion options
in the Zone
Properties
dialog box.

Generally speaking

The General tab of the Windows NT 4.0 DNS zone Properties dialog box has two essential functions. Like the Windows 2000 Server DNS options, this option allows you to specify the server as the primary or secondary record controller of the zone information. As we mention earlier in this chapter, in the section about configuring a Windows 2000 DNS server, if the server is the only DNS server on the network or it will host a new zone, you should config-ure it to host the primary zone.

"1 fight authority. . . ."

Figure 7-39 shows the SOA Record tab. The information on this tab configures the Start of Authority (SOA) record for the zone, as we mention earlier in this chapter, in the section "Working with Windows 2000 and Windows .NET Server."

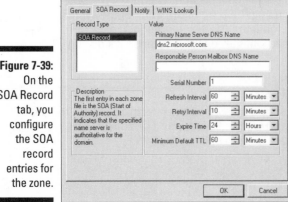

Figure 7-39:
On the
SOA Record
tab, you
configure
the SOA
record
entries for
the zone.

Sending notification

As with the comparable option in the Windows 2000 DNS server options, on the Notify tab you specify which DNS servers are notified when changes are made to this zone, as shown in Figure 7-40. To add a server to the notify list, enter the server IP address and then click the Add button. You can remove a server from the list by selecting it and clicking the Remove button.

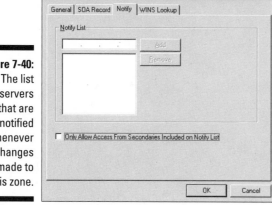

Figure 7-40:
The list of servers that are notified whenever changes are made to this zone.

WINS Lookup

You use the WINS Lookup tab to enable WINS resolution when DNS resolution fails. When you enable this option, WINS can be used as a last resort for name resolution. This option, as you may guess, requires that a WINS server be installed on the same server or another local computer.

Chapter 8

Unix Domain Name Servers

*L*ike the Microsoft Windows server products, many Unix systems include a DNS server you can use to deploy DNS. The DNS server included with most versions of Unix is most often a version of a common DNS server application, although some builds come with proprietary DNS servers. The most common, of the "common" DNS servers available for Unix, is Berkley Internet Naming Daemon, or simply BIND. In fact, it's uncommon to find a Unix DNS server running something other than BIND.

BIND was originally written at the University of California at Berkeley (surprised?), as one of the key applications to complement the Berkeley Software Distribution (BSD) version of Unix. BSD Unix, an extremely widely distributed version of Unix, is often used as a "reference product" for other development efforts.

The term *daemon* is used in Unix to describe a program that runs in the background and waits for connections. Essentially, it's the Unix equivalent of a service in Windows NT or Windows 2000.

BIND, like a great deal of other Unix software, including Unix itself, has a storied history. It was originally written for the ARPANET project (refer to Chapter 1) at Berkeley. Berkeley continued to maintain BIND for quite some time until version 4.9, and then its maintenance was taken over by Digital Equipment Corporation (DEC). Version 4.9.2 was the work of Paul Vixie, of Vixie Enterprises, and all versions since then have been under his control (he's now with the Internet Software Consortium, or ISC).

All references to BIND in this chapter are to BIND Version 9, and more specifically 9.2.0. Older versions may or may not share features in common with the version we discuss here.

Alas, this isn't a history book, so we take you directly to the part where you get your hands dirty! The first thing you may need to do is install BIND. If that's the case, you can install BIND in two ways: from binary packages and from source code. Although both methods have advantages, using the binary packages is generally much easier.

Binary packages are collections of executable files that are ready to run, although you need to ensure that the package is the correct one for your version of Unix. *Source code* is the code for the software; to make use of it, you would need to compile the source into a binary package. Most often, source code is used by people who have difficulty finding packages of their build of Unix or who want to make compile-time customizations to the software — it's something only experts should do.

Installing BIND the Easy Way

Packages are simple to install on most Unix systems. BIND packages are available for most distributions of Linux, Sun Solaris, HP-UX, and other common Unix OS distributions. In the examples in this book, Mandrake Linux 8.2 is used for the examples. The process for installing packages for your version of Unix will most likely differ slightly, and you may need to refer to the documentation for your system for additional guidance.

The most difficult part of installing BIND from packages is locating and downloading the correct packages. As noted, the package you use must match the "make and model" of your operating system. For example, packages for many different Linux distributions (including Mandrake) are available at `www.rpmfind.net`. This site is a central repository for, in particular, RedHat Package Manager (RPM) packages of all kinds, although many packages for Sun Solaris are at `www.sunfreeware.com`. Other package repositories exist for many different systems.

The first step is to retrieve the BIND package for your system. Because the system used in our examples is Mandrake Linux (which is based on the RedHat distribution), it uses RPM files.

1. **Using your Web browser, go to** `www.rpmfind.net`.

2. **Click the link labeled Go directly to the RPM database.**

    The main RPM repository page is shown in Figure 8-1.

    You can view the index of RPMs on the site in a number of ways: by distribution, by vendor, or by name, for example. The best way is to view the packages by name because packages for a certain distribution sometimes aren't under the correct distribution in the index.

Figure 8-1:
Navigating
the site —
here's the
main RPM
repository
page.

3. **Click the Index by Name link.**

   The Index by Name page, as shown in Figure 8-2, shows the number of
   packages starting with each letter.

   You're looking for the BIND package, so click the link labeled `n packages
   beginning with letter B`.

4. **Scroll down and locate the BIND packages (they're a lo-o-ong way
   down).**

   You then encounter the problem with packages: Notice that a number
   of different BIND packages are available. These different packages are
   different versions of the software and are for different distributions. As
   the time we wrote this book, the latest version of BIND was 9.2.0.
   Looking on the list, you can see that 9.2.0-8 is the latest version. The
   problem is that it isn't the version for Mandrake Linux — it's for Red Hat.
   The latest version for Mandrake is `9.2.0-6mdk`, as shown in Figure 8-3.
   The `mdk` indicates that it's for the Mandrake Linux distribution. You
   don't *have* to use the MDK ,version because other versions should work;
   with the MDK version, however, you know that it was built on the same
   system as the one you're using.

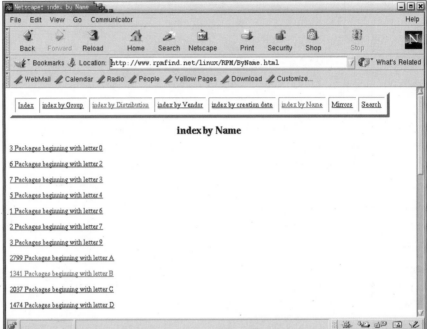

Figure 8-2:
This page shows the number of packages starting with each letter. Click a link to display a list of packages starting with that letter.

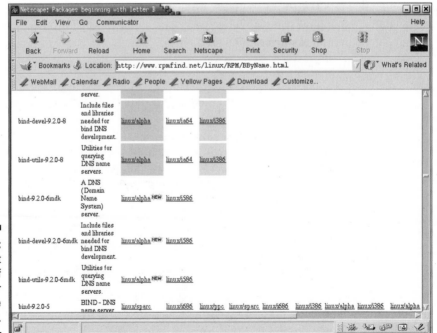

Figure 8-3:
The latest version of BIND for Mandrake Linux.

A more recent version of the software you're installing from packages (BIND, in this case) may be available, but it may not yet have a package in the RPM repository. If you want absolutely the latest version of the software, you may have to try to locate a package from the software developer's Web site or compile the software from source code (see the following section, "Getting to the Source"). You can find the latest version of the BIND distribution at the Internet Consortium Web site:

```
www.isc.org/products/BIND/
```

Two more small problems arise. First, a number of BIND packages are available, including `bind`, `bind-devel`, and `bind-utils`. The most important package is `bind` because it has the base functionality. `Bind-devel` is unnecessary unless you're programming or compiling applications that require integration with BIND. Finally, you should also have `bind-utils` because this package includes the BIND DNS client and the necessary configuration software.

The second small problem is that you need to know the architecture of your system. The sample system is Intel, so the `linux/i586` link is selected. If you're running a different CPU architecture (Alpha or ia64, for example), select the appropriate link.

5. **Click the appropriate architecture link for the bind-9.2.0-6mdk package and the package information page opens, as shown in Figure 8-4.**

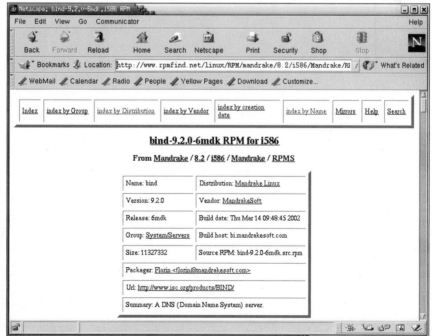

Figure 8-4:
The package information page shows details about the selected package.

6. **To download the package, use the package name link** (bind-9.2.0-6mdk RPM **for i586 in the example) and save the package to disk. Right-click the link and choose Save Link As or Save As, depending on your browser.**

   The procedure may differ if you're using a different Web browser.

7. **Go to the preceding page and click the appropriate architecture link for the** bind-utils **package and download it using the same procedure.**

   After the download is complete, both packages are ready for use on your system.

8. **In preparation for executing the packages, open a terminal window and navigate to the directory in which the packages were saved.**

   As you can see in Figure 8-5, the packages are in the current directory.

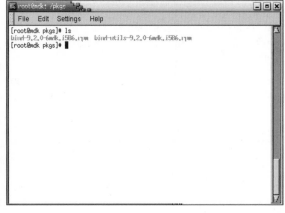

Figure 8-5:
The down-loaded BIND packages are in the working directory.

Now the rubber hits the road (so to speak): The installation process begins! When using Mandrake Linux (in addition to Red Hat and some other distributions), you use the RedHat Package Manager (RPM) to install the RPM packages.

Typically, RPM is used to install packages by typing **RPM -i** *<packagename>*, where *<packagename>* is the filename of the package to install; for example, filename.rpm. although this usage is recommended, it falls short in some cases. The -i switch instructs RPM to install the package, but if an earlier version of the package is already installed, the procedure doesn't work. A full discussion on the use of RPM is beyond the scope of this book, but you're far better off using the command RPM -Uvh *<packagename>* rather than -i because you don't encounter issues if an earlier version of the BIND server is installed. The -Uvh switches instruct RPM to upgrade any existing packages, and the -v and -h switches instruct RPM to display verbose information and a progress indicator, respectively.

Starting with the `bind-utils` package, install BIND using the `rpm -Uvh <packagename>` command for each of the two packages, as shown in Figure 8-6. The `bind-utils` package must be installed first, though, because the bind RPM package depends on it. Because the `-v` and `-h` switches are used, the package installation status is shown.

Figure 8-6:
The BIND packages are installed using the RPM utility.

Figure 8-7 shows the RPM command being used to verify that the packages are installed. Typing `rpm -qa` shows a list of all installed packages, and using the `grep` command makes it possible to search for only the packages in which you have an interest. Although the RPM command used to install the package showed that it was successful, you can use this `RPM -qa` command at any time to see whether a certain package is installed.

Figure 8-7:
Determining whether specific packages are installed.

Now that BIND is installed, you can move on to configuration. See the "Making Changes to BIND" section, later in this chapter, for more information.

Getting to the Source

Although you can install BIND by using packages, in some cases you may not want or be able to use precompiled packages for installation — for example, if recent (or any) packages weren't available for your system or if you want to make changes to BIND that can be made only at the time of compilation. Some people like to compile all software from source code to ensure that it's optimized for their systems.

Installing software programs like BIND from source code is fairly easy if the correct compiler and build tools are installed. Most systems come with them installed; if not, refer to your system documentation for more information. BIND is a well-developed application, and compilation goes smoothly on most systems.

The first step is to download the source code for BIND. The BIND source code is available from the ISC FTP site, at `ftp.isc.org`. These steps outline what you need to do to get hold of the source code:

1. **Using an FTP program of your choice, connect to** `ftp.isc.org`.

2. **Log on as user** `anonymous` **and use your e-mail address for a password.**

3. **Browse into the** `/isc/bind9` **directory.**

4. **Locate the latest version of the BIND and open the related directory.**

   The directory uses the BIND version as part of its name. For example, to find version 9.2.2 release candidate 1, open the folder named `9.2.2rc1`.

5. **Locate and transfer the appropriate source file.**

   For example, the source file for 9.2.2 RC1 is labeled `bind-9.2.2rc1.tar.gz`.

6. **Find the latest version of BIND.**

   We don't recommend, however, that you use the release candidate or beta versions (rc1, rc2, a1, a2, b1, b2, for example) because they may be unstable. Use only standard releases (9.2.0 or 9.2.1, for example).

   After you're in the directory for the latest BIND version, you should see two files: a `tar.gz` file and a `.asc` file. You need only the `.tar.gz` file.

   The .asc file contains a hash value that is used to verify the identity of the `.tar.gz` file. It's good practice to check the hash of the file you download and compare it to the value in the .asc file for security reasons but it isn't required.

7. **After you have downloaded the** `.tar.gz` **file, you can close the FTP client.**

8. **Locate the file, which should be in the current directory when you close the FTP client. You must then unzip and untar the file.**

   The file is compressed using the gzip utility and can be decompressed using the gunzip utility. The result is a `.tar` file that is a collection of files that aren't compressed.

   You use the `tar` utility to extract the files. If you're using the GNU version of the `tar` utility, as is standard on Linux, you can decompress and untar the file in one step.

9. **Type the command** tar -zxpvf *<file>* **to unzip and untar the file, as shown in Figure 8-8.**

   For example, you may type **tar -zxpvf bind-9.2.0.tar.gz**.

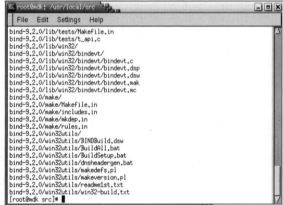

Figure 8-8:
Decom-
press and
untar files
compressed
with the
`gzip` utility.

After you have unpacked the downloaded file, you have a new directory. In this example, the new directory is `bind-9.2.0`.

10. **Change to that directory and type ls (the list directory contents command) to see the unpacked files, as shown in Figure 8-9.**

Whenever you install any software from source code, read the included `README` file.

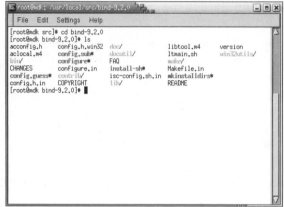

Figure 8-9:
The files
in the
downloaded
`.tar.gz`
file are
unpacked
in a new
directory.

Now you can begin to install the software. For BIND, the process is quite simple. The first step is to configure the source code, and then you can compile it. Configuring the source code is simple. Included with the code is a configuration script named `configure`. (Finally, something makes sense!) The `configure` script creates a configuration file that is used by the compiler to customize the compiled program for your system.

Follow these steps:

1. **Run the configure script by typing** ./configure **at a shell prompt, as shown in Figure 8-10.**

   The `./` in front of `configure` tells the shell that you want to run the `configure` script in the current directory.

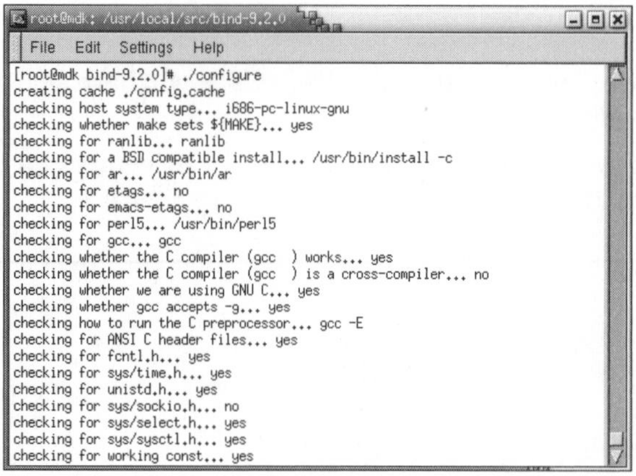

Figure 8-10:
Creating a
configu-
ration file
that's
used to
compile the
software.

After the `configure` script is complete, a `config.h` file is created. If you're familiar with C programming, you know that it's a header file containing all the configuration information for BIND. You can now compile BIND. The process is much simpler than it sounds.

2. **To compile the software, ensure that you're in the directory where the source code is located (if you just ran the `configure` script, you're already there) and type** make, **as shown in Figure 8-11.**

Figure 8-11:
The make
utility is
responsible
for com-
piling the
software.

```
root@mdk: /usr/local/src/bind-9.2.0                          _ □ x
 File  Edit  Settings  Help
[root@mdk bind-9.2.0]# make
making all in /usr/local/src/bind-9.2.0/make
make[1]: Entering directory `/usr/local/src/bind-9.2.0/make'
make[1]: Leaving directory `/usr/local/src/bind-9.2.0/make'
making all in /usr/local/src/bind-9.2.0/lib
make[1]: Entering directory `/usr/local/src/bind-9.2.0/lib'
make[2]: Entering directory `/usr/local/src/bind-9.2.0/lib/isc'
making all in /usr/local/src/bind-9.2.0/lib/isc/include
make[3]: Entering directory `/usr/local/src/bind-9.2.0/lib/isc/include'
making all in /usr/local/src/bind-9.2.0/lib/isc/include/isc
make[4]: Entering directory `/usr/local/src/bind-9.2.0/lib/isc/include/isc'
make[4]: Leaving directory `/usr/local/src/bind-9.2.0/lib/isc/include/isc'
make[3]: Leaving directory `/usr/local/src/bind-9.2.0/lib/isc/include'
making all in /usr/local/src/bind-9.2.0/lib/isc/unix
make[3]: Entering directory `/usr/local/src/bind-9.2.0/lib/isc/unix'
making all in /usr/local/src/bind-9.2.0/lib/isc/unix/include
make[4]: Entering directory `/usr/local/src/bind-9.2.0/lib/isc/unix/include'
making all in /usr/local/src/bind-9.2.0/lib/isc/unix/include/isc
make[5]: Entering directory `/usr/local/src/bind-9.2.0/lib/isc/unix/include/isc'
make[5]: Leaving directory `/usr/local/src/bind-9.2.0/lib/isc/unix/include/isc'
make[4]: Leaving directory `/usr/local/src/bind-9.2.0/lib/isc/unix/include'
gcc  -g -O2 -I/usr/local/src/bind-9.2.0 -I./include -I./../nothreads/include -I.
./include -I./../include -I./..        -W -Wall -Wmissing-prototypes -Wcast-qual -
```

The `make` utility is responsible for compiling the software, but doesn't perform the compilation itself. The `make` utility simply processes another script, `Makefile`, which runs the compiler.

After you have run the `make` utility, the software is compiled but not yet installed. Installing the newly compiled binary packages is as simple as the compilation process.

3. **At the shell prompt, type** make install. **This command installs the binary packages in the correct places.**

Although installing from packages requires two packages, one each for the base BIND applications and one for utilities, installing from source code requires only the one set of files. You can now move on to configuring BIND.

Making Changes to BIND

A couple of steps are involved in configuring BIND. The first few steps relate to getting BIND running, and the remaining steps relate to the now familiar concept of configuring DNS zones.

Getting BIND running

After BIND is installed, you still need to make changes to ensure that the daemon automatically starts when the system does. You can start BIND manually, but you probably will want it to start automatically if your network hosts will be using the BIND daemon for DNS services regularly. You can have BIND start automatically in one of two ways: Place it in a startup script or use inetd.

If you're familiar with Unix and Linux in particular, you may be familiar with inetd. It's a daemon that listens on the network for connections to the system. When inetd hears a connection on the network, it checks its configuration file (typically named inetd.conf) to see whether the network port (TCP/IP port number) on which the connection is communicating is on the list. If it is, inetd launches the appropriate process associated with the port number in the configuration file and connects the network connection and the application.

For some applications, inetd is a decent solution, but many heavily loaded servers don't use it because repeatedly spawning new processes consumes considerable system resources. If numerous connections are using a particular service, a better solution is to run the application at startup. In this case, rather than have inetd accept connections for the application, the application itself listens on the network for connections on that port.

In this book, we cover only the second method because inetd isn't configured on all Linux systems. Some systems, for example, use xinetd, which is configured in a significantly different manner from inetd.

Starting BIND is quite simple. The BIND program, called named, is installed in /usr/sbin by default. To start BIND, you can simply type **/usr/sbin/named**. BIND doesn't start if you haven't created the appropriate configuration files yet; when it's properly configured, however, this is how you initiate the BIND daemon.

BIND doesn't start unless a configuration file is created and configured for use. Without the configuration file, the BIND process immediately terminates.

To automatically start BIND, you just have to put the /usr/sbin/named command in a startup script. *Startup scripts* are run when the system first starts up. In Linux, startup scripts are typically located in the directory /etc/rc.d/. Look in that directory on your system for a file named rc.local — that file is the last startup script that is run when your system boots, and you should place in this any file any applications you want to run so that all the appropriate system services are running before your applications start. Place the /usr/sbin/named command at the end of the rc.local file, as shown in Figure 8-12.

```
root@mdk: /etc/rc.d                                                    _ □ ✕
 File   Edit   Settings   Help
 # want to make to /etc/issue here or you will lose them when you reboot.

 if [ -x /usr/bin/linux_logo ];then
        /usr/bin/linux_logo -c -n -f > /etc/issue
        echo "" >> /etc/issue
 else
        > /etc/issue
 fi
 echo "$R" >> /etc/issue
 echo "Kernel $(uname -r) on $a $SMP$(uname -m) / \l" >> /etc/issue

 if [ "$SECURITY" -le 3 ];then
        echo "Welcome to %h" > /etc/issue.net
        echo "$R" >> /etc/issue.net
        echo "Kernel $(uname -r) on $a $SMP$(uname -m)" >> /etc/issue.net
 else
        echo "Welcome to Mandrake Linux" > /etc/issue.net
        echo "-------------------------" >> /etc/issue.net
 fi
 fi
 touch /var/lock/subsys/local
 /usr/local/sbin/proftpd
 /usr/sbin/named
 [root@mdk rc.d]# █
```

Figure 8-12:
Place this
command
at the end
of the
`rc.local`
file.

That's all there is to it. BIND is now configured to start when the system starts. BIND is still at a point where it won't start, so read on. In the following section, we explain how to create and modify the BIND configuration files.

Changing BIND configuration files

As we mention earlier in this chapter, in order for BIND to start, a valid configuration file must be present. Also, if a keyword used in the configuration file is invalid (if you mistype it while editing the file, for example), BIND also fails to start. This situation can be a problem on a production DNS server because the incorrect syntax in the configuration file (if edited while the daemon is running) causes the DNS to stop responding.

If you're going to change your BIND configuration files, you should make the changes on a test server first to ensure that the changes don't have any undesirable effects. This step is vital on high-traffic production servers, such as those at ISPs, but it's less important on smaller DNS servers, where few users would be affected.

Two types of files are required for the operation of BIND:

- The BIND configuration file, typically called `named.conf`.
- A group of files called zone files. Inside the BIND configuration file is a list of zones hosted by the system. Those zones link to the zone files that contain the zone records. (For detailed information on zones and records, refer to Chapter 9.)

The BIND configuration file, usually named `named.conf`, is normally located in `/etc/`. If the file has a different name or is in a different location, you can point BIND to the file by using a command-line option when BIND is started. The BIND configuration file is quite complex, and the syntax must be exact or else BIND doesn't run.

The configuration file must have at least a few critical statements in place. The `named.conf` file always starts with an `options` section followed by zone definitions and an optional configuration area at the end of the file. Here's a sample `named.conf` file:

```
/*
 * Comments can be placed like this
 */

options {
        directory "/var/named";
};

zone "sample.tld" in {
        type master;
        file "sample.tld";
};

zone "sample_slave.tld" in {
        type slave;
        file "sample_slave.tld";
  1        masters { 192.168.1.1; };
};
```

This sample configuration file sets the zone file directory to `/var/named` using the `directory` option and then defines two zones. The `directory` option must be specified to tell BIND where to look for zone files. In most cases, zone files are stored in `/var/named` purely as a standard convention. You can place them in any directory you want.

You most likely need to create the directory `/var/named` (or whatever directory you choose for zone files). Type **mkdir /var/named** from a shell prompt to create the directory.

The zone entries in the configuration file tell BIND which zones it's hosting. Zones can be either master or slave zones (refer to Chapter 3 for a refresher on zone types). Master zones require zone files, and slave zone files are created automatically, but you must specify the DNS servers that are masters for the zone.

Before wandering too far off-track into zone files, find out more about the BIND configuration file. It can contain a wide variety of options. To see the complete list of options, type **man named.conf** from within a terminal session.

How to make cache

In one special case, you must create a special kind of zone. If you want to run a caching name server, you must create a root hints zone file. (We tell you more about this topic in a second.) A caching name server is the main type of DNS server used to service clients. A caching name server performs *recursive* lookups. Whenever a client asks the DNS server for a record and that server doesn't host that particular record, it queries the correct server and returns the record to the client. A caching DNS server, such as BIND, also keeps that record for a set period in order to serve the record without having to query the other server again.

The root hints zone entry must be added to the BIND configuration file:

```
zone "." in {
        type hint;
        file "db.cache";
};
```

The root hints file is normally named db.cache, but you can call it anything you choose. The root hints file contains a list of the root DNS servers. It must be kept up-to-date, but it's a fairly easy process. You can create the root hints file automatically using DIG:

1. **Change the directory to your zone file directory (typically, /var/named).**

2. **Type the command** dig @a.root-servers.net . ns > db.cache.

3. **Type** cat db.cache **to ensure that the file was created correctly.**

A typical root hints file should look like this:

```
; <<>> DiG 9.2.0 <<>> @a.root-servers.net . ns
;; global options: printcmd
;; Got answer:
;; ->>HEADER<<- opcode: QUERY, status: NOERROR, id: 7422
;; flags: qr aa rd; QUERY: 1, ANSWER: 13, AUTHORITY: 0, ADDI-
        TIONAL: 13

;; QUESTION SECTION:
;.                              IN    NS

;; ANSWER SECTION:
.       518400    IN    NS    B.ROOT-SERVERS.NET.
.       518400    IN    NS    J.ROOT-SERVERS.NET.
.       518400    IN    NS    K.ROOT-SERVERS.NET.
.       518400    IN    NS    L.ROOT-SERVERS.NET.
.       518400    IN    NS    M.ROOT-SERVERS.NET.
.       518400    IN    NS    I.ROOT-SERVERS.NET.
.       518400    IN    NS    E.ROOT-SERVERS.NET.
```

```
    .        518400    IN      NS      D.ROOT-SERVERS.NET.
    .        518400    IN      NS      A.ROOT-SERVERS.NET.
    .        518400    IN      NS      H.ROOT-SERVERS.NET.
    .        518400    IN      NS      C.ROOT-SERVERS.NET.
    .        518400    IN      NS      G.ROOT-SERVERS.NET.
    .        518400    IN      NS      F.ROOT-SERVERS.NET.

;; ADDITIONAL SECTION:
B.ROOT-SERVERS.NET.      3600000     IN     A     128.9.0.107
J.ROOT-SERVERS.NET.      3600000     IN     A     198.41.0.10
K.ROOT-SERVERS.NET.      3600000     IN     A     193.0.14.129
L.ROOT-SERVERS.NET.      3600000     IN     A     198.32.64.12
M.ROOT-SERVERS.NET.      3600000     IN     A     202.12.27.33
I.ROOT-SERVERS.NET.      3600000     IN     A     192.36.148.17
E.ROOT-SERVERS.NET.      3600000     IN     A     192.203.230.10
D.ROOT-SERVERS.NET.      3600000     IN     A     128.8.10.90
A.ROOT-SERVERS.NET.      3600000     IN     A     198.41.0.4
H.ROOT-SERVERS.NET.      3600000     IN     A     128.63.2.53
C.ROOT-SERVERS.NET.      3600000     IN     A     192.33.4.12
G.ROOT-SERVERS.NET.      3600000     IN     A     192.112.36.4
F.ROOT-SERVERS.NET.      3600000     IN     A     192.5.5.241

;; Query time: 99 msec
;; SERVER: 198.41.0.4#53(a.root-servers.net)
;; WHEN: Fri Apr 19 22:07:27 2002
;; MSG SIZE  rcvd: 436
```

Zoned out

Zone files are the second (and seriously important) configuration files required for the operation of BIND. A zone file is required for each master zone defined in the BIND configuration file. Slave zone files are created automatically through the zone-transfer process (refer to Chapter 3).

Zone files are fairly basic to work with, but can be tricky. The easiest way to find out about them is to look at a sample zone file and break it down from there:

```
$TTL 86400
@  IN SOA  dns1.sample.tld.      hostmaster.sample.tld. (
                    2001062501 ; Serial Number
                    21600      ; Refresh time
                    3600       ; Retry time
                    604800     ; Expire time
                    86400 )    ; Minimum TTL


        IN      NS      dns1.sample.tld.
        IN      NS      dns2.sample.tld.
```

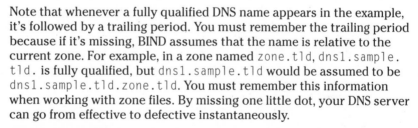

```
      IN    MX    10      mail.sample.tld.

            IN    A       10.0.1.5

www         IN    A       10.0.1.5
```

Check out this helpful list:

- ✔ **Zone TTL:** $TTL 86400, is used to set the time-to-live (TTL) value for the zone. This value controls the amount of time (in seconds) for which the zone is cached in other DNS servers and clients.

- ✔ **SOA record:** Following the TTL value (known as a directive) is the SOA, or start of authority, record. It's in place because the DNS server is authoritative for the domain. The SOA record defines certain characteristics about the zone:

- ✔ **Authoritative DNS server:** The first entry in the SOA record (dns1. sample.tld) is the primary DNS server that is authoritative for the domain.

- ✔ **Administrator e-mail address:** Next comes the e-mail address of the person responsible for the DNS server (hostmaster.sample.tld), usually known as the *hostmaster*.

Note that whenever a fully qualified DNS name appears in the example, it's followed by a trailing period. You must remember the trailing period because if it's missing, BIND assumes that the name is relative to the current zone. For example, in a zone named zone.tld, dns1.sample. tld. is fully qualified, but dns1.sample.tld would be assumed to be dns1.sample.tld.zone.tld. You must remember this information when working with zone files. By missing one little dot, your DNS server can go from effective to defective instantaneously.

- ✔ **Serial number:** The next item in the SOA record is the serial number. This somewhat arbitrary number must be incremented to a higher number each time the zone is changed. BIND uses the serial number to determine whether to reload the zone in memory.

The rest of the numbers in the SOA record are time, refresh, retry, expire, and minimum TTL values:

- ✔ **Refresh value:** The refresh value controls how often slave servers request updates from the master servers.

- ✔ **Retry value:** The retry value controls the interval at which a slave server tries to update from a master if the initial request fails.

- ✔ **Expire time:** The expire time causes the slave server to cease its role as an authoritative name server if the master servers cannot be reached.

✔ **Minimum TTL value:** The minimum TTL value indicates the absolute minimum amount of time that the zone information should be cached on any caching servers retrieving the zone information. This value ensures that remote DNS servers don't unnecessarily bog down your server with requests for new information.

Following the SOA record are the DNS records for the zone. (We discuss record types in more detail in Chapter 9). For now, keep in mind that three types of records are in the sample zone file:

✔ **NS records:** Specify the authoritative name servers for the domain

✔ **MX records:** Are responsible for forwarding mail for the domain

✔ **A records:** Point to actual servers.

You should now have a BIND configuration file and zone files in place. If everything is configured correctly, the BIND daemon (called `named`) should start when you restart your system. You can also start `named` manually by running the command `/usr/local/sbin/named` or its equivalent on your system if `named` is in a different directory.

Make It Go! No, Wait — Make It Stop!

Every time a change is made to a zone file or to the BIND configuration file, BIND must be restarted because BIND stores its configuration and zone information in memory for faster access. The configuration information is therefore retrieved from the configuration file only during the BIND startup process. The simplest way to restart BIND is to *kill* (a Unix term for ending a process) the `named` process and manually start the daemon again. The problem with this process is that it causes BIND to be unavailable during the period after you have stopped the process but before it has been restarted. That may not seem like much of a problem, but it's bad practice and may have a noticeable effect on a high-traffic DNS server.

A second and better method is to restart the `named` process using `the kill -HUP` command. This method sends to the `named` process a HUP signal that tells `named` to reload its configuration. Think of it as a minimalistic version of restarting the service. Although this method is a vast improvement over stopping the daemon, hold on your hat because it gets better!

You achieve the pinnacle of restarting by making use of the `rndc` utility. Included in BIND, it's used to control the `named` daemon and can be used to reload the BIND configuration data and zone files without stopping the `named` process. This way, requests are still fulfilled while the configuration files are being reloaded.

The rndc utility requires some configuration changes in order to be truly useful. In particular, because rndc can be used to restart remote DNS servers, it requires some security preconfiguration. In versions of BIND earlier than 9.2.0, the configuration of BIND to use rndc was fairly complex. The first step was to generate a key, add controls and key statements to your named.conf file, and then write a rndc.conf file.

Thankfully, the configuration of rndc for use with BIND is now far simpler for a basic BIND configuration. To configure rndc, type **rndc-confgen > /etc/rndc.conf**, which automatically generates the rndc.conf file, as shown in Figure 8-13.

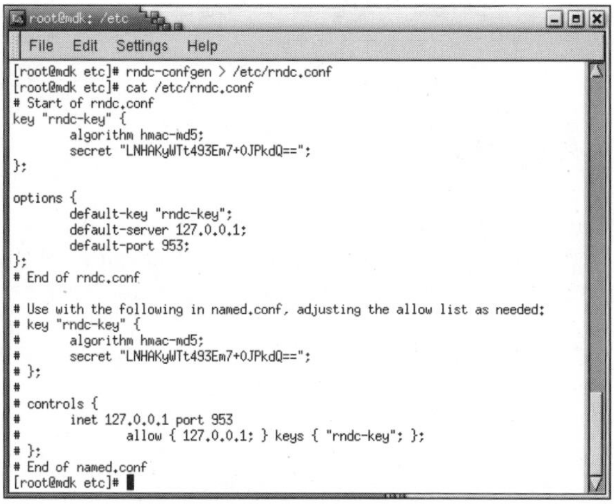

Figure 8-13: Automatically creating the rndc.conf file and the appropriate configuration information for the named.conf file.

```
[root@mdk etc]# rndc-confgen > /etc/rndc.conf
[root@mdk etc]# cat /etc/rndc.conf
# Start of rndc.conf
key "rndc-key" {
        algorithm hmac-md5;
        secret "LNHAKyWTt493Em7+0JPkdQ==";
};

options {
        default-key "rndc-key";
        default-server 127.0.0.1;
        default-port 953;
};
# End of rndc.conf

# Use with the following in named.conf, adjusting the allow list as needed:
# key "rndc-key" {
#       algorithm hmac-md5;
#       secret "LNHAKyWTt493Em7+0JPkdQ==";
# };
#
# controls {
#       inet 127.0.0.1 port 953
#               allow { 127.0.0.1; } keys { "rndc-key"; };
# };
# End of named.conf
[root@mdk etc]#
```

In addition to creating the rndc.conf file, you must make a change to the named.conf file. In the automatically generated rndc.conf file (refer to Figure 8-13), you must copy and paste into your named.conf file everything after the line #End of rndc.conf. This data should be added to the named.conf file after the options section but before any zone data occurs. You must also remove the hash mark (#) from each line except for the ones providing commentary about the directives that are used. The new named.conf file should look similar to the one shown in Figure 8-14.

Now that the changes have been made to the named.conf file, BIND must be restarted. At this point, you should use the killall -HUP named (or the pkill -HUP named on Solaris) command. If all goes well, this is the last time the command will have to be run because of a configuration file update. Running the killall command with the -HUP *signal* causes named to reload the configuration data, including the key and control statements, which allow rndc to function.

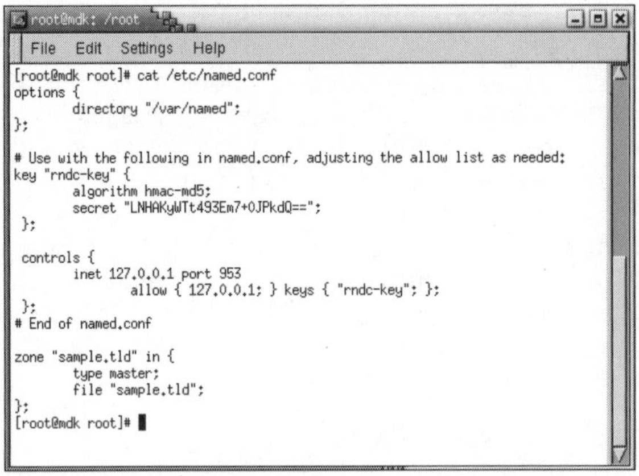

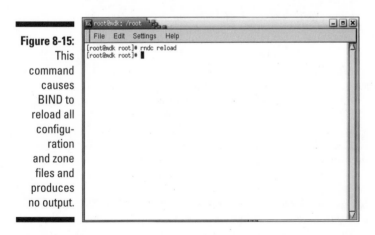

Figure 8-14:
For a new look, make a few changes.

RNDC Isn't a Rap Group

The `rndc` utility has many useful commands. The most common (especially considering the scenario presented in the preceding section) is the `reload` option. Running the command **rndc reload**, as shown in Figure 8-15, causes BIND to reload its configuration file and all zone files. Ideally, the `rndc reload` command should show no output, as shown in the figure. If any errors occur, however, they appear in the output.

Figure 8-15:
This command causes BIND to reload all configuration and zone files and produces no output.

Another way of using `rndc` was introduced in more recent versions of BIND 9.x. You can now make changes to a zone file and reload only that zone.

The command `rndc reload <zonefile>`, where `<zonefile>` is the zone file you want to reload, causes only that individual zone to be reloaded, and it saves the system the resources needed to reload the BIND configuration file and all associated zone files.

You cannot use the single zone reload feature of `rndc` to add zones. When you add a zone or make any other changes to the BIND configuration file, you must use the `rndc reload` command.

You can use a few other useful `rndc` commands. You can see a list of all `rndc` commands by running the `rndc` utility with no commands. Typing **rndc flush** causes the name server cache to be cleared of current entries. This feature is useful if a cached DNS record is known or suspected to be invalid. The `rndc status` command shows the status of the name server, as shown in Figure 8-16.

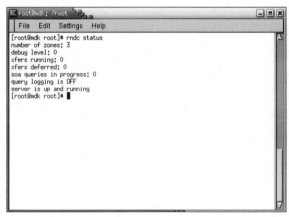

Figure 8-16: The name server status, including transfers and queries in progress.

Part IV

The Details: Setting Up Your DNS Zones

The 5th Wave   By Rich Tennant

"I assume you'll be forward-thinking enough to allow '.dog' as a valid domain name."

In this part . . .

*I*f you already have a DNS server in place, or after you have installed one, you have to populate it with useful data. If your server has information on it, information in this part of the book can help you to understand how it's arranged so that the DNS information can be properly interpreted.

These chapters explain what zones and records are and how they're used. The chapters also describe how to create your own zones and records and even how to create subdomains when your zones fill to the brim with records and become too large to handle easily.

Chapter 9

The Basics: Zones and Records

*T*he most basic configuration elements in a DNS server are zones and records. In earlier chapters of this book, we tell you how DNS works and how to install and configure a DNS server. We would be remiss if we didn't help you take a serious look at the concepts of zones and records because they really make DNS work.

First on the agenda are some definitions. A *zone* is essentially the name used for a domain in DNS. Each domain name is a zone and has a zone file. The *zone file* contains all the records for the zone. A *record* is the DNS information linking a name to an address. Records should be familiar to you if you have worked with databases.

Understanding DNS Zones

As we just mentioned, zones are essentially domains within a DNS server that contain records for that domain. The slight difference in definition between a zone and a domain, however, is that a domain can contain subdomains in a hierarchy, although each subdomain is defined as a separate zone. No hierarchy exists per se with zones, although they can be linked to one another. Zone information is stored in zone files, which are simply text files containing the zone data. Each domain and subdomain in your DNS server is a zone. These individual zones are essentially containers for the associated records

DNS has essentially two types of zones: forward lookup and reverse lookup. We describe them both in this section.

Forward lookup zones

Forward lookup zones are the zones a normal user comes across most often on the Internet. These zones are, from a purely superficial level, the more useful of the two zone types. Most users on the Internet continually interact with forward lookup zones as they use the network, but probably never interact directly with a reverse lookup zone.

The reason that forward lookup zones are used more commonly is that users can resolve a host name to an IP address. After a user enters a DNS name in her DNS client (browser or e-mail client, for example), the DNS client uses the forward lookup zone to determine the IP address associated with that DNS name. In many other cases, forward lookup zones are used.

Like all DNS zones, the forward lookup zone begins with an SOA record, followed by name server records that specify all the name servers (master and slave) for the zone. The remaining records in the zone usually include an MX record that specifies which host receives e-mail for the domain and a series of A records that reference host names to IP addresses. Of course, forward lookup zones can, and often do, contain other types of records.

Reverse lookup zones

A *reverse lookup zone* is a special type of zone used by DNS clients to determine a host name when the IP address is known. Although DNS can theoretically provide client services without a reverse lookup zone, the DNS standard requires that every A record have a corresponding record in a reverse lookup zone. DNS itself doesn't rely on having a reverse lookup configured for each host, but many applications, such as SSH and some secure Web applications, do rely on reverse lookups.

DNS Records

Records are the lowest-level component in a DNS server. Whenever your DNS client performs a DNS lookup, it's making a query that retrieves a record of some sort. (We describe the many different types of records in the following section.) Each zone file usually contains several individual records. The zone must contain at least a start of authority (SOA) record. Along with identifying the server as authoritative for a given domain, the SOA record contains additional information, such as time-to-live (TTL) values.

Although a zone can exist with only a SOA record, it wouldn't prove to be useful. If that were the case, no information other than the TTL values and other SOA information could be queried for that zone. Not surprisingly, in order for a zone to be useful, it must contain other records. Most zones contain name server (NS), mail exchanger (MX), and host (A) records, although a wide variety of record types are available. The following section lists all the down-and-dirty information about the possible DNZ record types.

Record Types

Many record types are available for use on DNS servers. Some, such as host records (A), are more common than others; some record types are hardly ever used in practice. The most common records include the ones in this list:

- ✔ **Start of Authority (SOA):** The SOA record must exist for every zone. It defines the attributes for the zone, such as the TTL values for caching, the zone administrator's e-mail address, and the master name server for the zone. The SOA record also contains a serial number that must be incremented each time the zone data is changed, which tells the DNS server that the zone data must be reloaded. Although the serial number is arbitrary, it always changes to a higher number each time the zone file is edited.

- ✔ **Name Server (NS):** Most zones contain NS records, which define authoritative name servers for the zone. Each name server, master or slave, should have a name server record in the zone file.

- ✔ **Mail Exchanger (MX):** Mail exchanger records have one use in a zone file: They instruct other systems about which system accepts e-mail for a given domain. All e-mail for a domain (@domain.tld) always goes to the same server or group of servers. A basic configuration consists of a single MX record with a value set to the mail server for the domain. You can also have a number of MX records pointing to different servers, for two reasons. When the records have equal preference values, they can be used to balance the load between two or more mail servers (if the servers are forwarders). With different preference values, the mail server with the preferred record gets all mail to the domain by default. Only if the highest preference server is down does the next most preferred server receive the mail. This process continues for as many MX records as are in the zone. This configuration is used for failover so that if the default mail server goes down, the secondary (or tertiary, or so on) mail server receives mail for the domain and holds it until the main mail server can retrieve it.

✔ **Host (A):** A host, or A, record is the most common type of DNS record. It's simply used to map a host name to an IP address. A records are used for just about everything on the Internet except for mail routing. Whenever you connect to a Web site, use a database, or ping another system, you're most likely using the A record for the target host. An A record simply takes the IP address value of the host it's referencing.

✔ **Canonical Name (CNAME):** A canonical name, or CNAME, record is a fancy way of describing an alias for a host. In many cases, you may want to have more than one DNS name for a host, including a Web site with more than one name. You can accomplish this task in two ways. The first is to use more than one A record with different names but the same IP addresses. This strategy poses a problem, however: If you change the IP address of the host, you need to change the IP address for each A record pointing to the same host. You can easily miss one when you have more than one, especially if the person making the change didn't create the records and isn't aware that more than one A record exists for the host. This problem is solved by using the other method of assigning more than one name to an address: CNAME records. To establish multiple host names for a system using CNAME records, you first set one A record for the host and then add CNAME records. The CNAME records have information that points requests to the CNAME back to the A record you previously defined. When the host's IP address subsequently changes, the single A record is changed and all the CNAME records automatically point to the new host.

✔ **Pointer (PTR):** A pointer record is essentially the opposite of an A record. Whereas an A record is used to provide an IP address when the client knows the DNS host name, a PTR record is used to provide a host name when the IP address is known. PTR records are used in reverse lookup zones.

✔ **Text (TXT):** A TXT record can contain any information. Unlike the other record types that require a specific type of value (name or IP address), a TXT record can have any value. The problem with TXT records, though, is that clients have almost no way to retrieve them unless the clients specifically request them using a command-line DNS client. Hardly any applications make use of TXT records.

✔ **Host Information (HINFO):** A HINFO record is similar to a TXT record in that it can have a freeform value. The HINFO record was originally used for a specific purpose — unlike the TXT record, which has no specific purpose. The HINFO record was intended to hold the hardware type, operating system type, and version of a host. You find that the HINFO record is seldom implemented, though: Administrators don't want to divulge any information about the hosts on their networks because it can be used by an attacker.

✔ **Service Locator (SRV):** The SRV record is designed to allow DNS clients to find specific services on the network, such as printers or file servers, rather than specific hosts. Although this record type isn't widely implemented, it does form a cornerstone of the Microsoft Windows Active Directory infrastructure. The SRV records allow a user to contact a service by knowing the service type rather than the specific host where the service resides (and using an A record).

✔ **IPv6 Host (AAAA):** The IP version 6 host record type is similar to the A record in that it maps a host name to an IP address value. The difference, though, is that an AAAA record is used to map a 128-bit IPv6 address to a host name rather than the traditional 32-bit IPv4 value in an A record. IPv6 has not seen the expected widespread implementation, though; a series of fixes have been made to IPv4 to extend the useful lifespan of its address space.

More DNS record types exist than just those in this list. In addition to the listed types, other record types are either nonstandard or standard and are rarely used. In the real world, most system administrators use only SOA, A, MX, and PTR records with the occasional CNAME thrown in for good measure. Records other than those are rare.

What is IPv6?

Internet Protocol version 6 is a replacement for the current king of networking protocols, IPv4. Although IPv4 has served the Internet well and has enough flexibility to accommodate the millions of network computers making use of it, some critical design flaws may become more serious issues as the number of networks sharing access to the Internet increases. The most notable problem is address exhaustion. IP addresses are broken into two groups: public and private. *Public* IP addresses must be unique among all hosts on the Internet. Frankly, they're all for the most part taken. New users and providers are limited to obtaining addresses from other address holders. This exhaustion may force providers to make do with fewer and fewer IP addressable devices, and various issues — from an inability to provide connectivity to congestion — may result. The answer is an addressing scheme with more address space and other enhancements.

The IPv6 addressing protocol has been slow to penetrate networks, and the final specifications for the protocol aren't yet set in stone. Many newer operating systems (Linux, Windows XP, and Apple OS X, for example) have support, or can be configured to support, IPv6. With this feature enabled, many sites allow IPv6-based connections. For all the details about the progress of the IPv6 protocol, check out the IPv6 Web site: www.ipv6.org. To make use of IPv6 on the Internet, you need to have support from the IPv6 backbone, or 6bone. For more information, see www.6bone.net.

Working with Windows

Microsoft Windows needs special consideration when you're configuring zones not found in other DNS servers. When you're using DNS Server services on Windows 2000 or later operating systems, you can have special zones, known as Active Directory-integrated zones. Information specific to these zones is at the end of this section. First, we tell you about generic zone configuration. All DNS configuration in Windows is done using the DNS snap-in: Choose Programs⇨ Administrative Tools from the Start menu.

Moving forward in Windows

To create a new forward lookup zone, follow these steps:

1. **Navigate to the Forward Lookup Zones container under the DNS server on which you want the zone in the DNS tool, right-click, and choose New Zone.**

   The New Zone Wizard appears.

2. **Click Next to continue past the introductory dialog box in the wizard.**

   The next dialog box is Zone Type, as shown in Figure 9-1. You must select the type of zone being created: primary, secondary, or Active Directory integrated, which is available only if the system is running Active Directory.

3. **In this example, select Primary and click Next.**

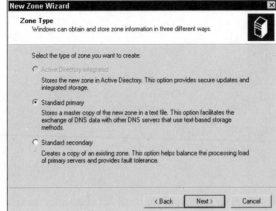

Figure 9-1:
Make a
decision
about the
new zone.

You have to name the zone. This name becomes the domain name for the zone.

4. Specify the name, as shown in Figure 9-2, and click Next to continue.

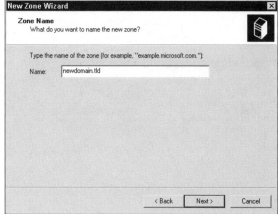

Figure 9-2:
Assign to the zone a name that will become the DNS domain name.

Now you must select a zone file to use, as shown in Figure 9-3. You almost certainly should create a new zone file as shown and accept the default filename. If you copied or backed up existing zone data from another system, though, you must copy that file to the `%systemroot%\system32\dns` folder and then select Use this existing file and specify the filename.

5. Select a zone file to use and click Next to continue.

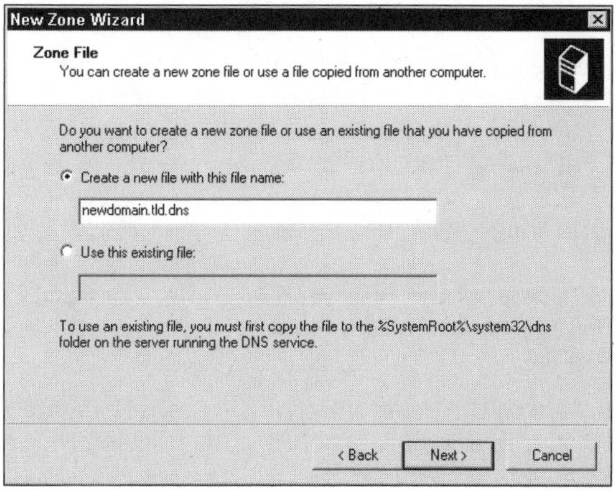

Figure 9-3:
Specify the DNS zone file to use to store the zone data.

The last dialog box in the New Zone Wizard shows a review of the information you have entered.

6. **Check Ensure that the review information is correct and click Finish to create the zone.**

Now that you have created your new zone, it appears under Forward Lookup Zones in the DNS snap-in. The zone created in these steps is shown in Figure 9-4.

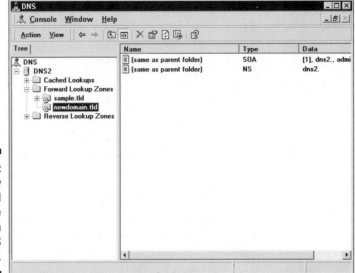

Figure 9-4:
The newly created zone appears in the DNS snap-in.

Adding records to the zone

As you can see, when you use the New Zone Wizard, two records are created automatically. The SOA record and NS record are required for all zones, so they're created for you. The zone now exists, and you can query it, but it's of no use because it contains no data. You must populate the zone with records.

To add a record to the zone, follow these steps:

1. **Locate in the left pane of the DNS snap-in, under Forward Lookup Zones, the zone in which to add a record. Right-click the zone, as shown in Figure 9-5.**

   You must choose from the menu the type of record to create. Choosing New Host, for example, adds an A record, and choosing New Mail Exchanger adds an MX record.

2. **For the sake of this example, choose New Host.**

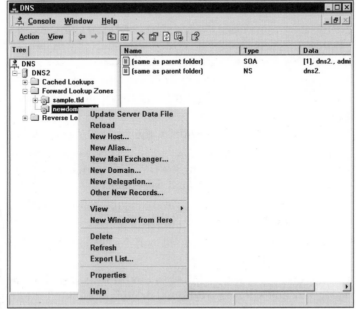

Figure 9-5:
Right-click a
zone to add
a variety of
records.

Figure 9-6 shows the New Host dialog box. The Location field, filled by default, shows the zone in which the A record will reside.

3. Fill in the Name field with the name of the host.

If you leave the Name field blank, the zone name is used as the host name, allowing you to assign an IP to the domain name (`newdomain.tld`, for example, rather than `host.newdomain.tld`).

Figure 9-6:
Adding an A
record to
the zone
in the
New Host
dialog box.

4. **Fill in the IP address field with the address to be assigned to the host.**

5. **Enable the Create associated PTR record check box if you want the pointer record for the host created automatically in the reverse lookup zone associated with the IP address.**

   This step saves you from having to go in later and add the PTR record manually. The reverse lookup zone for that IP address range must exist if you want to use this option.

6. **Set the time-to-live (TTL) value for the record, if you want.**

   This step is optional. By default, the record takes the TTL of the zone. This setting controls how long the record is cached by clients and caching DNS servers. The default value is usually acceptable.

7. **When you have filled in all the fields in the New Host dialog box, click the Add Host button.**

   The A record is added to the zone, and the Name field is cleared in the New Host dialog box.

8. **Add another A record by filling in the information in the New Host dialog box and clicking Add Host, or click the Done button if you're finished adding records.**

   Figure 9-7 shows the zone with the new A record in place.

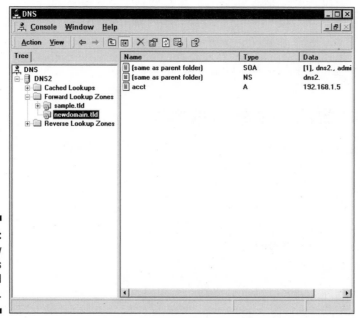

Figure 9-7:
The new record has been added to the zone.

You can follow the steps in the preceding section to add as many records as you want, but you may want to add a record that isn't on the menu when you right-click the zone.

Adding another record type

To add another record type, follow these steps:

1. **Right-click the zone in which to add the record.**

2. **Choose Other New Records.**

   The Resource Record Type dialog box appears, as shown in Figure 9-8.

3. **Select the record type to add, and click the Create Record button.**

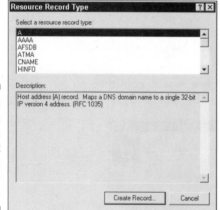

Figure 9-8:
Adding a
record type
that isn't
available on
the right-
click menu.

4. **Fill in the fields for the record as needed and then click OK.**

   The record is added to the zone.

As you can see from the Resource Record Type dialog box, you can use this method to add any record to the zone, including those listed on the menu when the zone is right-clicked.

Windows in reverse

After you have created forward lookup zones in your DNS server, you should add the corresponding reverse lookup zones. You should always have a reverse zone and PTR record for each host record in your DNS server.

In the following example, we show you how to create a zone and PTR record for the A record created in the preceding section, which was `acct.new domain.tld` pointing to `192.168.1.5`:

1. **In the DNS snap-in, right-click the Reverse Lookup Zones container under the correct DNS server and click New Zone.**

2. **Click Next to proceed past the introductory dialog box of the New Zone Wizard.**

3. **Select Standard Primary for the zone type and click Next.**

   You select Standard secondary if this DNS server was a slave server for the reverse lookup zone.

   This step requires you to specify the Network ID (subnet) for the reverse zone, as shown in Figure 9-9. In this step, you must specify the network portion of the IP addresses that will reside in the zone. The address in the example is simple because it's a standard Class C address. When you specify the address, the zone name is shown in the Reverse lookup zone name field automatically. If you want to manually specify the reverse zone name, you can select that option and type the zone name in the box. Specifying the network ID is much simpler, though, especially for a novice DNS administrator.

4. **Specify the subnet and click Next to continue.**

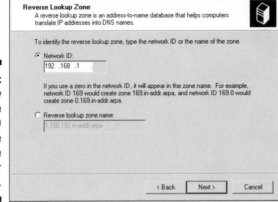

Figure 9-9:
Specify either the network ID or reverse lookup zone name for the zone.

You have to specify a zone file for the new zone, as shown in Figure 9-10. In most cases, you simply accept the default. If you have an existing zone file, though, you can select Use this existing file and specify the filename as long as the file is in the `%systemroot%\system32\dns` directory.

5. **Specify a zone file and click Next to continue.**

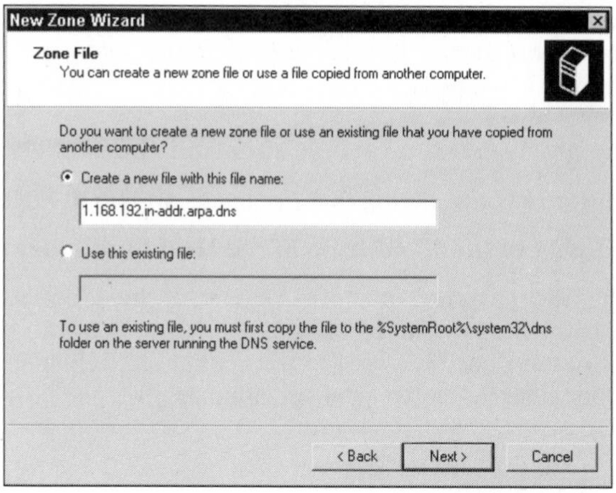

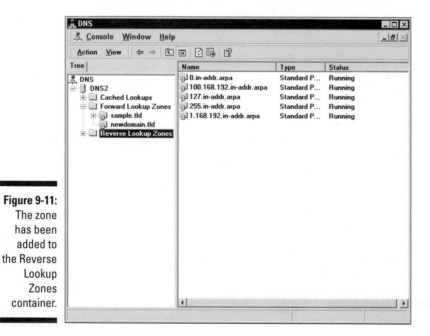

Figure 9-10:
Specify a
new or
existing
zone
filename.

You can review the selections you have made in the final dialog box of
the New Zone Wizard.

6. If you're satisfied with the settings, click Finish to add the zone.

The zone appears in the Reverse Lookup Zones container in the DNS snap-in,
as shown in Figure 9-11. Note that a number of reverse zones are created
automatically when the DNS server is installed, including those for the local
subnet, the `localhost` address (`127.0.0.0`), and the broadcast address
(`255.0.0.0`).

Figure 9-11:
The zone
has been
added to
the Reverse
Lookup
Zones
container.

Now you need to add a record to the reverse lookup zone to correspond with the host record you create earlier in this chapter, in the section "Forward lookup zones." Follow these steps:

1. **Right-click the newly created reverse zone and choose New Pointer.**

   The New Resource Record dialog box opens, as shown in Figure 9-12.

2. **Enter the host part of the IP address in the Host IP number box.**

   This is only the host part, not the network part, of the address. The complete IP address for the host in question is 192.168.1.5, and the reverse lookup zone is named 1.168.192.in-addr.arpa. The Host IP number will be is 5 as because the network is specified as 192.168.1 for the zone.

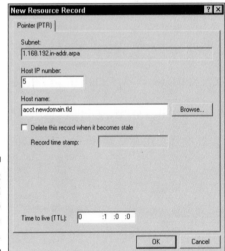

Figure 9-12:
Add a PTR record to the reverse lookup zone.

3. **Specify the host name.**

   It should be the same as the host name for the A record combined with the domain name for the forward lookup zone, as shown in the figure.

   The Delete this record when it becomes stale option is used to automatically clean up the DNS database and scavenge stale records. You rarely use this option unless you're using dynamic DNS. You don't want your manually configured records to be deleted automatically.

4. **Set the TTL for the record.**

   This setting controls how long the record is cached in caching DNS servers and client systems. Although the default value is inherited from the zone, you can customize it for the record.

5. **Click OK to add the record to the zone.**

   The new record appears in the zone, as shown in Figure 9-13.

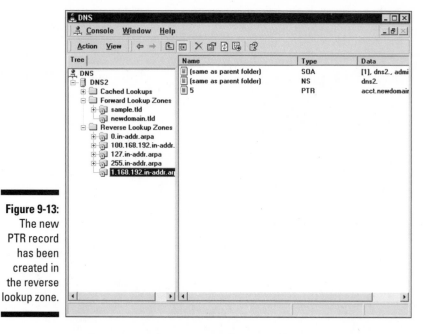

Figure 9-13:
The new
PTR record
has been
created in
the reverse
lookup zone.

You have created both a forward and reverse lookup zone and the associated record in each zone. You can now query these records from any DNS client if the rest of DNS is configured correctly. If you're working with an Internet DNS server, it must be registered with the root servers as the primary DNS server for the zone. You then can query the zone from anywhere on the Internet.

Making Use of Unix

Configuring DNS zones and records in Windows is a point-and-click process. Configuring zones and records in BIND, however, requires the manual customization of the BIND configuration file and the zone files themselves. Third parties have created tools specifically to add a graphical interface to the process, although most changes are still made by hand, by editing the files. (Appendix B describes one of these graphical interfaces — Webmin.)

Forward-looking Unix

Creating a forward lookup zone on BIND involves two steps: editing the BIND configuration file and creating the zone file. The BIND configuration file is typically located at /etc/named.conf. Open this file in your text editor of choice. You should find the file there, and it should look something like this:

```
options {
        directory "/var/named";
};

# Use with the following in named.conf, adjusting the allow
        list as needed:
key "rndc-key" {
        algorithm hmac-md5;
        secret "LNHAKyWTt493Em7+OJPkdQ==";
};

controls {
        inet 127.0.0.1 port 953
                allow { 127.0.0.1; } keys { "rndc-key"; };
};

zone "." {
        type hint;
        file "named.ca";
};

zone "0.0.127.IN-ADDR.ARPA" {
        type master;
        file "named.local";
};

zone "100.168.192.IN-ADDR.ARPA" {
        type master;
        file "named1.local";
};

zone "sample.tld" in {
        type master;
        file "sample.tld";
};
```

You can see a few things in this configuration file. First, the zone files are stored in the directory /var/named, the *working* directory. The DNS server is also configured to accept control connections from localhost using the specified key and is configured as a caching DNS server. It also has reverse zones for the localhost address and the local subnet as well as one zone, sample.tld.

To add a zone to the DNS server, add a line similar to the sample.tld zone directive in the example. You can add the new zone entry, which should look like the following example, anywhere after the controls section in the configuration file:

```
zone "newdomain.tld" in {
        type master;
        file "newdomain.tld.dns";
};
```

This file specifies a new zone named newdomain.tld with a zone file named
newdomain.tld.dns. This zone file is located by default in the working directory (/var/named). Under BIND, no differentiation exists between forward and
reverse zones either, so they're configured similarly in the configuration file, as
you see in the following section, "New reverse zones in Unix."

Now that you have added the zone directive to the configuration file, you need
to add the zone file. Switch to the DNS working directory (/var/named, in this
case) and open the zone file in your text editor. The zone file is newdomain.
tld.dns in this example. The file doesn't exist yet. You may want to copy an
existing zone file and edit it rather than start from scratch. The following
example shows what your zone file should contain:

```
@   IN   SOA     dns1.domain.tld. hostmaster.newdomain.tld. (
                        1               ; Serial
                        360000          ; Refresh
                        30000           ; Retry
                        3600000         ; Expire
                        360000  )       ; Minimum
    IN   NS      dns1.domain.tld.
```

Similar to the Windows example shown earlier in this chapter, this zone file is
enough to make the zone functional, but not enough to make it useful. First,
though, have a look at the sample zone file. The first line defines the SOA
record. The @ reflects the current *origin* of the zone (the zone name by default),
IN specifies an Internet record, and SOA defines the record type. The next field,
dns1.domain.tld., defines the primary master DNS server for the zone. The
hostmaster.newdomain.tld field defines the contact for the zone. This part
is an e-mail address, but the @ symbol is replaced by a period because the @
symbol has special meaning in a zone file. The attributes for the SOA record
must be in order, and they include the arbitrary serial number (which must be
incremented each time the zone is changed) and the TTL values for the zone.

The $ORIGIN directive sets the information that is appended to a name in a
zone file that isn't fully qualified. As you now know, a fully qualified name in a
zone file is suffixed with a period to indicate that it's fully qualified. When a
name isn't suffixed with a period, the value of the $ORIGIN directive is
appended. In addition, the @ symbol refers to the value of $ORIGIN. By default,
the value of $ORIGIN is the same as the zone name. By changing the value of
$ORIGIN part way through a zone file, you can change the domain name that's

appended to names that aren't fully qualified. You can use this value to implement subdomains by using the simple method we describe in Chapter 10 to set an $ORIGIN directive to the subdomain part way through your zone file. Every name following the $ORIGIN directive that isn't fully qualified is then in the subdomain because the new value of $ORIGIN is appended.

The second record in the zone file, the NS record, is also required. The NS records in a zone define the authoritative name servers for the domain. although this zone has only one NS record, most have two or more.

You have to add more records to the zone file in order for it to be useful to a client. As with the example we provide earlier in this chapter, in the section "Adding records to the zone," you can add an A record to the zone. To add the record, simply add the A record line to the end of the zone file:

```
acct        IN   A         192.168.1.5
```

Adding a record to the zone file is simple. The first field is the record name, which defines the host for an A record. IN indicates an Internet record (as most are), and A indicates the record type. Finally, the value field holds the IP address for the host.

Adding a record to a zone file in BIND is that simple. The key, though, is that you have to restart BIND when you make changes to the configuration file. When you're changing zone files, you can use the RNDC reload command to reload the zone data.

New reverse zones in Unix

Creating a reverse lookup zone in BIND is exactly the same as creating a forward zone: You first add a directive for the zone to the configuration file and then create the zone file. Unlike in Windows, though, no feature automatically creates the zone name. You need to determine the zone name yourself. In this case, you use the sample address in the A record: 192.168.1.5. The network address is 192.168.1, and the host address is 5. To create a reverse zone name, you reverse the order of the numbers in the network address and append the suffix in-addr.arpa. In this case, the zone name is 1.168.192. in-addr.arpa. The zone directive in the configuration file looks like this:

```
zone "1.168.192.in-addr.arpa" {
        type master;
        file "1.168.192.in-addr.arpa.dns";
};
```

Now you need to create a zone file for the reverse lookup zone. Although a reverse zone file contains SOA and NS records, just like a forward zone does, the remainder of the records in the zone are PTR records. The reverse lookup zone looks like this:

```
@   IN   SOA     dns1.domain.tld. hostmaster.newdomain.tld. (
                         1                ; Serial
                         360000           ; Refresh
                         30000            ; Retry
                         3600000          ; Expire
                         360000 )         ; Minimum
    IN   NS      dns1.domain.tld.
5   IN   PTR     acct.newdomain.tld.
```

As you can see in the example, a reverse zone file is the same as a forward zone file except that it has PTR records rather than A records.

Splitting the load: include statements

BIND allows you to use `include` statements in configuration and zone files. These simple statements allow you to split your configuration file or zone file into more than one file for ease of administration. You may want to put primary domains in one configuration file and secondary domains in another, for example.

The use of `include` statements is simple in both configuration and zone files. You still need the base zone and configuration files, but you use the `include` statements to link other files into the base files. With a configuration file, you use the `include` directive, as shown in this example:

```
options {
        directory "/var/named";
};

# Use with the following in named.conf, adjusting the allow
        list as needed:
key "rndc-key" {
        algorithm hmac-md5;
        secret "LNHAKyWTt493Em7+0JPkdQ==";
};

controls {
        inet 127.0.0.1 port 953
            allow { 127.0.0.1; } keys { "rndc-key"; };
};

include "forward.named.conf";
include "reverse.named.conf";
```

In this example, forward zones and reverse zones are contained in separate configuration files named `forward.named.conf` and `reverse.named.conf`. These files contain only zone directives defining zones and nothing else.

Using `include` statements in a zone file works slightly differently from using them in a configuration file, but the idea is the same. A zone file uses the `$INCLUDE` control statement:

```
@     IN  SOA     dns1.domain.tld. hostmaster.newdomain.tld. (
                          1               ; Serial
                          360000          ; Refresh
                          30000           ; Retry
                          3600000         ; Expire
                          360000 )        ; Minimum
      IN  NS      dns1.domain.tld.
Acct  IN  A       192.168.1.5
$INCLUDE cnames.newdomain.tld.dns
```

You can use the `$INCLUDE` statement in a zone file to include another file containing records, as shown in the example, but you can also use it in conjunction with the `$ORIGIN` statement to add subdomains to a zone. (Chapter 10 explains subdomains in detail.)

Chapter 10

Using Subdomains

*I*f you've read Chapter 9, you may recall that zones contain the records that are served to clients. At some point, however, your zone files become so full of records that they become unwieldy. It may not happen in a smaller office environment, but when you have a larger organization with multiple IP address ranges, you may need to consider splitting your zones into subdomains.

In Chapter 2, we explain that a domain is the highest-level name that belongs to you — for example, `domain.tld`. Subdomains encompass anything below that level, such as `sea.domain.tld`. Although this example may look like a host, it can also be a subdomain and contain hosts such as `ws1.sea.domain.tld`. You can name your subdomains anything you want. Common subdomains are named after business units or geographical locations. Your subdomains should have a name that is logical and somehow describes the records contained within.

Configuring Subdomains in Windows DNS

As in all configuration of the Microsoft Windows DNS Server, adding a subdomain is a fairly straightforward process. To build your subdomains under Windows 2000, follow these steps:

1. **Open the DNS snap-in by clicking the Start button and choosing Programs⇨Administrative Tools.**

2. **Locate the zone that will be the parent of the subdomain, as shown in Figure 10-1.**

3. **Right-click the parent domain and choose New Domain.**

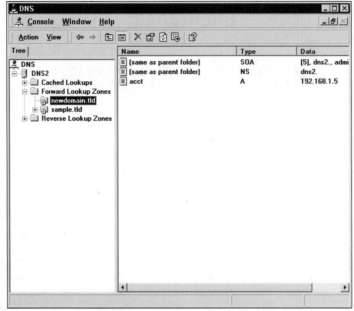

Figure 10-1:
Locate the
parent zone
for the
subdomain.

4. **In the New Domain dialog box, as shown in Figure 10-2, type the name of the new subdomain.**

   You need to type only the subdomain name as shown; you don't need to include the rest of the domain suffix.

5. **Click OK to create the domain.**

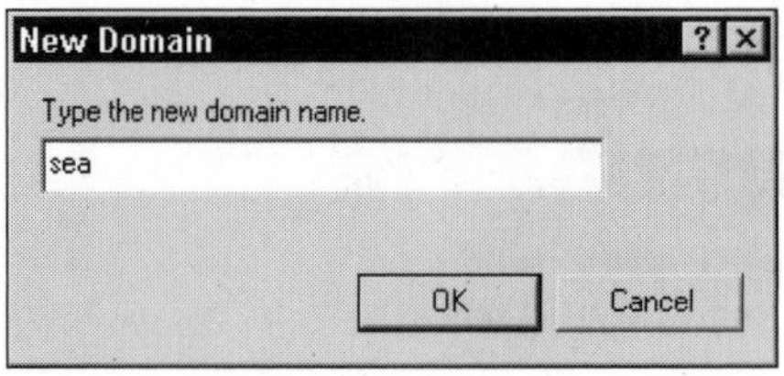

Figure 10-2:
What's the
subdomain
name?

The new subdomain is created, as shown in Figure 10-3. The subdomain appears as a container under the parent domain. You can add a record to the subdomain, just as you would with the parent domain.

To add a record to the subdomain, follow these steps (we also describe them in Chapter 9):

1. **Right-click the container in which to create the record.**

   In this case, it's the newly created subdomain.

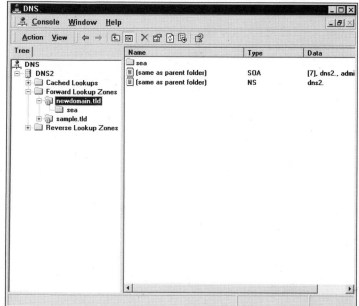

Figure 10-3:
The new subdomain has been created under the parent domain.

2. **Choose New Host to create a host (A) record or select another type of record to create.**

3. **Complete the New Host dialog box with the host name and IP address, as shown in Figure 10-4, and then click OK.**

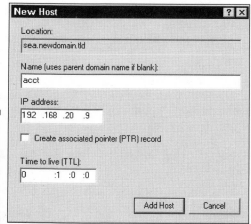

Figure 10-4:
Enter the host name and address for the new record.

The record now exists in the subdomain. By using the nslookup command (refer to Chapter 6) to query your server, you can see whether your tinkerings have accomplished what you have intended:

1. **Choose Run from the Start menu.**

2. **Enter** cmd **in the Open box and click OK.**

3. **Type** nslookup **and press Enter.**

4. **Use the command** SERVER <*address*> **to change the DNS server to the one on which you added the subdomain and record.**

5. **Type the DNS name of the record you created and press Enter (see Figure 10-5).**

   The IP address specified in the A record should be displayed, indicating that the subdomain is functioning correctly.

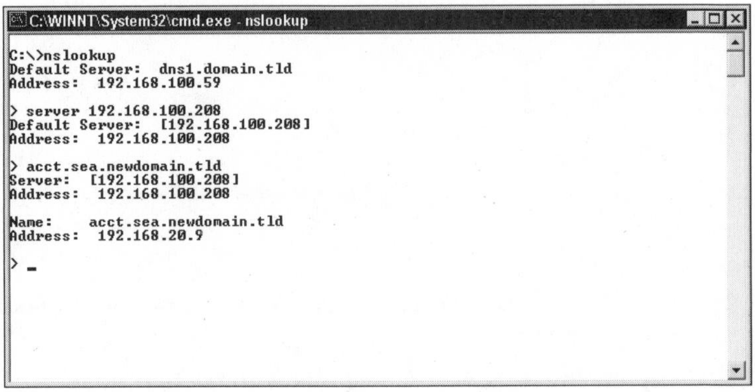

Figure 10-5:
Ensuring that the subdomain is working properly.

```
C:\WINNT\System32\cmd.exe - nslookup                              _ □ ×

C:\>nslookup
Default Server:  dns1.domain.tld
Address:  192.168.100.59

> server 192.168.100.208
Default Server:  [192.168.100.208]
Address:  192.168.100.208

> acct.sea.newdomain.tld
Server:  [192.168.100.208]
Address:  192.168.100.208

Name:     acct.sea.newdomain.tld
Address:  192.168.20.9

> _
```

In addition to creating a subdomain under a parent domain, as shown in the preceding example, you can create a subdomain under another subdomain. In the preceding example, the subdomain sea.newdomain.tld was created. But what do you do if you want to use business units in addition to geographical locations in your DNS namespace? Adding this organizational element is as simple as creating a subdomain in the preceding example.

Suppose that you want to create a domain for your company's engineering division. The following steps show you how to create the domain eng.sea.newdomain.tld and add a host named WS1:

1. **Open the DNS snap-in by clicking the Start button and choosing Programs⇨Administrative Tools.**

2. Locate the `sea.newdomain.tld` **subdomain you created earlier.**

3. **Right-click the** `sea` **container and choose New Domain.**

4. **Enter the name of the new subdomain, as shown in Figure 10-6, and click OK.**

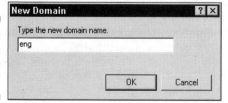

Figure 10-6:
What's
the new
subdomain?

If you launch the Windows 2000 DNS snap-in, you see the new subdomain as a container under the parent domain where you created it. You can now add a host or other record to the subdomain, as we explain in Chapter 9. Right-click the subdomain, choose New Host, and fill in the dialog box. The host appears in the subdomain container. Figure 10-7 shows NSLOOKUP being used to check the new host record and subdomain.

```
C:\WINNT\System32\cmd.exe - nslookup                          _ □ X

C:\>nslookup
Default Server:  dns1.domain.tld
Address:  192.168.100.59

> server 192.168.100.208
Default Server:  [192.168.100.208]
Address:  192.168.100.208

> WS1.eng.sea.newdomain.tld
Server:  [192.168.100.208]
Address:  192.168.100.208

Name:     WS1.eng.sea.newdomain.tld
Address:  10.52.202.105

>
```

Figure 10-7:
Ensuring
that the new
subdomain
and host
record are
working
properly.

Configuring Subdomains in BIND

Configuring subdomains in BIND is a more complex process than configuring them on a Windows 2000 server. In BIND, you need to set up the zone manually, whereas Windows is a graphically driven process. You can create subdomains in BIND in two ways:

✔ **You have only a few entries in a subdomain.** In this surprisingly simple method, the subdomain records are created directly in the parent domain zone file. Although this method makes creating the entries much easier, it has some shortcomings.

✔ **You have large subdomains.** This method, known as *delegating* the sub-domain, is fairly simple. It requires only that you create a new zone and add a few records in the zone of the parent domain. This method allows the administrator (you) of the name server on which the subdomain resides to make changes to the zone rather than require changes to be made on the parent domain's server. The subdomain may reside on the same server as the parent, but this method gives you the option to sepa-rate them. It also keeps the zone files less cluttered because you have two zone files — one for each domain (parent and subdomain) rather than only one zone file for both. If you end up having thousands of hosts, you will be thankful that you have small, organized zones to sort though in case you ever need to troubleshoot.

Taking the easy way out

To begin configuring a subdomain by using the simple method, first look at a standard zone file for the parent domain:

```
@          IN    SOA      dns1.domain.tld.
           hostmaster.newdomain.tld. (
                                1              ; Serial
                                360000         ; Refresh
                                30000          ; Retry
                                3600000        ; Expire
                                360000 )       ; Minimum
           IN    NS       dns1.domain.tld.
acct       IN    A        192.168.1.5
```

This example shows the zone file for a theoretical zone named newdomain.tld. Imagine that you want to create a host named ws1 for a remote site in your Seattle office, but you don't want it in the parent domain — you want it in a geographically based subdomain named sea. The host record looks like this:

```
ws1.sea      IN    A        192.168.100.109
```

Remember that when no trailing period appears after a name in a zone file, the zone name is appended. The result is that the sample host record points ws1.sea.newdomain.tld to 192.168.100.109, which is the required result. To add more subdomain records, continue this process. You can test your subdomain by using NSLOOKUP, as shown in Figure 10-8, or by using DIG (we describe both methods in Chapter 6).

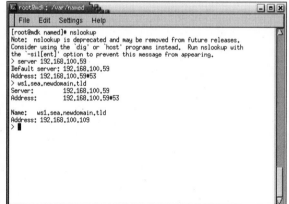

Figure 10-8:
Testing
the new
subdomain
record.

Serious subdomains

The simple method for creating subdomains we describe has shortcomings, as we tell you at the beginning of this section. What if you want to delegate the administration of the `sea.newdomain.tld` domain to another administrator with his own servers or to separate the `sea.newdomain.tld` domain out into a separate zone file on your DNS servers? This process isn't complex. Let's revisit the sample `newdomain.tld` zone file:

```
@           IN    SOA     dns1.domain.tld.
            hostmaster.newdomain.tld. (
                                1             ; Serial
                                360000        ; Refresh
                                30000         ; Retry
                                3600000       ; Expire
                                360000 )      ; Minimum
            IN    NS      dns1.domain.tld.
acct        IN    A       192.168.1.5
```

To add a subdomain named `sea`, you must tell other DNS servers and clients where to find the `sea.newdomain.tld` zone. You do that by creating name server (NS) records in the parent domain. The name server records looks like this:

```
sea         IN    NS      dns1.domain.tld
sea         IN    NS      dns2.domain.tld
```

You create an NS record for each DNS server that will host the subdomain. In this case, it's hosted on the same server as the parent domain. This change is the only one required in the parent zone. You now must add the subdomain's zone to the DNS servers that will host it. You do that by using the standard method in the BIND configuration file, adding a zone directive:

```
zone "sea.newdomain.tld" in {
        type master;
        file "sea.newdomain.tld";
};
```

Note that if the current server is a slave DNS server for the zone, the zone directive is different (refer to Chapter 9). Now that the zone directive has been added, the new zone file must be created. Nothing in a subdomain zone file is different from a parent domain zone file. The zone file should look something like this:

```
@           IN   SOA     dns1.domain.tld.
            hostmaster.sea.newdomain.tld. (
                                1           ; Serial
                                360000      ; Refresh
                                30000       ; Retry
                                3600000     ; Expire
                                360000 )    ; Minimum
            IN   NS      dns1.domain.tld.
            IN   NS      dns2.domain.tld.
ws1         IN   A       192.168.100.109
```

This example creates the ws1 host as a member of the subdomain, effectively accomplishing the same thing as the simple BIND configuration option. You can verify that the subdomain is working successfully using NSLOOKUP, as shown in Figure 10-8, or using the DIG utility.

With BIND, you can create multiple levels of subdomains by using either method. With the first method we describe, the subdomain host records simply have names such as ws1.acct.sea with as many levels of subdomains as you want.

Using the delegation method is somewhat more complex. You must "nest" the NS record for each subdomain in its immediate parent domain's zone file. The zone file for newdomain.tld would have an NS record for sea, and the zone file for sea.newdomain.tld would have an NS record for acct in order to get the subdomain acct.sea.newdomain.tld, for example.

You can also combine these two methods. You can, for example, have an NS record in the newdomain.tld zone file for acct.sea that points to the server containing the zone acct.sea.newdomain.tld. All records in the acct.sea.newdomain.tld zone then move to the acct.sea.newdomain.tld zone file, thus implementing the delegation method. Records for the subdomain sea.newdomain.tld can then move to the newdomain.tld zone file in the form name.sea because the sea.newdomain.tld subdomain using the simple non-delegation method isn't delegated.

Part V

Security and Advanced DNS Tricks

The 5th Wave By Rich Tennant

"Right here..., crimeorg.com. It says the well-run small-criminal concern should have no more than nine goons, six henchmen and four stooges. Right now, I think we're goon-heavy."

In this part . . .

In this part of the book, you find out how to use the advanced features of DNS, secure your DNS infrastructure, and troubleshoot your DNS system.

Although DNS is fairly simple at a superficial level, it has some high-level, complex features that facilitate lots of enhanced functionality. This functionality includes features that enable you to reduce the administrative overhead of the DNS servers and enable different DNS server systems to work together better. In addition, the security of your DNS servers is quite important. If your DNS infrastructure is compromised, you can end up with lost data, disrupted services, or other hassles.

Chapter 11

An Antidote for a Poisoned Cache: DNS Security

· ·

In This Chapter

▶ DNS security issues

▶ Securing DNS servers on Windows

▶ Securing BIND servers on Unix

· ·

*Y*ou would be extremely unwise to think of DNS as a service that doesn't require much in the way of security. Although the method for securing DNS isn't always obvious, it's important nonetheless. For instance, the act of compromising DNS security is often the first step in larger attacks, such as domain hijacking, in which a domain name is stolen, or the theft of e-mail. DNS security is also important in a corporate environment because an attacker could use an insecure DNS server to redirect traffic to an untrusted system. A secure DNS infrastructure is the first step in preventing this type of attack.

Potential DNS Security Issues

DNS has several major security issues. Some are important for all servers, and others are specific to certain functions, such as dynamic DNS. Both Microsoft Windows DNS and BIND provide a number of security features that can be used to customize DNS security for your environment.

Server security

One of the most important steps, if not the most important step, for DNS security is the security of the server itself. This issue isn't specific to DNS, but it's important nonetheless. The server must be secure to prevent malicious users from usurping the server and then compromising the DNS service.

The DNS server (hardware and operating software) should be carefully configured to minimize the potential risk from ill-intentioned network users (such as hackers). Ideally, DNS is the only application running on the system, especially if the DNS server is publicly accessible. A system running only DNS is more easily secured because the number of items that you have to ensure are secured against misuse is reduced. The other reason to isolate services on their own systems is attrition. If one system is compromised and it's running only DNS, that's a much better situation than the compromise of a system running DNS, a Web server, and an e-mail server.

After one application on a server is compromised, the security of the entire system is almost always lost. Hackers often install remote access and control applications if they can. Because this installation may or may not leave any evidence, you should back up data (not applications), format, and then rebuild the entire server from scratch if you determine that it was compromised.

Server security has three general components you need to be aware of:

- ✔ Physical security

- ✔ Operating system security

- ✔ DNS server application security

The first step to server security is hardware security. The servers should be in a secure location so that they cannot be accessed directly by unauthorized users. A good example of physical security includes placing the server in a secured room where only a few people have access. The next step involves securing the operating system itself. Although this step varies widely depending on your operating system, many security resources exist for all operating systems. Generally speaking, you should ensure that these three areas have been addressed:

- ✔ **Strong passwords:** Strong passwords should be at least six characters long, contain absolutely no dictionary words (names, places, or verbs, for example), include numeric characters, and not make use of repeating characters.

- ✔ **Restricting remote access authority:** Be sure to disable remote access (telnet, secure shell, terminal services, and remote desktop, for example) if they're not needed. If remote access services are needed, grant permissions to use these services only to users who need them.

- ✔ **Disable unused user accounts:** Some operating systems have anonymous or guest user accounts enabled by default. In most cases, these accounts serve no meaningful purpose and should be disabled or deleted.

- ✔ **Install patches and security updates:** New security risks are regularly identified. If you keep abreast of these updates, you can give yourself an edge against anyone who would take control of (or disable) your server.

Although you shouldn't use dictionary words, you can model your password after one. For example, the relatively weak password `dolphin` could become the much better `39d01ph1n6`. Notice that the middle of the new password uses character substitution (*o* becomes the numeral 0 and *I* becomes the numeral 1) to keep the password somewhat recognizable.

The final step for server security is configuring the security of the DNS server application. This process doesn't refer to a secure configuration of the DNS server but rather to running the DNS server application in a secure manner. By default, most DNS server applications run with full administrative privileges on a system using the system account in Windows and running as `root` in Unix. You can change the credentials of the DNS server application so that it runs at a lower privilege level. The importance of running the DNS server at a lower privilege level is that if it's compromised, it cannot be used to compromise the entire system. Near the end of this chapter, in the section "Running BIND in a jail," we discuss how to run BIND at a lower privilege level.

External and internal DNS

Some environments need to have a DNS server for only internal users — where no records are served to external clients. Other environments — such as ISPs (Internet Service Providers) — sometimes need an external DNS server to serve records to only outside customers. In the great majority of cases, though, the need exists to serve both internal (LAN) and external clients. Each of these scenarios has different security requirements.

External DNS doesn't require much in the way of specialized configuration. The external DNS server should be located outside the firewall or in a firewall-controlled DMZ. The reason is that access to the server can be restricted and, if it's compromised in any way, it doesn't threaten the internal network resources. Regardless, you still don't want to have to continually rebuild your DNS server, so it should be thoroughly secured.

A *demilitarized zone,* or *DMZ,* is a network that is separate from an internal LAN but is also behind the firewall and not on the public network. The DMZ is used to isolate servers that can be accessed by external users in case one of these servers is attacked and compromised. The attacker can use the compromised system to attack any other systems in the DMZ, but can't attack any systems on the internal network because the DMZ is isolated.

An internal DNS server is configured somewhat differently. You should still configure it in a secure manner, but because it's located within the private network, the server is protected by the (presumed) firewall that conceals the rest of the network. If recursion is enabled on the internal DNS server, the firewall should be configured to allow outgoing connections enabled on the DNS port (53) so that the DNS server can retrieve records from other DNS servers.

When you're required to provide both internal and external clients with DNS resolution, as in the case in which a company hosts its own DNS for a Web site or e-mail, you should have two sets of DNS servers. One set for external clients should be located in the DMZ as just explained and should host only the zones and records that are absolutely necessary. Internal DNS servers are located in the internal network and serve internal clients. This separation of internal and external DNS servers limits the possibility of information leaks and DNS poisoning, as described in the following section.

Poisoned DNS

The goal of many attacks against DNS servers is spoofing. Normally, a DNS request is served by an authoritative DNS server for a domain. *Spoofing* occurs when an attacker intercepts a DNS request and sends a manufactured (spoofed) response to the client. The client can be either a DNS client or a DNS server performing recursion. By spoofing the DNS response, the client then has an incorrect DNS entry, which is cached. This process is known as *cache poisoning* because the cached spoofed response is reused until the time-to-live (TTL) value expires.

The term *poisoned* is used because the false record (the poison) is injected into the system at one point and spreads throughout the system, affecting other points. This situation happens especially when a DNS server's cache is poisoned because it may serve many clients whose DNS caches are also poisoned.

Although intercepting individual DNS requests poisons both individual DNS servers doing recursion and individual clients, sometimes an attacker wants to cause the poisoning effect on a larger scale. In this case, he can use one of a few methods to poison the authoritative DNS server for a domain. In this case, every time a request is made for the domain, the poisoned record is returned to the client.

Typically, cache poisoning is done on the client side. The attacker is located at a point where he can intercept the DNS traffic from a specific client and spoof to that client any DNS entries he wants. DNS server poisoning, on the other hand, is done on the server end. DNS server poisoning can be done by either intercepting all requests at the server and spoofing the DNS responses or poisoning the server itself by changing the records.

Although cache poisoning is normally done by intercepting DNS requests and injecting false responses or falsifying zone transfers, it can also be done if dynamic DNS updates are enabled on the server. Dynamic DNS entries can typically be added by any system and then subsequently modified or deleted by only that system. This situation causes two problems in that any system can add a record to a zone and an attacker can modify a record if security is weak. Dynamic DNS should be enabled for only private workstation networks and should never be enabled for servers. Keep dynamic DNS disabled except in a zone with only workstations.

Leaky seals

An *information leak* is any security vulnerability that causes private information (such as the host-to-IP mapping on your DNS server) to end up in the hands of an unauthorized person. Although an information leak vulnerability isn't usually the mechanism used in direct attacks against your network, they do provide an attacker with valuable information about the configuration of your systems. They can therefore be used to find vulnerabilities for a later attempt at disabling or intruding into your network. Information is power, and when it comes to securing your network, you should keep all the power to yourself.

DNS has a couple of information leak vulnerabilities inherent in its design, including the domain listing function `ls` in `nslookup` and zone transfers. The ls function is used to list all hosts in a domain. Almost no modern DNS servers respond to the `ls` command though, so it isn't much to worry about.

Zone transfers are worth worrying about. They're used to transfer all the zone data for a specific zone to a slave server for that zone. Without zone transfer security, though, anyone can perform a zone transfer and get a list of all hosts in the zone. Restricting zone transfers is one of the key tenets of DNS security. Zone transfers should always be restricted so that only the slave server or servers for a particular zone can perform a zone transfer. Zone transfers are restricted either by the IP address of the systems allowed to perform transfers or by encryption keys so that any system with the proper key can perform a zone transfer.

Securing DNS on Windows

Windows DNS from Windows 2000 and later has extensive security features, even including zone-based ACLs.

Restricting zone transfers

Restricting zone transfers is one of the first steps to DNS security. Restricting zone transfers stops the information leak that occurs when unauthorized users transfer zones from your servers. Using a zone transfer, an attacker can get a list of all the systems in the domain with little effort. With this list, he can choose the systems he wants to attack rather than have to use the more difficult method of network mapping. Restrictive zone transfer policies are just one method of keeping your network layout away from prying eyes.

Unfortunately, Windows by default sets zones to be transferable by anyone. It's also unfortunate that zone-transfer policies are set on a per-zone basis. If you have a number of existing zones, changing them all to a more restrictive policy involves a great deal of work. New zones are configured as they're created, saving more work later on.

To set the zone transfer configuration on a zone, follow these steps:

1. **Open the DNS Management snap-in by clicking the Start button and choosing Programs⇨Administrative Tools from the menu.**

2. **Navigate using the left pane and locate a zone under either Forward Lookup Zones or Reverse Lookup Zones, as shown in Figure 11-1.**

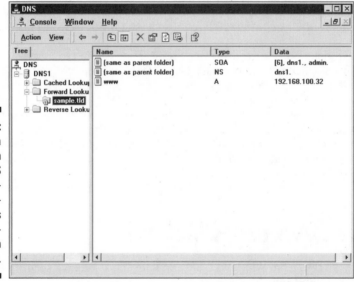

Figure 11-1:
Select a zone in the DNS management snap-in to set its configuration properties.

3. **Right-click the zone and choose Properties from the pop-up menu.**

4. **Click the Zone Transfers tab in the zone Properties dialog box, as shown in Figure 11-2.**

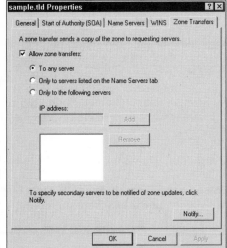

Figure 11-2:
Setting
zone-
transfer
policies —
the default
setting
allows
any zone
transfer.

5. **Set the zone-transfer policy for the zone.**

The default setting allows zone transfers to any server, which is obviously too lax. Two other options are available for zone transfers:

• **Only to servers listed on the Name Servers tab:** Selecting this
option allows zone transfers to any system with an NS record for
the zone (any other name servers for the zone). This option typically is the one you select because any secondary DNS servers for
this zone are listed on the Name Servers tab and these are the only
servers requiring zone transfers.

• **Only to the following servers:** Selecting this option allows zone
transfers to only the explicitly listed servers. If you have secondary servers for the zone, you must add their IP addresses to
this list by clicking the Add button. Unlike in the preceding option,
any servers on the Name Servers tab aren't automatically allowed
zone transfers; the servers must be explicitly specified.

6. **Disable zone transfers.**

Choose this option if the zone has no slave DNS servers, such as when
you're using only one DNS server or multiple master DNS servers.

You use the Notify button, at the bottom of the Zone Transfers tab, to
configure the DNS NOTIFY message that is used when zones are modified (see Chapter 12).

7. **When you're finished, click OK to save the zone-transfer configuration
and close the zone Properties dialog box.**

Restricting interfaces

Another security setting for a Windows DNS server, although it's less commonly used, is interface restriction. You can have the DNS server answer DNS queries on only one or a set of network interfaces rather than all interfaces on a system (the default). This feature isn't useful if your DNS server has only one interface (as most do); if your DNS server is attached to multiple (multi-homed) networks, however, you may want to provide DNS service to only one interface or a few.

To restrict the interfaces on which DNS provides service, follow these steps:

1. **Open the DNS Management snap-in by clicking the Start button and choosing Programs⇨Administrative Tools from the menu.**

2. **Locate the DNS server name in the left pane and then right-click and choose Properties.**

   The server Properties dialog box opens, as shown in Figure 11-3.

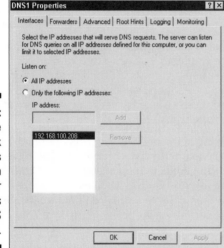

Figure 11-3:
Setting the network interfaces on which the server listens for DNS queries.

On the default tab, Interfaces, you configure on which interfaces the server listens. By default, the server listens on all IP addresses and therefore on all interfaces.

3. **To specify the addresses on which the server listens, first select the Only the following IP addresses option.**

All addresses assigned to all interfaces on the system appear on the list by default.

4. **Select an address and click the Remove button to exclude that address from receiving DNS services.**

5. **To add an address not on the list, enter the address in the IP address box and click the Add button.**

6. **When the list of IP addresses is configured to your liking, click OK to save the changes and close the server Properties dialog box.**

Zone ACLs

In Windows, Active Directory (AD) -integrated DNS zones can have access control lists (ACLs). These ACLs restrict who can make changes to the zone, which can help add security to specific zones and allow for the delegation of zone maintenance to users other than the administrator. This feature is useful if you want to allow a branch office or group administrator to add their systems to their zone.

Remember that ACLs can be set only on Active Directory-integrated zones, and the feature is available by default when AD-integrated zones are in use.

To configure the ACL for a zone, follow these steps:

1. **Open the DNS Management snap-in by clicking the Start button and choosing Programs⊏>Administrative Tools from the menu.**

2. **Locate the zone to configure in the left pane. Right-click the zone and choose Properties.**

3. **Click the Security tab in the zone Properties dialog box, as shown in Figure 11-4.**

   If you see no Security tab, the zone isn't an Active Directory-integrated zone and an ACL cannot be configured.

   Permissions are inherited by default from the parent object, which is typically fairly far up the Active Directory tree. If you want to change the ACL on a specific zone, you must disable this behavior.

4. **Deselect the Allow inheritable permissions from parent to propagate to this object check box.**

   You see the dialog box shown in Figure 11-5.

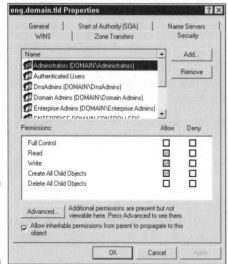

Figure 11-4:
Configuring
an ACL for
the zone.

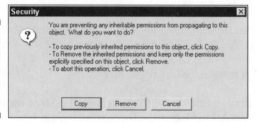

Figure 11-5:
Keep them
or discard
them? You
decide.

You have to choose whether to keep the old permissions that have been inherited and copy them to the new ACL or remove the inherited permissions and start from scratch. You probably should keep the inherited permissions because you simply add the users to whom you want to give access and leave in place the existing administrative users and groups or change permissions for users on the existing list.

5. **In that case, click the Copy button. To remove the existing permissions, click Remove.**

6. **To change permissions, select the user from the list and change the permissions in the Permissions box:**

   • **Read:** The user can view zone data and configuration information.

   • **Write:** The user can add, modify, and delete zone data.

- **Create All Child Objects:** The user can create child objects, such as subdomains, under the current zone.

- **Delete All Child Objects:** The user can delete child objects, such as subdomains, under the current zone.

7. **If you need to add a user to the list, click the Add button and select the user in the Select Users, Computers, or Groups dialog box and click OK. To remove a user from the list, select the user and click the Remove button.**

8. **When you have completed the process of setting permissions, click OK to close the Zone properties dialog box.**

You can configure permissions for the entire DNS server by right-clicking the server in the left pane and choosing Properties and then clicking the Security tab. This procedure works the same as for an individual zone, except that the permissions are effective for all zones. For permission to function, the DNS server must be integrated with Active Directory.

Dynamic DNS security

Dynamic DNS is another feature that is enabled by default for Active Directory-integrated zones, although it isn't enabled by default for nonintegrated zones. Dynamic DNS updates present a security vulnerability because an attacker can pollute the DNS zone information.

Active Directory-integrated zones and nonintegrated zones have different security requirements. With nonintegrated zones, no security measure is available except for some basic rules. Dynamic DNS shouldn't be enabled for nonintegrated zones unless absolutely necessary.

Active Directory-integrated zones use security measures to avoid rogue updates. Only authenticated users may submit DNS updates using a security method known as GSS-TSIG for transaction security.

To change dynamic DNS settings:

1. **Open the DNS Management snap-in by clicking the Start button and choosing Programs⇨Administrative Tools from the menu.**

2. **Locate the zone to configure in the left pane, right-click, and choose Properties.**

   The zone Properties dialog box opens to the General tab, as shown in Figure 11-6.

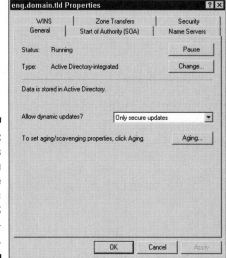

Figure 11-6:
On this tab, you determine dynamic DNS configuration.

3. **Select the dynamic DNS setting by using the Allow dynamic updates drop-down box.**

   The following three settings are available on an Active Directory-integrated zone; only two are available on a non-integrated zone:

   • **No:** Dynamic updates are disabled.

   • **Yes:** Dynamic updates are enabled and security isn't required. Avoid this setting.

   • **Only secure updates (only Active Directory-integrated zones):** Dynamic updates are enabled and GSS-TSIG security is required.

4. **Click OK to save the changes and close the zone Properties dialog box.**

Save the planet — stop cache pollution

The Secure cache against pollution option is a server-wide option used to attempt to avoid cache pollution caused by incorrect DNS responses. The Secure cache against pollution option causes the server to discard rather than cache any DNS responses that are not in the domain in the DNS request. For example, if the DNS request is for www.domain.tld and a referral is returned to www.rogue.tld, that referral isn't cached. When the option is disabled, any referrals are cached.

Referrals are used to pollute the DNS server's cache by attaching unrelated DNS records to the referral.

To enable the Secure cache against pollution option:

1. **Open the DNS Management snap-in by clicking the Start button and choosing Programs➪Administrative Tools from the menu.**

2. **Locate the DNS server for which you want to enable the option in the left pane, right-click, and choose Properties.**

3. **Click the Advanced tab, as shown in Figure 11-7.**

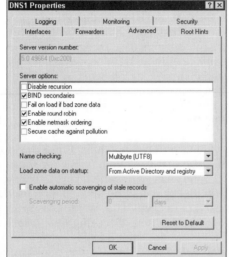

Figure 11-7: On this tab, you set the Secure cache against pollution option.

4. **Select the Secure cache against pollution check box.**

5. **Click OK to save the changes and close the server Properties dialog box.**

Securing DNS (BIND) on Unix

Although you can secure BIND on a Unix system in many ways, you should take a few important steps on every system, as described in this section.

Transaction signatures and control security

Transaction signatures (TSIG) is a method of securing DNS data by using encryption with a shared secret key. A *shared secret key* is simply an encryption key configured on both ends of the connection so that both parties must know the same key. TSIG is used to secure zone transfers, dynamic updates, and control functions, such as restarting the name server.

Using codes: Encryption

Encryption is the process of converting plain text into ciphertext. *Ciphertext* isn't readable by any party who doesn't have the correct key to decrypt it. Although you can use a variety of encryption algorithms, their common feature is that they take two pieces of input, the data and a key, and produce ciphertext. Without both the key and the ciphertext, getting the plain text data is nearly impossible. The term "nearly impossible" is used because many encryption algorithms are susceptible to attack. Although the process is usually quite difficult, you can get the plain text data from the ciphertext without the proper key. Encryption algorithms are often a compromise in that they may be susceptible to a certain attack, but that attack is so difficult that the time it would take to carry out would be so large that the attack would be of no value.

Two basic types of keys are in encryption algorithms: those that use shared secret keys (symmetric) and those that use public/private-key pairs. Shared secret keys must be shared among each party who wants to encrypt or decrypt data. With public-/private-key pairs, the public key is used to encrypt data, and the private key is used to decrypt data. We discuss the advantage of this arrangement in the following section, "Securing zone transfers."

The biggest problem in *cryptography* (the study of encryption) other than the design of a secure encryption algorithm is key exchange. In a shared secret key algorithm, the person encrypting data must be able to send the key to the recipient of the data. Although the data is encrypted and can be sent over a clear channel, the key must be kept secure or else the data gets compromised. You can send the key in somewhat secure ways (by way of a secure courier, for example), but these methods are often slow and unwieldy.

The public-/private-key pair solution addresses the problem of key exchange. The recipient of a message generates a pair of keys, one public and one private. The recipient keeps the private key secure and sends out the public key to anyone who wants to send some encrypted data. The sender encrypts the data by using the public key, and the recipient decrypts the data by using the private key. Although the mathematics behind the way a public-key algorithm works are complex, the private key is the only way to decrypt the data; the public key is useful only for encryption. Most modern encryption algorithms are hybrid systems in that they use slower public-key encryption to exchange a shared secret key and then use that key in a faster symmetric algorithm for the data-encryption process.

Another type of cryptographic algorithm is known as a *one-way hash function*. This type of function is used by TSIG for DNS security. A one-way hash function uses input (typically data and a key) to create some output, known as a hash. This output is much smaller than the original input, but is still large enough to have a high probability of being unique. This hash can be generated by two parties using a shared secret key and some known data, and then the two parties can compare hashes and determine whether the data has been altered in transit.

For more advanced information on encryption, get a copy of the book *Applied Cryptography: Protocols, Algorithms, and Source Code in C,* by Bruce Schneier (Wiley Publishing, Inc.). This book explains the basics of cryptography and then proceeds to more advanced topics.

TSIG is fairly easy to configure in BIND. You must first generate a shared secret key and then configure the key in the configuration file. To generate a key on a BIND 9 system, issue the following command and replace ⟨*hostname*⟩ with the name of one of the systems using the key. although this value is arbitrary, it assigns a name to the key. You should use a name that describes the zone name or host name:

```
dnssec-keygen -a HMAC-MD5 -b 128 -n HOST <hostname>
```

This example generates two files in the current directory: K⟨*hostname*⟩+157+n.key and K⟨*hostname*⟩+157+n.private. Note that the value n is a hash value of the key itself and is used simply for identification. Open the .private file and you see a value such as Key: 62+ZgLvjjofGXWsM8OjKZw==. You need to insert this value in the BIND configuration file in a key statement. The key statement should immediately follow the options statement:

```
options {
        directory "/var/named";
};
key "eng.domain.tld." {
        algorithm hmac-md5;
        secret "62+ZgLvjjofGXWsM8OjKZw==";
  };
key "rndc-key" {
        algorithm hmac-md5;
        secret "LNHAKyWTt493Em7+OJPkdQ==";
  controls {
        inet 127.0.0.1
                allow { 127.0.0.1; } keys { "rndc-key"; };
  };
```

After keys are defined, you can use them for zone-transfer and dynamic-update security, as discussed later in this chapter. Keys can also be used for control security. BIND 9 uses a utility named rndc to control the DNS server.

The rndc utility can be used to restart the server, reload zone files after an update, flush the DNS cache, and more. It doesn't work without a key defined in the configuration file, though.

The advantage of using rndc is that it allows the remote control of a BIND DNS server. With no security in use, however, anyone can start and stop any DNS server he wants. For this reason, rndc isn't enabled by default. To allow the use of rndc, follow these steps:

1. **Create a key using the** dnssec-keygen **command, as shown a little earlier in this section; name the key** rndc-key.

    The complete command is

    ```
    dnssec-keygen -a HMAC-MD5 -b 128 -n HOST rndc-key
    ```

2. **Add the key to the BIND configuration file, as shown in the preceding code listing.**

3. **Add a** controls **statement to the BIND configuration file, as shown in the preceding code listing.**

    The values are shown in this list:

    - The inet address defines the IP address on which you want the server to listen for control commands. Change it to an address on your system or leave it at 127.0.0.1 to listen only locally. To listen on all addresses, use the value *.

    - The allow address defines the IP addresses that are allowed to send commands to the DNS server. The value 127.0.0.1 allows only local commands. You can also specify external systems as long as you separate the addresses with semicolons. Using a value of any allows all systems to send control commands as long as they have the correct key.

    - The keys value specifies the keys used to allow control commands to be sent to the system. The values here (separated by semicolons) refer to the names of keys defined in the key statements earlier in the configuration file.

4. **Restart the DNS server.**

5. **Configure the client.**

    On the system that will send the commands to BIND using rndc, you must create a configuration file. This file is typically /etc/rndc.conf and must look like this:

    ```
    key "rndc-key" {
            algorithm hmac-md5;
            secret "LNHAKyWTt493Em7+OJPkdQ==";
    ```

```
};
options {
        default-key "rndc-key";
    default-server 127.0.0.1;
};
```

This `rndc.conf` file uses a `key` statement that is the same as the one in the BIND configuration file shown earlier in this chapter. The `options` statement simply defines the default key that is used and the default server to which `rndc` sends commands. You can also add more keys to the `rndc.conf` file if you have other servers you want to control.

Now that you have configured `rndc`, you can begin to use it. The `rndc` utility is a simple one. You can type `rndc` for a list of all `rndc` commands. The most common `rndc` commands are `rndc reload` and `rndc restart`, which reload the zone files after a change and restart the DNS daemon after a change to the configuration file, respectively. You can also type `rndc reload <zone>` to reload only a specific zone file.

When you're using keys, the BIND configuration file (typically `named.conf`) and the `rndc` configuration file (`rndc.conf`) should be set to a permission level at which they're readable only by their owner because they contain keys that can allow a malicious user to perform unauthorized updates or zone transfers or control the DNS server. Use the command `chmod 600 <file>` to set the permissions on these files. As a result, only the owner of the file and `root` can read and write to the file.

Securing zone transfers

BIND also allows zone transfers to all clients by default. You should restrict zone transfers for all zones to only your slave DNS servers (if any). Just add an `allow-transfer` substatement to each zone or to the entire server. You most likely want to disable all zone transfers by default in the BIND configuration file and allow zone transfers as needed in the zone files. You may also want to allow zone transfers to your known slave servers globally and allow or disallow zone transfers to other systems on an as-needed basis in the zone files.

To disable zone transfers globally, add the following lines to the `options` section of your BIND configuration file — typically, `/etc/named.conf`:

```
options {
      allow-transfer { none; };
};
```

If you want to allow zone transfers to your known slave servers globally, replace none with the IP addresses of those servers separated by semicolons:

```
options {
        allow-transfer { 192.168.1.2; 10.0.0.4; };
};
```

Now that you have configured zone transfer policies globally (although it isn't required), you can configure zone transfers on a zone-by-zone basis. In the BIND configuration file, under the zone statement for the zone you intend to configure, you must add an allow-transfer substatement:

```
zone "sample.tld" {
        type master;
        file "sample.tld";
        allow-transfer { none; };
```

This example disables all zone transfers for the zone. You can add the IP addresses of the servers which are allowed zone transfers to the allow-transfer substatement separated by semicolons:

```
zone "sample.tld" {
        type master;
        file "sample.tld";
        allow-transfer { 192.168.1.2; 192.168.1.3; };
```

You can also allow zone transfers based on the TSIG keys, as explained in the preceding section. As long as the key is defined in a key section in the configuration file, you can allow zone transfers to any server with the appropriate key by specifying the key name this way:

```
allow-transfer { key eng.domain.tld.; };
```

Some slave server setup is also required when using TSIG for zone transfers. You must add the appropriate key statement to the configuration file to define and specify the key and then add a server statement:

```
server 192.168.100.2 {
        keys { eng.domain.tld.; };
};
```

The server statement tells the slave server that whenever it contacts the specified server, it must use the specified TSIG key.

Restricting interfaces

As with DNS on Windows, you can also restrict the network interfaces on which BIND responds to queries. You may want to do that on a *multi-homed* system, which is one with more than one network connection. You may not want to provide DNS service to an external network, or you may want to provide different DNS services to different subnets.

With BIND on Unix, you can *bind* the DNS server to one IP address and start another *instance* of BIND running on another IP address. Each instance of the DNS server can use a different database. This strategy allows you to have more than one virtual DNS server running on a single server, which is useful if you have a small network and want to have different DNS databases for internal and external clients. Running multiple instances of BIND on one system is as simple as starting the first instance of BIND with the command `named -c <configfile1>` and the second instance with the command `named -c <configfile2>`. You have to ensure that each instance of BIND is configured to listen on a unique IP address, though; otherwise, they don't both start.

To configure your DNS server to listen on only specific interfaces, you need to add a `listen-on` substatement to the configuration file. This statement resides in the `options` section of the configuration file because it's a global option for the DNS server. The `listen-on` substatement requires an IP address or list of addresses:

```
options {
      listen-on { 192.168.100.2; 10.0.0.2; };
};
```

In addition to restricting the interfaces on which BIND provides service, you can restrict the IP addresses that are allowed to query the server or specific zones. This process is as simple as adding an `allow-query` substatement in the `options` statement, as just shown. This example restricts which hosts can query all zones to those within the `192.168.100` subnet:

```
options {
      allow-query { 192.168.100/24; };
};
```

The IP addresses in the `allow-query` substatement can be specified in network address/mask format, as shown, or as individual addresses. Multiple addresses or networks are separated by semicolons. Zone-specific `allow-transfer` statements override the global settings. A value of `any` can be assigned to the `allow-query` statement in a zone to allow anyone to query the zone if a global restriction is in place. The `allow-query` substatement is added to the `zone` statement in the BIND configuration file like this:

```
zone "sample.tld" in {
      type master;
      file "sample.tld";
      allow-query { 192.168.100/24; 10.0.0.5; };
};
```

Dynamic DNS security

Dynamic DNS is disabled by default in BIND. You need to add an `allow-update` substatement in a `zone` statement to allow dynamic updates. This process makes dynamic updates fairly secure unless you allow any system as follows:

```
DON'T DO THIS: allow-update { any; };
```

You can allow updates based on one of two parameters: IP addresses or TSIG keys. TSIG keys are the most secure method because you can spoof an IP address, but you need to have the TSIG key to forge a false update when you're using TSIG security. A zone allowing updates from IP addresses looks like this:

```
zone "sample.tld" in {
        type master;
        file "sample.tld";
        allow-update { 192.168.100/24; };
};
```

This example allows updates from anywhere in the `192.168.100.0` subnet. Allowing updates using TSIG keys is equally simple as long as the key has been defined in the BIND configuration file, as discussed earlier in this chapter, in the section "TSIG and Control Security." The zone statement looks like this:

```
zone "sample.tld" in {
        type master;
        file "sample.tld"
        allow-update { key eng.domain.tld.; };
};
```

Any system with that key now can send updates to the server. BIND 9 can also use the `update-policy` substatement in a zone statement to control who can perform dynamic updates. This fairly complex substatement uses TSIG keys, as shown in this example:

```
update-policy { grant host1.eng.domain.tld. self
            host1.eng.domain.tld.; };
```

This update policy allows the system with the `eng.domain.tld.` key to update its own records, specified by `self`. You can use the `update-policy` statement to grant or deny almost any dynamic update policies, but a discussion of them is beyond the scope of this book. More documentation is available on the Internet and in more advanced DNS books. Here's another useful example:

```
update-policy { grant *.eng.domain.tld. self
            *.eng.domain.tld.; };
```

This statement allows any system with a key suffixed by `eng.domain.tld.` to update its own DNS records.

Controlling access

An *access control list (ACL)* in BIND is referring to something different from the ACL feature we mention earlier in this chapter, in the section "Securing DNS on Windows." An ACL refers to a list of IP addresses or networks (or both) that are assigned a name. ACLs are defined in the BIND configuration file and are used when you're using the same IP addresses several times in statements such as `allow-query` and `allow-transfer`. If you've read this entire chapter, you have seen an ACL in action; the `any` ACL is automatically understood to mean all IP addresses. In addition to `any`, BIND has the predefined `none`, `localhost`, and `localnets` ACLs. Although `none` is obvious, `localhost` refers to all IP addresses assigned to the DNS server, and `localnets` refers to the networks of all IP addresses assigned to the system. An ACL is defined in the configuration file this way:

```
acl "internal" { 192.168.100/24; };
```

This ACL can now be used in any statement that requires an IP address value, such as the `allow-transfer` substatement:

```
zone "sample.tld" in {
        type master;
        file "sample.tld";
        allow-transfer { internal; };
};
```

Running BIND in a jail

Unix allows you to do some special things in the area of security. In an attack on your system, an attacker typically compromises some process on your system and then uses that compromised process to move throughout the file system on the server and add, remove, or take files as he wants. Unix allows you to confine a process to a directory using the `chroot()` function. When a process is jailed in this manner and is compromised by an attacker, the attacker cannot move anywhere beyond the jail directory in the server's file system.

Jailing the BIND server is a complex process. You must create a user for BIND, create a directory in which to jail the daemon, copy all required files into that directory, and then configure BIND to start using that user and directory. This process works only for BIND 9. While reading through the procedure, consider that although the root of the system is /, you're changing the root for the BIND process to `/var/named`. The BIND process thinks that `/var/named` is the root of the file system.

To run BIND in a jail:

1. **Create a user for BIND.**

   The username for BIND is typically `named`. When you create the named user, it shouldn't be assigned a functioning shell and should be assigned a home directory of the directory in which you jail BIND. On Linux, use this command:

   ```
   useradd -d /var/named -s /bin/false named
   ```

2. **Create the jail directory for BIND if it doesn't exist.**

   Typically, you use `/var/named`:

   ```
   mkdir /var/named
   ```

3. **Create the required directories in the jail — typically** `etc`, `dev`, `var`, `var/run`, **and** `var/named`.

   If you use any other directories for logs or zone files or anything else, they must also be created here:

   ```
   mkdir /var/named/etc
   mkdir /var/named/dev
   mkdir /var/named/var
   mkdir /var/named/var/named
   mkdir /var/named/var/run
   ```

4. **Change the owners of these directories to the** `named` **user:**

   ```
   chown named etc dev var var/run var/named
   ```

5. **Copy the BIND configuration file to the** `/var/named/etc` **directory and copy your zone files into the correct directory.**

   If you keep your zone files in a directory other than `/var/named`, change the second `cp` command to suit your system:

   ```
   cp /etc/named.conf /var/named/etc/named.conf
   cp /var/named/* /var/named/var/named/
   ```

6. **Ensure that the** `named` **user owns the configuration file:**

   ```
   chown named /var/named/etc/named.conf
   ```

7. **Make the special device files** `null` **and** `random` **in** `/var/named/dev`:

   ```
   mknod /var/named/dev/null c 1 3
   mknod /var/named/dev/random c 1 8
   ```

8. **Change the owner of those device files to** `named`:

   ```
   chown named /var/named/dev/null /var/named/dev/random
   ```

9. **Configure** `syslog` **to allow logging from the jailed BIND process.**

   You must have a fairly recent version of `syslog`. By default, a jailed process cannot write to the system log. This issue is relevant only if you're not using log files specified in a logging statement in your BIND configuration file. To do this, you must change `syslog` so that it starts using the switch `-a <jaildir>`. In many versions of Unix, the `syslog` daemon is started by a file named `/etc/init.d/syslog`. In many newer versions of Linux, including Linux RedHat 7.2 and Mandrake 8.0, a file named `/etc/sysconfig/syslog` is used to pass options to the `syslog` daemon. In this file, a variable named `SYSLOGD_OPTIONS` is set to `-m 0` by default. Change this line to read

   ```
   SYSLOGD_OPTIONS="-m 0 -a /var/named/dev/log"
   ```

   This line is just an example, so it may vary depending on your operating system.

   If you have a version of `syslog` that doesn't support the `-a` option, you must make BIND log to files in the `jail` directory using a logging statement in the BIND configuration file (`/var/named/etc/named.conf`, in this case). When you're specifying the path to these files, remember that `/` in the configuration file refers to `/var/named` because of the `chroot()` function. To log to `/var/named/var/log/namedlog`, you specify

   ```
   logging {
           channel file {
                   file "/var/log/namedlog";
           };
   };
   ```

10. **Change the file that starts BIND to use the new configuration.**

    In Linux, BIND is often started in `/etc/rc.local` with the command `/usr/sbin/named`. Change `/usr/sbin/named` to

    ```
    /usr/sbin/named -u named -t /var/named
    ```

    This command instructs `named` to start using the user `named` and `chroot` automatically to the `/var/named` directory. The daemon is now running in a jail.

If you follow these steps, `named` should be running and providing service. If it's compromised, it doesn't allow the attacker to access other files on your system.

Chapter 12

What Else Can DNS Do?

In This Chapter

▶ Dynamic DNS and scavenging

▶ DNS round robin load balancing

▶ DNS zone change notification process

▶ Incremental zone transfers

*I*n the first 11 chapters of the book, only the more basic features in DNS are described. Although we have briefly mentioned some more advanced concepts, this chapter examines more advanced features in detail. For a service that is designed (basically) to link IP addresses with host names and service types, the number of advanced tricks available for tweaking DNS operation is surprising.

For the purposes of this chapter, basic features include the process of serving records from manually configured zone files using a manually configured configuration file. All DNS servers share this core set of features as required by the standards organization that maintains the DNS specifications.

Advanced features refer to those features that perform functions above that of the basic DNS service. A number of advanced DNS features are discussed in this chapter, although they're not supported on all DNS servers. Microsoft Windows 2000 and later DNS servers and BIND 9 on Unix support almost all the listed features. Any variation is noted.

A Dynamic Scavenger

Traditionally, records were added to DNS zones manually. Each host would receive an entry in the zone file and in the event that the host IP addresses changed, the zone file would need to be changed manually. For a site with hundreds or thousands of hosts within the DNS domain, maintaining records in the face of these types of changes becomes an incredibly involved task.

To a large extent, much of the more complex DNS maintenance is still done manually, although an advanced DNS feature, dynamic DNS, can be used to reduce the amount of manual configuration that's required. This feature is especially useful for registering workstations in DNS where the required DNS client configuration is relatively simple. In fact, Windows 2000 and newer workstations are configured to use dynamic DNS automatically.

Before you leap in with both feet, you need to know something: To use dynamic DNS, support for this feature must exist on both the client and the server. This statement may sound somewhat remedial, but a mixture of devices are commonly found on a network. The Microsoft Windows 2000 and later DNS server and BIND 8 and 9 support dynamic DNS to some extent. Microsoft Windows 2000 and newer clients support dynamic DNS registration, and Unix clients for dynamic DNS registration are available.

Understanding Dynamic DNS

Dynamic DNS is a fairly simple process as implemented in Microsoft Windows. When a host registers or updates its DNS information, the process occurs in an orderly manner:

1. The client uses its configured DNS servers to determine the authoritative (master) DNS server for the domain being updated by requesting the SOA record for the domain. The client's DNS servers are sometimes authoritative for the domain, but that's often not the case, which makes this step important.

   The client sends an UPDATE message to the DNS server provided in Step 1. The UPDATE message contains the requested changes or registration to the DNS record.

2. The authoritative DNS server inspects the UPDATE message and determines whether the update should be allowed. For a number of reasons, an update request may be denied, as we mention a little later in this section. If the update request is accepted, the DNS server makes the change to the zone.

3. If the update fails, the client then uses an NS (name server) query to find other DNS servers for the domain because the SOA record in Step 1 contains only one DNS server. If other servers are returned by the NS query, the client attempts the dynamic DNS update on those servers in order. If they all fail, the update isn't performed.

If you're interested in reading technical protocol definitions, the DNS UPDATE message is described in IETF RFC 2136.

A number of criteria allow dynamic DNS record updates to occur. Typically, new records can be added by any system or host, but only the system that registered the record in the first place can make changes. In Microsoft Windows DNS, two types of updates can be used: secure dynamic updates and unsecured dynamic updates. A secure dynamic update uses Access Control Lists (ACLs), which list the users, groups, or computers that have the required access to update a record. Secure dynamic update is available only for Active Directory-integrated zones and is required by default with these zones.

Zones that aren't Active Directory-integrated use unsecured dynamic updates, and Active Directory integrated zones can be changed to allow unsecured updates too. If unsecured dynamic updates are in use, any host can update DNS records. By default, workstations first attempt an unsecured dynamic update; if that update is rejected, a secure dynamic update is attempted.

Enabling dynamic DNS on a Windows server

Dynamic DNS in Windows 2000 and later (it isn't available in earlier versions) is enabled on a zone-by-zone basis. To enable dynamic DNS for a zone, first open the DNS snap-in by clicking the Start button and choosing Programs⇨ Administrative Tools. In the left pane of the DNS snap-in, locate and select the zone for which you want to enable dynamic DNS and then choose Properties from the Action menu. The Zone Properties dialog box opens, as shown in Figure 12-1.

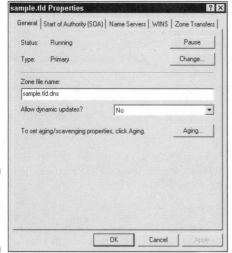

Figure 12-1:
Enabling
dynamic
DNS.

The option labeled Allow dynamic updates? on the General tab of the Zone Properties dialog box is used to enable or disable dynamic DNS. This option is set to No by default, and changing the setting to Yes enables unsecured dynamic updates to hosts using the DNS server for domain services. If the zone is an Active Directory integrated zone, the default setting allows only secure dynamic updates. Again, the secure updates are available only with an integrated Active Directory implementation.

Dynamic DNS and BIND

On a BIND 9 DNS server, dynamic DNS is also configured on a zone-by-zone basis. Two methods allow dynamic updates in BIND, and both are configured in the configuration file for individual zones. The two options are `allow-update` and `update-policy`.

Making sense of TSIG keys

BIND has a feature named *transaction security,* or *TSIG.* TSIG keys are used for update security in the next two sections. TSIG uses secret keys that must be configured on both the client and the server. On the server, TSIG keys are defined by using key statements in the configuration file. A key is defined this way:

```
key workstation1.sample.tld. {
    algorithm hmac-md5;
    secret ?/dkdYjLoO8GdrJK/wgxMBQ==?;
};
```

Although the key name is arbitrary, using the client's fully qualified domain name (FQDN) is a useful convention. Secret keys can be generated by using the `mmencode` command because they must be base 64 encoded. Type the command **echo <*secretkey*> | mmencode** at a shell prompt, where `<secretkey>` is the plain text you want to use for the key and the encoded secret key is shown. If you know the plain-text `<secretkey>`, you can generate the key on the client and the server by using the preceding command, and you don't need to copy the encoded key between the two systems.

allow-update

The simplest way to allow updates in BIND is with the `allow-update` option. This option allows the specified hosts to update DNS entries. In the configuration file, a zone entry set to allow dynamic updates look like this:

```
zone "sample.tld" in {
        type master;
        file "sample.tld";
        allow-update {192.168.100.0/24;};
};
```

The `allow-update` option that is shown allows all systems on the `192.168.100.0/24` network to send dynamic updates to this DNS server for the `zone sample.tld`. You can also specify more than one IP address or range as long as they're separated with a semicolon and a semicolon appears after the last address.

In addition to allowing updates based on source addresses, you can allow updates based on TSIG keys. This method is far more secure because source IP addresses can be spoofed.

Spoofing an IP address involves sending a network packet with a false address. You can write software that overrides the default network behavior of a system (which is to use the system's IP address as the source) and use any IP address as the source.

To use TSIG keys for update security, use the option `allow-update {key workstation1.sample.tld.;};`. You can also specify multiple keys by using a semicolon to separate each one.

update-policy

The `update-policy` zone option, new in BIND 9, provides more configuration options for dynamic updates. To use the `update-policy` option, you must have TSIG keys configured because source IP addresses cannot be used. The `update-policy` option can be used to grant or deny update access using keys, although access is denied by default. The `update-policy` option is configured as shown:

```
zone "sample.tld" in {
        type master;
        file "sample.tld";
        update-policy {
            grant workstation1.sample.tld self
        workstation1.sample.tld.;
            grant admin.sample.tld. name sample.tld;
            grant *.sample.tld self *.sample.tld. A;
        };
};
```

Individual rules are specified with the `update-policy` option. For example, a general form of the `update-policy` directive looks like this:

```
update-policy [grant or deny] <key> <nametype> <name> <types>
```

The *<key>* field refers to the TSIG key defined earlier in the configuration file used for the rule. The *<nametype>* field specifies the type of update that can be made. The *<nametype>* field can be either `name`, which matches the rule to the name field; the `subdomain` option, which allows the rule to be used to update any subdomains of the domain in the `name` field; or `self`, which allows the rule to be used for a system to update only its own record.

Although the `name` field isn't used when the `self` name type is specified, something must still be in the name field, as shown in the example.

The `<name>` field is used to control what entries can be updated by a client with a matching `<key>`. Finally, the optional `<type>` field can be used to restrict the record type that can be updated.

In the preceding code example, three rules are being applied with the `update-policy` option. The first rule allows the system with the key `workstation1.sample.tld.` to update any of its own records. The second rule grants the key `admin.sample.tld.` the access to update any records in the `sample.tld` zone. The last rule grants all systems with keys ending with `sample.tld.` permission to update their own A records. (The advantage of using the FQDN for key names becomes clear in this example.)

Keeping things fresh

The DNS scavenging feature on Microsoft Windows DNS servers is typically used with dynamic DNS. Scavenging can also be used with manually configured DNS records but it's rarely useful.

The scavenging feature is responsible for removing old, or "stale," DNS records. This feature is important when you have a large environment and numerous dynamic DNS clients. As these clients register in DNS and some clients eventually change host names, change domains, or are removed from the networks, some dynamically created records are left in the DNS server. Over time, this situation causes the zone files to grow. These large zone files cause problems because they consume lots of disk space and cause the DNS server to operate more slowly.

Dynamic DNS records are removed automatically whenever computers are removed from the network properly. Only when the system is removed improperly do the DNS records get left in the server and become stale.

Luckily, scavenging removes these stale records. Scavenging isn't enabled on Microsoft Windows DNS by default because using scavenging effectively requires some understanding of how the DNS server is being used by clients. A one-size-fits-all approach isn't a good idea when the topic is scavenging. Scavenging relies on another process, aging, which is configured on a zone-by-zone basis. *Aging* is responsible for determining which records have passed a user-determined threshold (usually a period in which some kind of update must occur) and thus need to be removed. The problem with scavenging occurs when aging is configured incorrectly and records that are still valid are removed. This is the primary reason that scavenging is disabled by default.

Dynamic DNS records have a value known as a timestamp. The timestamp is initially created when the record is registered in the DNS server. The client then occasionally refreshes the timestamp. If the client doesn't refresh the timestamp, it indicates that the client may have gone offline, and the record becomes stale and a target for scavenging. Manually configured DNS records don't have this timestamp.

Configuring scavenging is a twofold process, first configuring zone aging and then configuring scavenging in the DNS service configuration. Both configurations are done using the DNS snap-in on Windows 2000 and later operating systems. Scavenging isn't supported on systems running Windows NT 4.0 or other earlier versions. To begin, open the DNS snap-in, choose Start➪Programs➪ Administrative Tools, and click the DNS icon.

Zone aging settings

Now that you have the DNS snap-in open, double-click the server name entry in the left pane and double-click the Forward Lookup Zones container to expand its suboptions. You should see a list of zones in the left pane. Select the zone for which you will enable aging, and choose Properties from the Action menu. From the General tab of the Zone Properties menu, click the Aging button. This step opens the Zone Aging/Scavenging Properties dialog box, as shown in Figure 12-2.

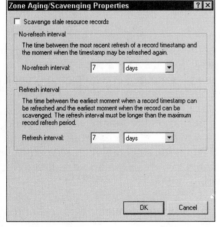

Figure 12-2:
Enabling and configuring scavenging on a zone-by-zone basis.

To enable aging and scavenging on the zone, select the Scavenge stale resource records check box. The two refresh intervals can be set as well. By default, both are set to seven days. The first interval is the no-refresh interval. This is the amount of time that must pass after a record timestamp is refreshed before it can be "refreshed" by the host again. The second interval is the refresh interval, which defines the maximum period a host has to refresh its DNS record timestamp. If it fails to do so before this interval expires, the record is marked as eligible for scavenging. After you click OK to close the Zone Aging/Scavenging Properties dialog box and click OK to close the zone Properties dialog box ,the changes are saved.

To better understand how the aging intervals work, an example is in order. After a specific record is added or its timestamp is refreshed, the timestamp cannot be refreshed again for the amount of time defined by the no-refresh interval. After the no-refresh interval expires, the record can be refreshed. If the record isn't refreshed in the amount of time defined by the refresh interval after the no-refresh interval expires, the record can be scavenged. If both intervals are set to 7 days as the default, the record can be refreshed 7 days after the last refresh. If it has not been refreshed after 14 days, it can be scavenged.

In addition to configuring scavenging for individual zones, you can configure zone-level scavenging settings for all zones at one time. This feature is rarely used because scavenging is normally used only for zones with dynamic DNS enabled and dynamically updated records. To set scavenging for all records, select the server in the left pane of the DNS snap-in and choose Set Aging/ Scavenging for all zones from the Action menu. This action opens the Server Aging/Scavenging Properties dialog box. This dialog box is functionally identical to the dialog box used to set scavenging on a zone, as we mention earlier in this section, except that it sets scavenging for all zones.

Scavenging for everyone

What happens if you want to enable scavenging at the server level? With the DNS server snap-in open, select the server in the left pane of the and choose Properties from the Action menu. In the server Properties dialog box, click the Advanced tab. To enable scavenging on the sever, select the check box labeled Enable automatic scavenging of stale records, as shown in Figure 12-3.

You configure the scavenging period on the Advanced tab. The scavenging period controls how often the scavenging process runs. By default, scavenging occurs every seven days. When the scavenging process runs, all records in zones with scavenging enabled for which the no-refresh and refresh intervals have passed are removed.

You can also run the scavenging process manually. If you want to run scavenging (if you make changes to aging and want to force scavenging of expired zones, for example), you can do it from the DNS snap-in. Select the DNS server in the left pane of the snap-in and choose Scavenge stale resource records from the Action menu.

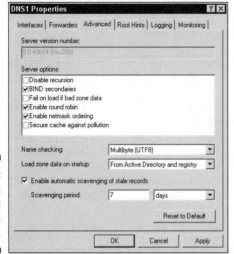

DNS1 Properties

Interfaces | Forwarders | Advanced | Root Hints | Logging | Monitoring

Server version number:

5.0 49664 (0xc200)

Server options:
- [ ] Disable recursion
- [x] BIND secondaries
- [ ] Fail on load if bad zone data
- [x] Enable round robin
- [x] Enable netmask ordering
- [ ] Secure cache against pollution

Name checking: Multibyte (UTF8)

Load zone data on startup: From Active Directory and registry

[x] Enable automatic scavenging of stale records

Scavenging period: 7   days

Reset to Default

OK   Cancel   Apply

Figure 12-3: Enabling scavenging on the server.

Feel the Burn: Handling Heavy Loads

Imagine that you have one basic Web server with static content and no database connections, but it's getting pummeled with Web requests and the resulting server load is high.. When it comes time to upgrade the server (hopefully before it gives up the ghost), you have a number of options. The most obvious option is to upgrade the existing server to something more powerful. You can choose another method, though, that allows you to add another Web server in addition to the existing server, which is often a cheaper and less invasive (because your original server is mostly untouched) way to provide additional capacity. The process of having more than one server providing the same service simultaneously is known as load balancing.

Don't confuse load balancing with failover, although the two terms are sometimes used interchangeably. *Load balancing* refers to the division of network traffic between two or more servers providing the same service, and *failover* refers to the ability to redirect traffic to another server in the event that a server fails.

Load balancing can be implemented in a number of ways. Many devices are made specifically for the purpose of load balancing and can monitor a huge number of statistics, such as query times and even actual server load as reported by utilities on the system. These statistics are then used to determine the "weighting" for the load on each server. Basically, if one system is twice as fast as the other system (in a two-server load balancing environment), an appropriate portion (two-thirds) of the load is sent to that server with the other portion going to the slower server.

DNS provides its own load balancing method: DNS round robin. DNS round robin is quite simple and has no way of measuring the load on any of the servers. You simply provide a list of servers for the same record, and DNS responds to each request with the next server in the list and loops back to the beginning. If you have two servers, for example, the first DNS query results in the first server on the list, the second DNS query results in the second server on the list, the third query results in the first server again, and so on. This example is a bit of an oversimplification. The DNS round robin changes the order in which the servers process (or receive) requests. If you have three servers with the addresses 1, 2, and 3, the first query would return 1, 2, 3; the second query, 2, 3, 1; the third query, 3, 1, 2; and so on. So, some users are shuffled to Web server 1, some to 2, and others to 3. This system breaks the incoming traffic (all bound for a single Web site in the example) across multiple servers.

Although most operating systems use only the first returned server address, this behavior causes round robin to not work properly on some systems, such as Microsoft Windows, that choose the DNS entry from the list based on subnet priority. If you're using DNS round robin and one of the systems is on the same subnet as your Microsoft Windows workstations, those workstations always use that server, and the round robin is ineffective.

The round robin is on the window

Configuring a record for round robin DNS processing in Microsoft Windows 2000 and later is simple. (The process for adding a host record is discussed in Chapter 7.) To configure round robin, simply add another host record using the same name and the new IP address instead.

Open the DNS snap-in by choosing Start➪Programs➪Administrative Tools. Locate and select in the left pane the zone in which the record is created. The existing records are shown in the right pane. If it doesn't already exist, create the first host record by choosing New Host from the Action menu. Specify the name and IP address and click Add Host to create the record. Next, use the New Host command and specify the same name but a different IP address; then click Add Host. Two records now have the same name, as shown in Figure 12-4. You can create a number of records for round robin, if you want.

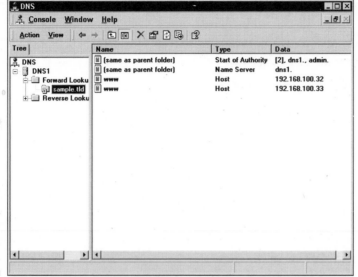

Figure 12-4:
Multiple records with the same name have been created for round robin DNS.

Configuring round robin DNS on BIND

Configuring round robin DNS on BIND is done in the zone file for the particular host you want to change. A normal zone file looks like this:

```
$TTL 86400
@  IN  SOA  dns1.sample.tld.    hostmaster.sample.tld. (
                    2001062501 ; Serial Number
                    21600      ; Refresh time
                    3600       ; Retry time
                    604800     ; Expire time
                    86400 )    ; Minimum TTL


       IN  NS     dns1.sample.tld.
       IN  NS     dns2.sample.tld.

       IN  MX  10 mail.sample.tld.

       IN  A      10.0.1.5

www    IN  A      10.0.1.5
```

To enable round robin DNS for this zone, you simply add IP addresses to the record, as shown here:

```
www   IN  A      10.0.1.5
      IN  A      10.0.1.6
```

You can add a number of IP addresses to the record.

Sending Notice

DNS zone change notification, or NOTIFY, is a DNS feature that's useful when you have a master NS server and any number of slave servers. Normally, a slave server performs a zone transfer each time the refresh time of the zone expires. This transfer can cause a problem if the zone is modified on the master DNS server. The zone file on the slave servers is out of synchronization until the refresh time expires.

NOTIFY is a solution to this problem. When a zone on a DNS server with notification enabled is modified, the DNS server sends a NOTIFY message to all DNS servers listed with name server (NS) records in the zone. This message causes the servers to perform a zone transfer for the modified zone immediately, and the changes are updated on all slave servers.

NOTIFY is enabled by default on Microsoft Windows DNS BIND. You can change a number of NOTIFY settings, though.

Using NOTIFY on Windows 2000 and Windows .NET

NOTIFY configuration is done on a zone-by-zone basis in Windows. Open the DNS snap-in by choosing Start⇨Programs⇨Administrative Tools. Locate and select a zone to configure in the left pane and choose Properties from the Action menu. Select the Zone Transfers tab and click the Notify button to open the Notify dialog box, as shown in Figure 12-5.

The default settings are shown in the Notify dialog box. By default, all servers with a name server (NS) record in the zone are notified. By deselecting the Automatically notify check box, no servers are notified when changes are made to the zone. The other available option is to configure manually the servers that will receive NOTIFY messages. By selecting the option labeled The following servers, entering an IP address, and clicking the Add button, you can manually specify a list of servers to be notified. This technique is useful if servers are configured as zone slave servers and don't have NS records in the zone, although that is a rare case.

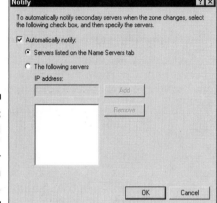

Figure 12-5:
Configuring
NOTIFY
settings for
a zone in
Windows.

Working with NOTIFY on BIND

BIND also sends NOTIFY messages by default, though the configuration of NOTIFY is slightly different in BIND. NOTIFY is enabled and disabled at the server level, but additional servers can be configured for notification at the zone level.

Notification is enabled and disabled in the server configuration file (typically /etc/named.conf) in the Options section. Here are the contents of a typical configuration file:

```
/*
 * Comments can be placed like this
 */

options {
        directory "/var/named";
};

zone "sample.tld" in {
        type master;
        file "sample.tld";
};

zone "sample_slave.tld" in {
        type slave;
        file "sample_slave.tld";
        masters { 192.168.1.1; };
```

This example causes notification behavior in the default manner, which is enabled. Changing the file and explicitly enabling notification (as shown in the following example) would have no additional effect (it's still enabled):

```
options {
        directory "/var/named";
        notify yes;
};
```

To disable notification, you must set the `notify` option to the value of `no`. The following example shows a sample configuration that would disable notification:

```
options {
        directory "/var/named";
        notify no;
};
```

One other (final) setting is available with the `notify` option. Setting the option to `explicit`, as shown next, forces notification to occur only between the servers defined with the *also-notify option* in the options or zone directives. The servers with NS records in other zones aren't notified:

```
options {
        directory "/var/named";
        notify explicit;
};
```

Configuration files can also make use of the `also-notify` option. You can use it to specify a list of servers to notify in addition to those with NS records in the zone. If you set the `notify-explicit` option, though, only the servers specified by `also-notify` are notified and not the servers with NS records in the zone.

You configure the `also-notify` option in the configuration file as follows:

```
/*
 * Comments can be placed like this
 */

options {
        directory "/var/named";
        also-notify {192.168.100.44;};
};

zone "sample.tld" in {
        type master;
        file "sample.tld";
        also-notify {10.1.1.39;};
};

zone "sample_slave.tld" in {
        type slave;
        file "sample_slave.tld";
masters { 192.168.1.1; };
```

In the sample configuration file, the server 192.168.100.44 is notified every time any zone is modified in addition to the servers with NS records in the specific zone. The server 10.1.1.39 is notified whenever the sample.tld zone is modified in addition to the servers with NS records in that zone.

Moving in Increments

Normally, whenever zone transfers take place, the slave server transfers the entire contents of a zone each time. The incremental zone transfer (IXFR) protocol allows a slave server to transfer only the part of the zone that has changed rather than the entire zone. On very large zones, this protocol can save a significant amount of time and bandwidth.

IXFR can be used only on zones that have a change history. Under Windows, most zone transfers can be done using IXFR. In BIND, only dynamically updated zones and slave zones that have been transferred using IXFR can be transferred to a slave server using IXFR. Manually configured zones and slave zones transferred using the traditional zone transfer process cannot be transferred using IXFR. This isn't a major disadvantage to IXFR because dynamically updated zones are normally the largest zones because they have large numbers of workstations (typically). Manually configured zones are often much smaller.

IXFR is used automatically by both Windows and BIND 9 servers when requesting a zone transfer from the master server. If the zone cannot be transferred using IXFR, the master server sends the entire zone using a traditional full zone transfer (AXFR).

Split DNS

Split DNS is something you can do only on BIND because it isn't supported under Microsoft Windows. Split DNS is a way of designing a DNS architecture where internal systems have different access to DNS records from external users. Two sets of DNS servers are required for this design, one each on the external and internal networks. The internal DNS servers accept queries from internal clients and contain records for internal servers. All other requests are forwarded to the external DNS servers. The external servers may be queried by all clients, internal and external. The servers contain records for externally accessible servers. The external DNS servers should be accessible from both the outside and inside of the private network. As you can see, this arrangement goes a long way toward securing the local network because external clients cannot even query the server that is hosting information about internal hosts. You can still determine internal DNS information through other methods, but this still is a worthwhile practice to limit the amount of information about your network that is publicly accessible. External users may still be able to get you internal host information, but they have to work for it.

This configuration is used because the same zones are stored on both the internal and external DNS servers. The internal servers contain all records for the zones, and the external servers contain only records that external clients can access.

The configuration of split DNS is fairly complex, especially when e-mail must be delivered to internal servers. The internal servers are configured to forward all requests that cannot be served from their own zone files to the external servers using the forward only and forwarders{<server>;} options. The servers are also configured to accept queries only from internal clients and the external DNS servers. The servers can also host zones that are specific to the internal network, and those zones can be restricted to internal clients using the zone-specific allow-query option. The external servers are configured to accept any DNS queries.

Here's an example of the internal DNS configuration:

```
/*
 * Internal split DNS configuration
 */

/* Internal systems */

acl internal {192.168.100.0/24;};

/* External DNS Servers */

acl externaldns {10.1.1.1; 10.1.1.2;};

options {
        directory "/var/named";
        forward only;
        forwarders {10.1.1.1; 10.1.1.2;};
        allow-transfer {none;};
        allow-query {internal;external;};
        allow-recursion {internal;};
};

zone "sample.tld" in {
        type master;
        file "sample.tld";
        allow-query {internal;external;};
};

zone "sample_internal_only.tld" in {
```

```
                type master;
                file "sample_internal_only";
                allow-query {internal;};
        };
```

Here's an example of the external DNS server configuration:

```
/*
 * External split DNS configuration
 */

/* Internal systems */

acl internal {192.168.100.0/24;};

/* External DNS Servers */

acl externaldns {10.1.1.1; 10.1.1.2;};

options {
                directory "/var/named";
                allow-transfer {none;};
                allow-recursion {internal;external;};

};

zone "sample.tld" in {
                type master;
                file "sample.tld";
};
```

Assuming that the mail server is on the internal network, some configuration is necessary in order for mail to be accepted from the outside. You can configure the mail exchanger (MX) records on the external servers to point directly to the internal mail server, but that isn't always possible. Using a wildcard MX record, the external servers can accept all mail for the internal domains and forward it to the internal servers. For this process to work, the external DNS servers must be configured to use only the internal servers for DNS resolution. The zone contains a line like this:

```
*    IN    MX    10    external.sample.tld.
```

This line causes mail coming from an external mail server to be accepted by the external DNS server external.sample.tld. The external DNS server then locates the proper mail exchanger. The reason that this method works is that the external server is using the internal server to resolve names and can therefore see servers on the internal network, including the proper mail exchanger configured in the sample.tld zone file on the internal DNS server. If the external DNS server needs to resolve a DNS name that isn't hosted by the internal DNS server, the internal server forwards the request to the external server, which resolves the name. The process is convoluted, but it's the only way to forward mail through the split DNS architecture. Figure 12-6 shows a diagram of how the split DNS architecture works. Note that only one external and one internal DNS server are shown, although it's good practice to use at least two of each. This method doesn't change the configuration of the systems.

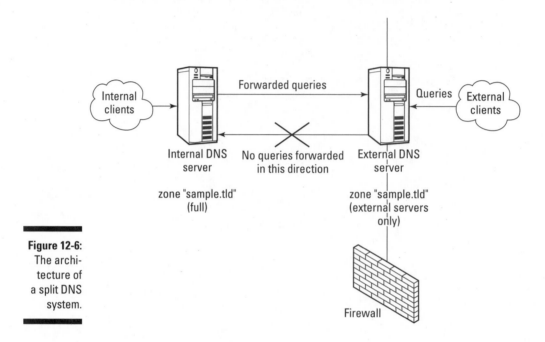

Figure 12-6:
The architecture of a split DNS system.

Using DNS and WINS

When you're using Windows-based DNS services, you can integrate WINS with DNS so that if DNS lookups fail, WINS is used. This feature is used only for A records and is truly useful only if WINS is widely deployed on your network and (for one reason or another) you aren't using dynamic DNS. In this scenario, you would probably benefit from having WINS as a backup in the event that DNS resolution fails.

WINS integration can be enabled for forward or reverse lookup zones.

If normal DNS resolution fails, WINS integration for forward zones works by separating the host name from the domain suffix and querying the configured WINS servers for that host. If the WINS server can resolve the host, the address is returned to the DNS server and then to the client. Reverse WINS resolution works by sending a "node adapter status request" directly to the IP address being queried and appending a fixed DNS name to the returned host name.

Forward zone WINS integration

To enable WINS integration, you must add a WINS record to the DNS zone to be integrated. After the record is added, queries that fail in this zone fall back to WINS. The record is added from the DNS snap-in you find by choosing Start➪Programs➪Administrative Tools. Locate and select the zone to which the WINS record will be added. Choose Properties from the Action menu and click the WINS tab, as shown in Figure 12-7.

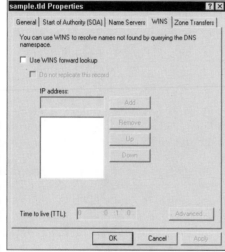

Figure 12-7:
Adding
a WINS
record to
the zone
for WINS
integration.

To enable WINS integration, follow these steps:

1. **Enable the Use WINS forward lookup check box.**

2. **Enter the IP address of each of your WINS servers in the IP Address box.**

3. **Click the Add button.**

You can control the order of the WINS servers by selecting a server in the list and using the up- and down-arrow buttons. The closest WINS server (preferably on the local network) should be at the top of the list. Servers can be removed by selecting them from the list and clicking Remove.

The WINS resource record (RR) type is specific to Microsoft Windows DNS. If you're using any other DNS server applications as slave servers for this zone, make sure that you check the Do not replicate this record box. If you don't, zone transfers will fail because the WINS record is invalid on the other DNS servers.

From this tab, you can also set the TTL for the WINS record. The TTL informs clients and servers that retrieve this record how long to keep it in their cache.

The format of the TTL field is days:hours:minutes:seconds. The default TTL setting is one minute. You can also configure advanced TTLs for the WINS zone by clicking the Advanced button to open the Advanced dialog box, as shown in Figure 12-8.

Figure 12-8:
Configure
advanced
TTL values
for the
WINS
record.

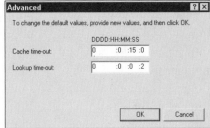

The Advanced dialog box has two TTL settings: Cache time-out and Lookup time-out. The Cache time-out controls how long the record information should be cached by clients. The Lookup time-out controls how long the DNS server waits for a response from the WINS server.

After you have enabled WINS integration and added WINS servers to the list, click OK to close the zone Properties dialog box. The WINS record is created and appears in the right pane, as shown in Figure 12-9.

Reverse zone WINS integration

WINS integration for reverse zone lookups is somewhat of a misnomer. Rather than use the WINS servers for reverse lookups, which isn't possible because WINS doesn't maintain IP address information, the DNS server sends a "node adapter status request" to the IP address being queried. The system then provides its NetBIOS host name to the DNS server. The DNS server appends the domain name to the host name and returns the response to the client.

To configure WINS lookups on a reverse zone, select the zone in the left pane of the DNS snap-in and choose Properties from the Action menu. Select the WINS-R tab from the zone Properties dialog box, as shown in Figure 12-10.

You must first enable reverse WINS integration by selecting the Use WINS-R lookup check box. As with a forward zone, you must select the Do not replicate this record check box if you're using as slave servers for this zone any DNS servers other than Microsoft Windows 2000 or later.

You must also specify a domain name in the Domain to append to returned name box. This domain is appended to the host name returned by the WINS-R lookup, and the complete name (host plus domain) is returned to the requesting client.

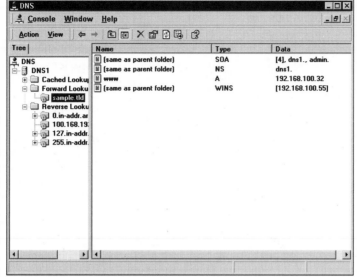

Figure 12-9:
After WINS
integration
has been
enabled for
the zone,
a WINS
record is
added.

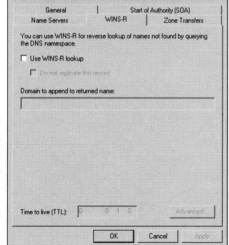

Figure 12-10:
Configuring
WINS
integration
on a
reverse
zone.

WINS-R integration has one major shortcoming: You can specify only one domain name for WINS-R lookups in a given reverse zone. With this limitation, all WINS-R lookups for a given reverse zone (and therefore an entire subnet) have the same domain appended. This is often no problem on a network of workstations using the same domain name, but it can become a problem if you have systems on the same subnet with different domain names. If you're in the small subset of users who require WINS-R integration, however, it probably won't be a problem.

You can also set the TTL (Time To Live) values for the WINS-R record. The TTL value on the WINS-R tab controls the amount of time (days:hours:minutes: seconds) that the record may be cached on clients and other DNS servers. By clicking the Advanced button, you can configure the Cache time-out, which controls how long clients may cache the record information, and the Lookup time-out, which controls how long the DNS server waits for a WINS response.

Also in the Advanced dialog box for a WINS-R record is the Submit DNS domain as NetBIOS scope option. NetBIOS scope is a specialized process that allows you to separate NetBIOS services on your network. It allows a certain set of systems (one scope) to access a specific set of NetBIOS services and another set of systems (another scope) to access different services. If you choose this option for the WINS-R record, the appended DNS domain is sub-mitted as the NetBIOS scope identifier. This option should be selected only if you're using NetBIOS scope on your network.

After you have configured the WINS-R record, click OK to close the zone Properties dialog box. The WINS-R record is added to the reverse zone and appears in the right pane, as shown in Figure 12-11.

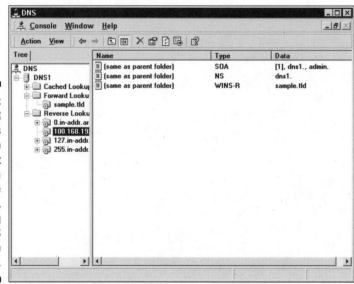

Figure 12-11:
The WINS-R record is shown in the right pane for a reverse lookup zone, indicating that WINS integration is active.

Chapter 13

"It Doesn't Work!" (Troubleshooting)

In This Chapter

▶ Troubleshooting tips for Windows DNS

▶ Troubleshooting tips for BIND on Unix

Simple DNS configuration changes that aren't implemented correctly can lead to dire consequences. Because you will probably need to hunt down a problem and fix it sooner or later on your DNS server, this chapter spends some time on the topic of troubleshooting. There's no sense in beating around the bush, so dive right in!

One fairly common problem with DNS servers is that after a change is made and the server is restarted (if necessary), the whole server or portions of the DNS service, such as individual zones, no longer work. When that happens, the problem is normally caused by syntax errors in the DNS configuration. This type of issue is a configuration problem, resulting from human error — the single largest contributor to DNS server dysfunction. Of course, problems can occur with DNS that result from something other than configuration issues, but that's the exception and not the rule. BIND 9, for example, can be operated with static information and requires only the configuration file in order to run. The Windows DNS service is susceptible to a few more problems but is also still quite stable.

With both Windows DNS and BIND, the procedures for isolating configuration problems are quite similar. In both cases, you should first investigate the DNS server's logs to try to zero in on the source of the issue and determine when it began. In many cases, the logs indicate the precise cause of a problem and, in the case of the BIND logs, indicate the exact line in the file where the problem exists. If the log file doesn't give you the information you need, start doing some investigation of your own. By using the command-line DNS tools and inspecting zones and configuration files, you can eliminate most common problems, even if they're not obvious in the log files or if login isn't operational. Although errors resulting from configuration issues and bad syntax are generally logged, data errors — such as mistyped addresses or names — don't cause the kinds of errors that are logged. You have to find those problems the old-fashioned way: by searching one file at a time.

Troubleshooting Microsoft Windows DNS

Because logging obviously can be helpful, this section starts by describing the process for examining DNS log files. Unless you're certain that another source exists for whatever issue you're experiencing, checking the log files should almost always be your first step. As with most log files in Windows, you view the log events with the Event Viewer snap-in. To open the log for DNS, follow these steps:

1. **Click the Start button and choose Programs⇨Administrative Tools to open the Event Viewer menu.**

   The Event Viewer opens, as shown in Figure 13-1.

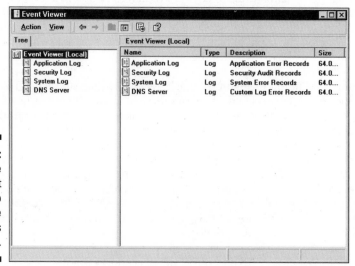

Figure 13-1:
Use the Event Viewer to view the Windows event log.

The event log contains all events logged by the system. Almost all applications, in addition to Windows itself, log their events to the event log.

2. **To view DNS log events, click the System Log container and look for events with DNS as the Source field, as shown in Figure 13-2.**

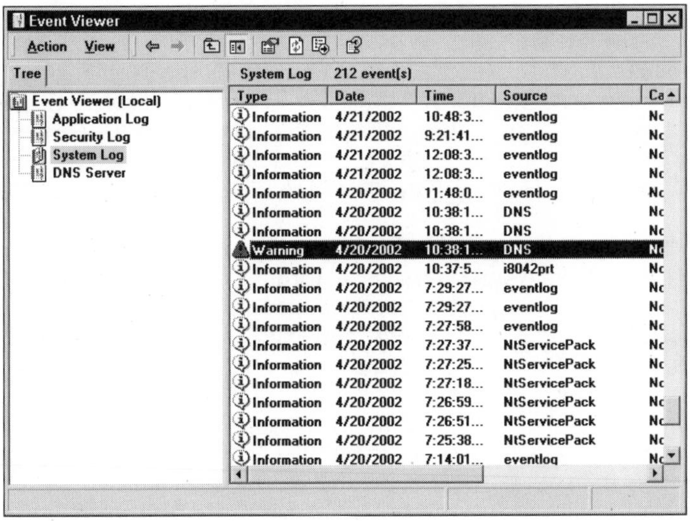

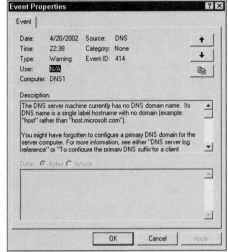

Figure 13-2:
DNS events
are denoted
by DNS in
the Source
field.

In the Event Viewer, you can see a certain amount of information about the specific event, including its severity and the date and time of its occurrence. If that's not enough information for you, check out detailed information about the event by double-clicking a specific entry. The Event Properties dialog box is displayed, as shown in Figure 13-3.

Figure 13-3:
Detailed
information
about the
events listed
in the Event
Viewer.

As you can see, the Event Properties dialog box shows detailed information about the event. The description of the event gives you information about the event, including basic instructions on how to fix the problem in some cases. You can also press the up- and down-arrow buttons to move through the Event Log and look at each event's details in the Event Properties dialog box rather than exit from the Event Properties dialog box each time and double-click a new event. However you choose to do it, this task can be truly tedious.

A number of events related to DNS may show up in the Event Viewer. They range from informational messages informing you when the DNS server starts to generate errors all the way to when the DNS service fails. In most cases, the Description field in the Event Properties dialog box gives you all the information you need to solve the problem.

Unbelievable as it sounds, in some cases you cannot solve the problem you're having by using only the Event Viewer. Depending on whether the problem is data related or server related, you can take a couple of routes. If you suspect that the server itself is the issue, the best reference is Microsoft Product Support Services: Point your browser at support.microsoft.com, as shown in Figure 13-4. This site is useful because it allows you to search the Microsoft Knowledge Base.

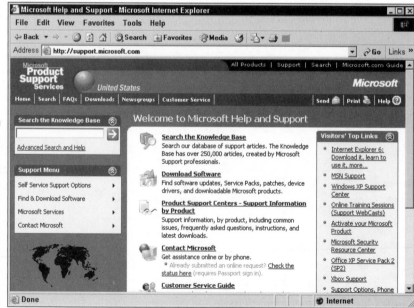

Figure 13-4: Search the Microsoft Knowledge Base whenever you have problems with Microsoft products.

You can search the Knowledge Base in two ways:

- ✔ **Quick search:** Do a quick search using the Search the Knowledge Base box in the upper-left corner of the page. Enter the text for your search and press Enter.

- ✔ **Advanced search:** Use the advanced search page, as shown in Figure 13-5. To get there, click the Search the Knowledge Base link on the main page or click the Advanced Search and Help link in the Search the Knowledge Base box in the upper-left corner of the page.

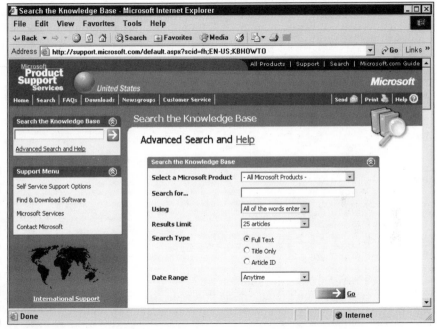

Figure 13-5:
Use the
Advanced
Search and
Help page to
search the
Knowledge
Base more
specifically.

The Advanced Search page is useful if you want to do a more narrow search of the Knowledge Base. For example, if you use the Search the Knowledge Base text box on the main Product Support Services page to search for a DNS problem, you receive results for all versions of Microsoft Windows. You can use the Advanced Search page to search for articles about only the product you're using. Select your product from the drop-down box and enter in the Search for text box the words you want to search for. You can also use the other options to narrow your search.

The Knowledge Base search feature is especially useful in combination with the Event Viewer because you can search for specific event ID numbers in the Knowledge Base. Simply use the event ID as the term for the search, and you probably will get information about your issue the first time.

After you have specified the terms for your search, click Go. The Web site searches the Knowledge Base for relevant articles, and a summary is returned, as shown in Figure 13-6. The summary of relevant articles shows the article title and a brief description of each article.

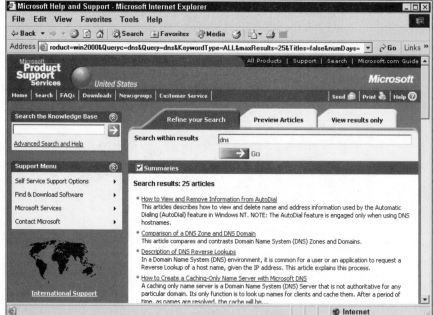

Figure 13-6:
A summary of results shows the title and a brief description of each relevant article.

Browse through the summary pages (you may have more than one page of results). If you see an article you want to view, simply click the article title. The Knowledge Base article is displayed, as shown in Figure 13-7.

You see a few key links in all the articles:

- **Article number:** The Knowledge Base article number is shown at the top of the article and is always in the form Q*xxxxxx*. This number is useful later as a quick reference back to the same article because you can enter it as the search criteria when you search the Knowledge Base and quickly find it again.

- **The information in this article applies to:** This section of the Knowledge Base article tells you to which Microsoft products the article is relevant. Many features are consistent across versions of products and even totally different products, so some articles are relevant to a number of different products.

- **Summary:** The summary gives a brief overview of the contents of the article.

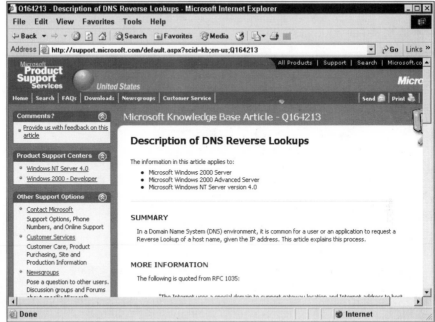

Figure 13-7:
A sample
Knowledge
Base article.

➤ **More information:** This section, the heart of the Knowledge Base article, contains the article contents.

➤ **For more information:** At the bottom of some Knowledge Base articles is a section containing links to other relevant articles. This section lets you view the other articles relevant to a specific problem without having to find them in the search results.

If the problem you're having is related not to the DNS service itself but rather to data in your DNS server, you need to do some investigation to find the problem. The most useful tool in Microsoft Windows for finding data problems is NSLOOKUP, which we describe at length in Chapter 6. Use NSLOOKUP to examine the record that you suspect to be faulty. What does the server tell clients about the domain that is having trouble? These kinds of questions can be answered with the NSLOOKUP tool. After you locate the problem using NSLOOKUP, you can most often correct it by using the DNS snap-in.

Troubleshooting BIND

If you're using BIND, making mistakes that require troubleshooting is easier to than it is in Microsoft Windows DNS. The reason is primarily that the manual editing of configuration files leaves you wide open for typographical errors. BIND doesn't always fail completely, though: If a zone file is bad, that zone isn't loaded, although the rest of the server continues to run properly. Luckily, BIND has excellent logging that makes troubleshooting this kind of issue quite easy.

As with Windows, the first place to look when troubleshooting BIND is in the log files. The log files in BIND are configurable, though, so they may not always be in the expected location. Check your BIND configuration file for a logging directive. If this directive is present, it specifies the location of log files for the server. If the directive isn't present, log entries are written to the syslog daemon, as is the default.

Most Unix and Linux systems run a *daemon* (that's a background process, not a creature from the underworld) named syslog. The only job of the syslog process is to accept log entries from other applications and write them to a log file. Some implementations of syslog are quite flexible and allow you to separate log entries into different files depending on their source. In most cases, however, all log entries are written to a common file.

To view the log file, you must first know its location. In Linux, the log created by syslog is at /var/log/messages; in Sun Solaris, it's at /var/adm/ messages. This location varies depending on the type of Unix system you're running, so consult the documentation for your system. When you have located the log, you can use a few useful utilities to view it, such as more, tail, and grep; these standard Unix utilities are on virtually every system in some form or another:

- ✔ more: Allows you to view a file one page at a time starting from the beginning. This utility is useful if you want to browse through the entire file.

- ✔ tail: Lets you view only the lines at the end of the file. By default, tail usually shows the last ten lines of a file, although you can instruct tail to show as many lines as you want.

- ✔ grep: Searches for patterns in a file. You can use grep to search for the term named in your log file, for example, and see only DNS server-related entries.

From a shell on your system, change to the directory where your log files are located, typically /var/log/ by default. Type the command more *messages*, replacing *messages* with the name of your log file if it's different. To use more, press Enter to move one line through the file and press the Spacebar to move down an entire page. Figure 13-8 shows an example of the more command being used to view the log file on a Linux system running BIND.

In the log file, you're looking for entries logged by BIND. These entries begin with named, which is the name of the daemon that logged them. In this figure, you can see a number of log entries from named, although they're purely informational.

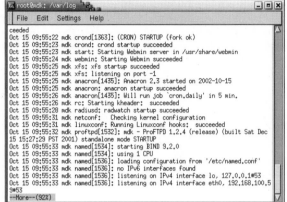

Figure 13-8:
Using
the more
command to
view the log
file in Linux.

The second way to view the log file is by using `tail`. It can be used in a few useful ways. The first is to simply type the command `tail messages`. This command displays the last ten lines of the log file, as shown in Figure 13-9.

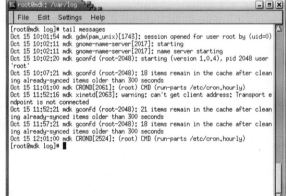

Figure 13-9:
Using
the tail
command to
show the
end of a file.

As you can see in the figure, no `named`-related log entries are in the last ten lines of the log file. You can also type `tail -x messages` (replace *x* with the number of lines you want to view) to view more than the last ten lines of the file. Note that technique this may not work with all versions of `tail`, although it does work with the GNU version of `tail` that is included with Linux. Consult the `man` page for your version of `tail` if it doesn't work.

One more way to use `tail` is by using the command `tail -f messages`, as shown in Figure 13-10. The `-f` switch, which stands for follow, causes `tail` to show the last ten lines of the file in addition to any new lines added to the file. Note in the figure that you're not returned to the shell prompt. As long as the `tail -f` command is running, any new log entries appear on the screen.

This situation is useful because you can keep a shell window open for monitoring in the corner of your screen while you're working on your DNS server, and you can see what's happening in real time. Press Ctrl-C to interrupt the `tail -f` command.

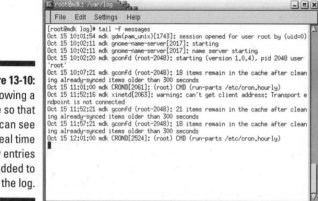

Figure 13-10:
Following a file so that you can see in real time any entries added to the log.

The final way to view the log file is by using the `grep` command. The proper use of `grep` is `grep <pattern> <file>`, where *<pattern>* is the text you're searching for in *<file>*. In this case, you use the command `grep named messages` to find all DNS-related log entries, as shown in Figure 13-11.

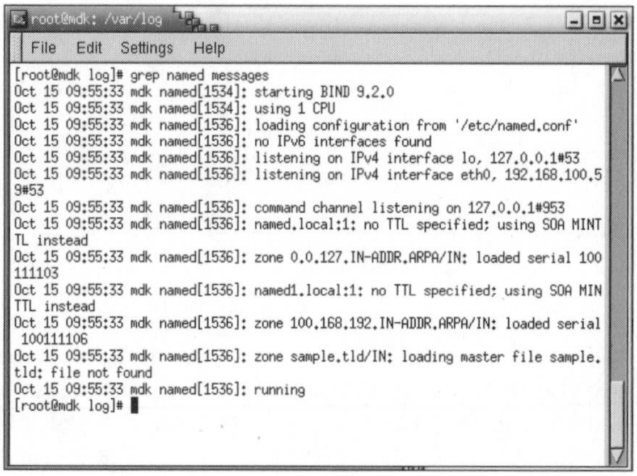

Figure 13-11:
Using `grep` to find all DNS-related log entries.

Now that you know how to view the log files, you can look at the log data and determine what is happening on the server. Separating informational, warning, and error messages in Unix is more difficult than it is in Microsoft Windows because they're not denoted as such. Look at the sample output of the `grep` command shown in Figure 13-11. The first seven log entries, from `starting BIND 9.2.0` to the `command channel listening` message, are informational. They're explaining the process that BIND is experiencing as it starts. The ninth and eleventh messages are also informational: they're informing you that the specified zones have been loaded. The last message, `running`, informs you that the BIND startup process is complete.

Three messages aren't informational. The eighth and tenth messages (no TTL specified) are warnings that no explicit TTL was specified for the zone and that the TTL specified in the SOA record is being used instead. Although this isn't a problem that causes the zones to fail, it isn't proper practice, so a warning message is logged. You should fix problems resulting in warning messages, although it isn't absolutely necessary. Leaving them as is, however, can lead to bigger problems down the road.

The remaining message is an error message: `file not found`. This message is explaining that in trying to load the `zone sample.tld` described in the BIND configuration file, the specified `zone file sample.tld` could not be found in the zone files directory. It's an error message because it causes the zone to not be loaded. You must fix this error before the zone will function. Note, however, that the failure of one zone doesn't cause the entire server to fail.

As you can see, working through log files where BIND is in use can also be a tedious process. To reduce the sheer number of items you must examine, you can forward the DNS logging information to a separate file (away from the common system log) by altering the logging directive. In addition, you can invest in a third-party log analyzer to parse and sort the log file entries by any of a number of criteria. These kinds of tools are often available from the Unix or Linux vendor whose product you're using.

When an error occurs in a zone file or the BIND configuration file, the logged message often indicates the line number on which the error occurred. You can then quickly edit the zone or configuration file and repair the error.

Unlike in Microsoft Windows, no central repository for troubleshooting information exists for BIND. Microsoft has an extensive Knowledge Base that is useful for its integrated products; when you're using BIND on some version of Unix or Linux, however, you can't look for information in any specific place.

The most useful place to look for information about troubleshooting BIND is on an Internet search engine, especially using Google (`www.google.com`). Simply enter the problem you're having with BIND and browse the results. You may be surprised at how many other administrators have had the same problem. Google searches standard Web sites; even more useful, however, are mailing lists that have been archived to the Web. Google finds in these mailing list archives some hits that often contain useful answers.

Another useful support resource if you're administrating BIND is the bind-users mailing list, from the Internet Software Consortium, which maintains BIND. You can find information for signing up for the list at this URL:

```
www.isc.org/services/public/lists/bind-lists.html
```

The bind-users list is a relatively high-volume list on which anyone using BIND can ask questions and solve problems. Another list, named bind-announce, is used only to send out announcements pertaining to BIND.

Another troubleshooting method for BIND is the use of the command-line tools NSLOOKUP and DIG, as described in Chapter 6. Using NSLOOKUP or DIG, you can locate data problems in your DNS server. These problems appear whenever you attempt to retrieve records from a zone in your server. If a major problem occurs in the zone, an error occurs and no data is returned. Using one of these tools would have located the problem shown in Figure 13-11, where the sample.tld zone file couldn't be found, because an error would be returned if you attempted to retrieve a record from the sample.tld domain.

Part VI
The Part of Tens

The 5th Wave — By Rich Tennant

@RICHTENNANT

NO INTERNET ADDRESS

PLEASE

In this part . . .

This part provides a number of lists, each consisting of ten (more or less) interesting facts about DNS. Some of these lists can help you to design a manageable DNS server infrastructure. You can read any of the lists as either an interesting curiosity or a reference for building your own systems.

Chapter 14

Ten DNS Services and Resources

● ●

In This Chapter

▶ Services that depend on DNS

▶ Web sites with DNS information

● ●

According to statistics, nearly 550 million people worldwide use the Internet. Of these 550 million people, only a few even know that DNS exists, although it provides a vital infrastructure for the entire Internet. Without DNS or some other naming service, the Internet would be all but worthless because a huge number of IP addresses are available. Without names, you could remember only a few Web sites and e-mail addresses.

Services That Need DNS

The services listed in this section are important either directly or indirectly to the majority of Internet users. Without DNS, none of these services would be useful in a practical sense.

The World Wide Web

The Web is the most obvious place that DNS is used, and it's transparent to the user. When you open your Web browser and type an address, such as www.yahoo.com, you don't have to concern yourself with the IP address of the Web server hosting the Yahoo! Web site.

The advantage of using DNS on the Web is that servers can be moved around, and only the DNS record must be changed. The client, using the DNS name, always contacts the server that you, as the administrator, want it to contact. You can build a new Web server, ensure that it's functional, and switch traffic to the new server without the user's knowledge.

The second advantage of DNS and Web servers is that DNS allows one name to point to more than one server, through a process known as DNS round robin (refer to Chapter 12). More than one host record (A) is created for the same host with different IP addresses, and the DNS server automatically provides each address in a round-robin fashion to fulfill client requests. This system provides a low-cost method of spreading a load across multiple servers, although it's not appropriate for all environments.

E-mail

E-mail has been reported to be the most widely used application on the entire Internet. E-mail provides a method for users all over the world to talk to each other for the cost of the Internet connection or time spent at an Internet café.

DNS provides an integral part of e-mail in more than one capacity. First of all, when you're using an e-mail client, it usually uses DNS to send messages to the e-mail server and retrieve messages waiting on the server. Even when Web-based e-mail is being used, DNS is used to connect to the Web-based mail application.

The second and more important way that DNS is used is in the transfer of e-mail from server to server, or *mail relaying.* The mail server software, or Mail Transfer Agent (MTA), looks in the queued e-mail at the domain name of the recipient's e-mail address and locates the Mail Exchanger (MX) record for that domain in DNS. The MX record instructs the MTA where to send the e-mail message. The MTA then uses the SMTP protocol (typically) to relay the message to the recipient's e-mail server. Refer to Chapter 4 for more information about how DNS facilitates e-mail and other applications.

Games

Many computer games support play against other users across the Internet. These games normally have proprietary network code and a central game server. Clients use DNS to contact the game server transparently, and the server enables the players to play together.

Instant messaging

Although e-mail may be the most common application on the Internet, instant messaging (IM) is probably experiencing the fastest growth. If the person you want to talk to is online, your message appears on her desktop as soon as you send it. Services such as MSN Messenger, AOL Instant Messenger (AIM), and Yahoo! Instant Messenger are being adopted as both personal and professional tools for instant communication.

Instant messaging uses DNS in a fairly simple manner. DNS is used by the IM client to locate the IM server's IP address. After the client and server connect, the connection is *persistent* (it never disconnects), so DNS isn't required again. Instant messages aren't forwarded from server to server as they are with e-mail, so DNS has no other use.

The DNS addresses of the servers are usually hard-coded into the IM application. The advantage to using DNS in this case is that the IM server can be moved around and only the DNS record needs to be changed. No changes are necessary on the client side.

Microsoft Active Directory

Traditionally in Microsoft Windows NT 4.0 and earlier versions, the Windows Internet Naming Service (WINS) and NetBIOS broadcasts were used for contacting other computers on the network, and the limited list of services was kept in the domain controller database and WINS. Only primary and backup domain controllers (PDCs and BDCs) were kept on the list.

In Windows 2000 and later, Microsoft has moved from the domain controller model to Active Directory. *Active Directory* is a set of services based on the Lightweight Directory Access Protocol (LDAP) and on DNS as well as on a number of proprietary services. All client computers running Windows 2000 or later automatically register their names and addresses in DNS. Active Directory also uses DNS to maintain a complete list of services available on the network in SRV records. This system replaces the incomplete and often unstable service and computer listings in WINS.

Multiple-tier applications

A multiple-tier application refers usually to an application that runs on the World Wide Web and uses several layers of services. These *tiers* usually include the front-end Web server to which the end user connects, a back-end database server, and at least one application, or *middleware,* server in between. This application server is responsible for parsing and formatting data from the database and passing it to the Web server, which serves it to the client. The client can also submit to the Web server some data that is then parsed by the application server, formatted, and stored in the database.

Multiple-tier applications normally use DNS in their communication between tiers. The use of DNS rather than IP addresses allows specific servers in the system to be replaced seamlessly if the need arises. This way, a new server can be put in place, the DNS record can be changed, and after the DNS caches time-out, the new server is used and the old server can be removed. This process is facilitated even further by using short cache time-outs on the records and zones for the multiple-tier application. This arrangement reduces the amount of time it takes for the DNS caches to update.

System administration

In most companies, the system administrator is easily overlooked. She typically is called only when something bad happens and is off doing other work the rest of the time. DNS makes the life of a system administrator (sysadmin) much easier. A sysadmin has much more interaction with a system than a user does. The sysadmin connects to a system using telnet or SSH if it's a Unix system or a remote control application if it's running Windows or with an FTP client for moving files.

With a good DNS implementation, a system administrator needs to remember only the host name and domain of the system rather than have to reference a list of IP addresses every time he needs to do some work on a system. This situation makes the sysadmin more efficient and makes his job a little easier.

Finding More Information

The dynamic entity DNS changes occasionally. It has a wide range of uses and could undergo a redesign or have new features added to its specification. Changes can be made to the original RFC (check out the IETF Web site link in the following section), or custom changes can be made to DNS applications that deviate from the standard. Either way, you probably can benefit from knowing about them. This section lists three Web sites that provide additional information about the use, development, and administration of DNS.

BIND on RedHat Linux

```
www.redhat.com/support/resources/tips/dns/bind.html
```

Because you may want to make use of BIND services on Linux — and chances are good (if the usage statistics are correct) that you will be using some derivative of RedHat — this Web site should prove to be quite a handy tool. The site covers a variety of configuration issues and how-tos.

DNS and Active Directory

```
www.microsoft.com/windows2000/techinfo/reskit/
         deploymentscenarios/scenarios/dns_02_sir.asp
```

If you intend to make use of Windows 2000 Server or .NET server, you will probably encounter the contorted cousin of DNS: Active Directory. The DNS/Active Directory Web site can be quite useful if you find that you're in a quandary while trying to make your DNS server and Active Directly "play nice" together.

The Web site

```
www.ietf.org/
```

The Internet Engineering Task Force (IETF) is the clearinghouse for the standards used on the Internet. Among other things, this Web site allows you to access the Request For Comment (RFC) documents that define the accepted and proposed standards for a variety of Internet-related topics. Many RFCs also document communications between agencies and related topics. The main Web site has an RFC Pages link you can click to search by RFC number or to browse an index of RFCs. First, take a look at RFCs 1034 and 1035 because they focus on the DNS basics. You can also find interesting information in RFCs 1101, 1183, 1348, 1383, and 1535.

Chapter 15

Ten Things Even Experienced People Do to Make DNS Break

*I*t's time for an author confessional. One of us has been working as a senior-level system administrator, including working with DNS on both Unix and Windows, for quite a while. He has made changes to configuration and zone files on production DNS servers that provide services to hundreds of clients and caused the servers to stop responding. That's not the worst dumb mistake he has ever made, but those are stories for another day.

The key here is that everyone, including experienced systems administrators, make mistakes that cause DNS to break. If you're working with a DNS server, you'll probably make some mistakes too. The reason that breaking DNS is so common is that it is extremely picky when it comes to configuration files, especially BIND on Unix. By reading over the list in this chapter, you may be able to avoid making these simple but easily overlooked mistakes.

Syntax, Syntax, Syntax

All versions of BIND on Unix are picky about the syntax of their configuration files. *Syntax* defines how entries made in the DNS configuration files must be formatted. In the case of DNS, syntax requires the precise use of specialized punctuation. The most important thing to watch in DNS, and the most common cause of problems, is the syntax of configuration and zone files. Make sure that all semicolons are in place and that the SOA record is formatted correctly. Sometimes, even spelling mistakes or typos cause problems. If the syntax in the configuration file is incorrect, DNS doesn't start. If the syntax in a zone file is incorrect, that zone isn't loaded. These errors are almost always recorded in the server's log files and usually even indicate the line number with the error in the file.

Forget the Trailing Period

Several record types — including NS, MX, and CNAME records — accept DNS names as data. DNS looks at names in zone files in one of two ways:

- **Relative names** are considered relative to the zone in which they're contained (hence, the name). With a relative name such as www inside a zone named domain.tld, the domain is appended to create the final fully qualified domain name (FQDN) www.domain.tld. This action is important for records such as CNAME because if you want to create a CNAME record pointing to www.domain.tld within the domain.tld zone file, you can simply specify www as the record value.

- **Absolute names** are treated differently. If you want to create a CNAME record for www.domain.tld within a different zone, you obviously cannot use www as the record value because it appends the domain name of the zone in which the record is contained. For this record, the value is www.domain.tld. Note the trailing period. It's vitally important because it indicates that the name is absolute.

The problem with forgetting the trailing period is that DNS thinks that the name is relative rather than absolute. Consider a CNAME within a zone named dnsfordummies.tld. If the CNAME record value is www.domain.tld with no trailing period, the record returned to the client is www.domain.tld.dnsfordummies.tld because without that period, the domain is appended to the value.

Fail to Keep Your @ in Order

The record name @ is used to reflect a record with the same name as the current zone origin. By default, the origin value is set to the name of the zone. (For an explanation of how origin directives work in zones, refer to the section in Chapter 9 about forward-looking Unix.) For example, in a domain named `domain.tld`, an A record named @ would be for `domain.tld` by default. An at-sign (@) is often used to assign IP addresses to the domain name with no host name, which allows Web users to type **domain.tld** rather than **www. domain.tld**. A few rules regarding @ records aren't well documented, though. The main rule is that an @ record may not be CNAME. It *must* be an A record, or else the zone doesn't work. Also, a CNAME record shouldn't be assigned a value of @. Rather, create two A records — one for @ and one for the other name. (For more information about these record types and the rules for their use, check out the section in Chapter 9 about record types.)

Mix Names and IP

This kind of mistake is quite common. Mixing names and IP may look like a silly mistake, but in a busy office or Internet Service Provider (ISP), a person can easily get distracted and make mistakes. DNS uses three major record groups:

- Records that take IP address values, such as A records
- Records that take name values, such as CNAME
- Records that take other information, such as TXT records that can contain anything

Other types of records, such as MX and NS records, can take both name and IP address values, but those aren't an issue because they can use either one. In addition, SOA records take a variety of information.

Attempting to use a name value for a record such as A or attempting to use an IP address value for a record such as CNAME causes lookups for the zone to load improperly or not at all. Ensure that you always use the correct type of value for a record. If a DNS server is behaving as though it doesn't have a record that you're sure is supposed to be there (either a name or an IP), checking the A or CNAME record format is a good place to start.

Don't Apply Changes

DNS servers store configuration and zone data in memory. Because of this behavior, changes to DNS files aren't reflected until the files are reloaded into memory. Some DNS servers require a restart after any changes are made to zone or configuration files, and others can be reloaded without restarting the DNS application by using a specific utility. Regardless of the procedure (which you should be familiar with), by ensuring that the changes you have made are loaded and active, you can save yourself from lots of headaches. Making a configuration change that appears to have no effect can leave you wanting to pull your hair out in frustration.

Don't Increment

Each zone file (refer to Chapter 9) begins with a start of authority (SOA) record. The SOA record contains a serial number for the zone file. Although this number is arbitrary, each time a zone file is modified the serial number must be changed to a value higher than before. It doesn't matter whether you increment it by one or one million — it just needs to be a larger value. Obviously, you wouldn't want to increment it by one million every time you change the zone file because you would run into a size limitation on the field — but you could. Incrementing the serial number tells the DNS server application that the zone has changed and causes the slave servers to transfer the new zone data.

Forget That Pointing Is Okay

Failing to add corresponding PTR records isn't so much a mistake as it is bad practice. You can add an A record in a zone without adding the corresponding PTR record in the reverse lookup zone file, and DNS still functions properly. The problem arises, however, with other applications that use reverse lookups. A number of applications don't function properly when a system doesn't have a proper reverse lookup address defined. For this reason, every time you add an A record, you should add a corresponding PTR record in the reverse lookup file for the IP address. If you change the address for an A record, the reverse lookup should also be changed. If you have a problem that results from a missing PTR record, identifying it can be quite difficult because the zone appears to work for the majority of other DNS-dependent services.

Timeout: Long and Short

The SOA record for a zone contains four time values:

- ✔ **Refresh:** Controls how often a slave DNS server checks the master server for updates.

- ✔ **Retry:** Controls how often the slave checks for updates from the master if a check for an update is unsuccessful.

- ✔ **Expire:** Controls how long the secondary server keeps the zone while the master DNS server isn't responding; this setting eliminates excessively stale records.

- ✔ **Negative caching TTL (minimum TTL in older versions of BIND):** Controls how long a server may cache a negative response from the zone.

In addition, newer versions of BIND use a value in zone files named $TTL. The $TTL value defines how long records from this zone are cached by other servers.

All these values are important in determining DNS behavior. If they're low values, the master server gets flooded with requests from the slave servers for updates, and all the servers face higher traffic from clients that aren't keeping records in the cache for long. As a result, they request updates more often. If the values are too high, however, the client-cached records and secondary DNS server-cached zones become stale. That is, if changes are made to the zone, they aren't reflected at the client, and the changes are unavailable, probably causing a service outage. Find a balance for these values based on factors in your environment, such as the frequency of zone changes and the amount of traffic to your DNS servers. Because different zones can have different values, zones that are updated often may have shorter values, and more static zones may have longer values.

Use Unannounced Servers and MX Records

The first version of this problem, unannounced slave servers, is less common and less of an annoyance than the second, unannounced MX records. Unannounced slave servers occur when a DNS administrator configures his server to be a slave for some zone where the DNS administrator for the primary server is unaware that the slave is being added. In this case, the primary server typically isn't set up for the unannounced slave, and zone transfers are requested but not carried out. You shouldn't set up your DNS server as a slave unless you're sure that the primary server is also properly configured.

The second version of the problem is with unannounced MX records. When you're configuring an MX record, the mail server to which the MX record points must also be configured to accept mail for the domain. An unannounced MX record occurs when a DNS administrator configures an MX record to point to a mail server without informing the administrator of that mail server. The mail server is then sent all messages addressed to that domain, but isn't configured to handle it, so in most cases it's dumped into the postmaster account or discarded. Before configuring an MX record, ensure that the mail server is configured to accept mail for the domain.

Chapter 16

The Top Ten Tips for Maintaining a Manageable DNS Server

Although DNS is a relatively simple application, this simplicity can encourage bad habits among administrators that may lead to problems in the future. This issue is especially prevalent on a BIND DNS server running on Unix, and the server can easily become disorganized with massive zones and randomly placed records. Similar issues arise on Windows servers with a lower frequency, but some of the tips in this chapter would indeed apply to Windows-based DNS servers. After a server becomes disorganized in this way, it becomes virtually impossible to maintain properly. You can follow a number of tips to make maintaining your DNS server easier.

Slice It Up with Subdomains

As the number of network hosts increases, making use of DNS subdomains becomes an attractive, if not essential, tool for managing DNS information. The unfortunate truth is that many DNS domains are a barely organized cluster of hosts. Some of these domains may contain tens of thousands of hosts. By planning the namespace as a first step (refer to Chapter 2), you can prevent potential organizational issues. You should decide how to divide the namespace and therefore which subdomains you will have. In all except the largest cases, a single layer of subdomains is enough. These subdomains can be based on geographical location, business function, or some other identifiable grouping.

Save Yourself the Legwork

DNS administrators commonly build each zone file from scratch and by hand. This practice is a good thing if only a few zones are on a DNS server. When many zones are on a server, though, you might save yourself from some needless suffering if you use a standard zone file template rather than build each one by hand.

This zone file template is similar to your regular zone files. The start of authority (SOA) record is mostly filled out, and all the other appropriate records are in place, but they have no values. When you're creating a new zone, you simply open the zone file template, add the correct values, and save the result to a new file that becomes the zone file.

Keep Things Consistent

You must maintain a consistent look and feel across all your zone files. The tip in the preceding section, about using a standard zone file template, contributes significantly to consistency in zone files. This consistency greatly eases the administrative burden of BIND DNS. One common headache with BIND occurs as the result of an administrator's inadvertently either editing the wrong zone file or making a change to a zone file using incorrect data or syntax.

Keeping consistency in your zone files requires consistency in

- **How the file is organized:** You can quickly find the correct records to change without needing to do a search on the file.

- **How the data is presented:** Keeping the data in a consistent format helps reduce syntax- and entry-related problems.

Section Zone Files

Sectioning zone files can help with administration. Zone files can have essentially any layout you want, as long as they start with the start of authority (SOA) record. Other than that, the records can be in any order so that you can group records in logical, rather than random, sections. In large zone files, you can simply navigate to the correct section and then find the record you're looking for or add a new record rather than have to search the entire zone file (although most text editors have search operations).

Comment Your Code

Just like programming or scripting languages, zone files can contain comments. *Comments* are used to explain the purpose of certain records, note when changes were made, and keep sections of zone files separate. Comments in zone files are prefixed by semicolons, like this:

```
@   IN   SOA   dns1.domain.tld. postmaster.dns1.domain.tld. (
                   100111106      ; Serial
                   360000         ; Refresh
                   30000          ; Retry
                   3600000        ; Expire
                   360000 )       ; Minimum
    IN   NS        dns1.domain.tld.
;PTR Record for local system
1   IN   PTR       localhost.domain.tld.
;PTR Record for Name Servers
59  IN   PTR       dns1.domain.tld.
60  IN   PTR       dns2.domain.tld.
```

Batteries Not Included (include Statements)

Include statements (which we describe in Chapter 9 and which have nothing to do with batteries) are used to separate a single zone or configuration file into multiple files for ease of administration. Using `include` statements is an extreme example of sectioning zone files (refer to the section "Section Zone Files," earlier in this chapter). You use an `include` file whenever you have a long configuration file, such as when you have a large number of zones or zones with quite a large number of records.

An `include` statement is simple to use. In a BIND 9 configuration file, simply add this statement:

```
include "filename";
```

The file that's specified must contain configuration directives, just like a standard configuration file. Those directives, although stored in a separate file, are treated as part of the original configuration file.

Using `include` statements in zone files is a little different. The `include` statement in a zone file looks like this:

```
$INCLUDE filename
```

When you use the $INCLUDE statement in a zone file, everything in the specified file is treated as part of the original zone file.

Back Up in Case You Blow Up

Many administrators are guilty of failing to adequately cover their bases when making configuration changes. Make the following line your mantra: "Make a backup copy before making configuration changes." If you know that your current configuration works, you should make a copy of that file (named.conf.11012002, for example) before you edit the original to make changes. That way, if the changes tank your DNS server, you have a quick way to switch back to the original configuration. This strategy is equally valid for any configuration file, the BIND configuration, zone files, and the RNDC configuration.

Make a Log and Check It Twice

An important task that many administrators fail to do regularly is to check the DNS server log files, for both Microsoft Windows DNS and BIND on Unix. Checking the server logs regularly is important on both systems because that's where you find evidence of configuration problems on the server. Little issues now may balloon into big issues in the future. The configuration problems may also have gone unnoticed simply because nobody has accessed a certain zone yet.

To check the DNS server logs in Microsoft Windows, you must use the Event Log Viewer. Click the Start button and choose Programs➪Administrative Tools➪Event Viewer. In the left pane of the Event Viewer, select the DNS Server object, as shown in Figure 16-1.

The events relevant to the DNS server are shown in the right pane of the Event Viewer. Each event has a severity indication of either information, warning, or error. An error designation indicates a complete failure, a warning designation indicates an event that could contribute to a loss of service, and an information designation denotes an event that isn't detrimental to system performance. To view an event, double-click it in the right pane. The Event Properties dialog box appears, as shown in Figure 16-2.

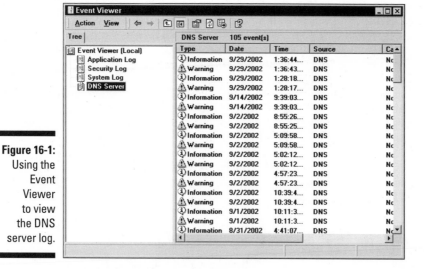

Figure 16-1:
Using the
Event
Viewer
to view
the DNS
server log.

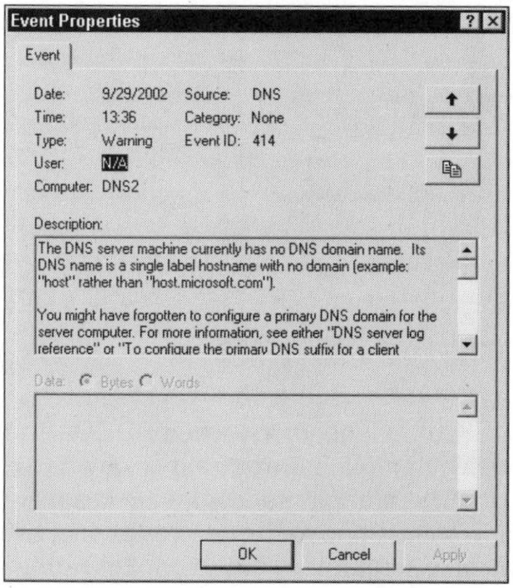

Figure 16-2:
The details
for a
selected
event.

The Event Properties dialog box shows the specific information for the event and, in the case of an error or warning, often provides suggestions for how to repair the problem. After the problem has been rectified, the event doesn't appear again in the Event Viewer.

For BIND running on Unix, the logs are stored in a text file. Depending on how your BIND configuration file is set up, the logs may be stored in a variety of places. By default, BIND uses the Unix syslog facility to store DNS log entries in the system log. This file, typically /var/log/messages in Linux and /var/adm/messages in Solaris, varies with other versions of Unix.

You can send the logs for BIND to other files by using a logging directive, though, which directs BIND to another location in which to put the log files. If a logging directive is in the BIND configuration file on your system, you must look in the specified files for log information.

The /var/log/messages file from a Linux system running BIND 9 is shown in Figure 16-3. The command cat /var/log/messages was used to view the file, although you can also use the more or tail command.

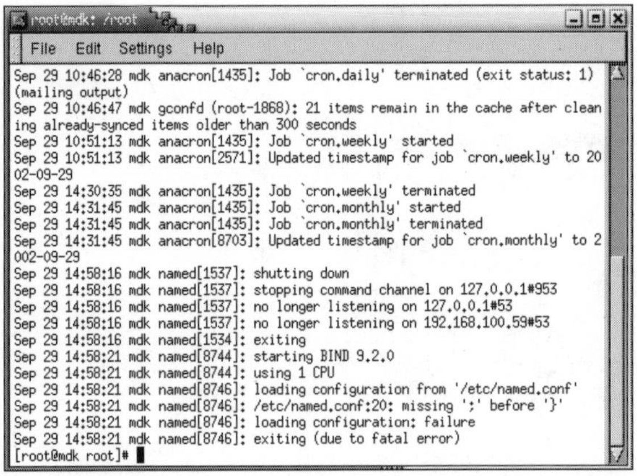

Figure 16-3:
This file
from a
BIND 9
system
shows
errors
starting with
the DNS
server.

As you can see in the figure, a problem occurred when BIND was started. When BIND 9 starts successfully, minimal information is saved to the log. Although configuring BIND is fairly difficult, its logging makes fixing any mistakes fairly easy. In the third-from-last line in the messages file, BIND indicates the specific error (a missing semicolon) in the configuration file and specifies that the problem is on Line 20 of the file. You can then simply open the configuration file, navigate to Line 20, and add the missing semicolon.

Chapter 17

The Top Ten DNS Server Design Considerations

*N*ot everyone has the experience necessary to design solutions for infra-structure-level applications, such as DNS (or for Web and mail, but that's another book topic). If you follow a basic set of guidelines, though, you can have a stable and scalable DNS server without much hassle. Stability and scalability are the two qualities that all architects strive for. Of course, DNS servers can be implemented in other ways; every system administrator seemingly has her own tricks for configuring a system. Keep in mind that every clever trick you use in configuring a system is one more headache you have when you're troubleshooting the system later on. Strive for simplicity, and your sanity will thank you.

Keeping the Server Secure

Security is paramount when you're configuring a DNS server. (Refer to Chapter 11 for an extensive description of DNS security.) You may think that security is truly important only in an Internet Service Provider (ISP) setting, to avoid Web page hijacking or e-mail spoofing, but it's equally important in a corporate setting. DNS security is quite important in an ISP. If an intruder gains access to your DNS server, he can point A records to other servers containing defaced Web pages, which is as good as gaining access to the original Web server itself and defacing the page. The intruder's access can also be used to change the MX record for a domain, which has even worse consequences. By pointing the MX record to a mail server, the intruder controls and even takes ownership of the domain by submitting changes to the domain registry. Note that this insecurity is not so much a fault in the DNS infrastructure as it is the fault of the domain administrators who use MAIL-TO as an authentication method for their domains.

DNS security is equally important in a corporate setting, although it has a more subtle importance. The problem in a corporate environment is the same as in an ISP: An intruder can change DNS records to point to a server he controls. In this case, he can steal important data by making users think that it's going to a real server when it's really going to the rogue server. Remember that most attacks on corporate networks come from inside the corporation, so DNS security is important even if you have a firewall or even no Internet connection.

DNS does not run in a vacuum. Not only does your DNS service need to be secured, but the operating system you use and the physical server also need to be thoroughly examined and tested. Even if you have secured the DNS services properly, all is for naught if a network intruder can gain administrative- or root-level control of the server that is hosting DNS.

Perhaps most obvious, you should physically secure the server in a location where only authorized users can gain access. You should also restrict, using operating system policies, nonadministrative personnel from being able to log on to the server. Regularly check with your operating system vendor for software updates and security alerts. The security of the server that is hosting DNS is your top priority — if you let it slide, you'll probably regret it.

In Case of Emergency

When planning out your DNS infrastructure, you always need to have at least two DNS servers for the purpose of redundancy. If one server goes down, the other one can still serve clients. DNS servers in many cases aren't redundant, but that situation is absolutely not recommended. If you're using a single DNS server and it fails, you will probably get the unenviable task of answering lots of nasty phone calls.

You can provide DNS redundancy in two ways:

✔ **Master/slave:** In the traditional master/slave DNS relationship, (one or more) DNS slave servers load zone data from the master server on startup and at intervals specified in the start of authority (SOA) record for each zone. This method of redundancy has one huge advantage: When a zone file is changed, the changes are automatically propagated to the slave servers. This process normally happens as soon as the changes are made if the NOTIFY DNS feature is supported, and it happens after the time interval in the SOA record if NOTIFY is not supported.

The master/slave DNS server relationship has a disadvantage also: If the master goes down, the slave is restarted, and the zone data cannot be transferred. Also, if the master goes down and isn't restored by the time the DNS record becomes stale (because it cannot update from the master server), the zone is no longer accessible.

✔ **Multiple master:** If you're more concerned with having DNS available at all times rather than having the convenience provided by a master/slave configuration, you can use a multiple master configuration. This concept is simple: All DNS servers are master servers for each zone. The most difficult part of having multiple master DNS servers comes when a change is made to a zone file or the DNS configuration. The change must be made to every master DNS server and isn't automatically propagated.

Don't Put All the Eggs in One Basket

The location of the DNS servers is important for a number of reasons. (This section overlaps slightly with the preceding two sections.) Most environments use two DNS servers — a master and a slave or two masters if they're caching only — although no limit exists on the number of servers you can have.

You must consider two separate but related issues for the DNS server location:

✔ **Placement in relation to a firewall:** In most cases, internal DNS servers are placed on the internal network, and externally accessible servers are placed in the demilitarized zone (DMZ) of the firewall, which is secure but also accessible from the public network. If you have only one set of DNS servers for both internal and external DNS (although that arrangement isn't recommended), you should place them in the DMZ and have internal users access them from the internal network rather than place them in the internal network and open a hole in your firewall for external DNS requests.

✔ **Placement on your network segments geographically or in some other logical fashion:** You have a number of reasons to place your DNS servers on separate network segments and separate locations —primarily, redundancy. If one network segment goes down, or even an entire location is lost because a disaster of some sort, you still can provide DNS service. In addition, performance increases for internal DNS servers may result if you configure systems to use the local DNS server first and use the remote DNS server if the local server is down. Having at least one internal DNS server at each geographical location is common practice.

Less Is More

When it comes to system architecture, two schools of thought are prominent: minimization and consolidation. Once considered antiquated thinking, consolidation (putting many applications on one large server) is coming into style again as the footprint of the data center (the amount of space taken up by all servers) is becoming an issue. Placing numerous applications on one expensive, high-capacity server is often cheaper and saves on the monthly cost of having numerous cheaper servers.

For applications such as DNS, minimization is the way to go. *Minimization* refers to having a smaller server with only one application — in this case, DNS. DNS is an ideal candidate for minimization because it makes the maintenance of the system easier and can provide more security. DNS also allows the system to be scalable because no other applications are competing for resources.

When you're planning for minimization, no applications other than DNS should be running on the server. Most operating systems come with a variety of network services that run by default, and all they should be disabled. This arrangement also makes the system much more secure because DNS is the only way to attack. If unnecessary applications are running on the system, they provide more targets for an attacker.

Thanks for the Memory

Random Access Memory, or RAM, is probably the most important consideration in selecting hardware for your DNS server. When the DNS service starts, the entire DNS database of zone files is loaded into memory for speed purposes. Serving a record from memory is much faster than serving it from disk. Cached DNS records are also stored in memory. For this reason, the amount of RAM on the server must be at least equal to the size of the DNS database plus the amount of RAM required by the operating system. This amount is typically not an issue because even the cheapest systems come with at least 128MB of RAM, and many come with 256MB. Most servers have 512MB or more. Having a DNS server with a database of zone files measuring more than a few megabytes is quite uncommon. Even in large ISPs, a large DNS database would be split over multiple servers, each with a portion of the DNS zones or even on specialized DNS hardware to minimize the load on the DNS servers. Still, whenever you're choosing hardware, consider the size of your DNS database and the amount of traffic your server will have. (More traffic means more cached records if caching is enabled.) Choosing twice as much memory as you think you need is always prudent, especially because memory prices are lower than ever.

Processing Power!

The central processing unit (CPU) you choose for your DNS servers also makes a difference in the performance of your DNS infrastructure. Small DNS servers with no requirements other than serving zones and caching don't require much CPU power. DNS servers are often run on older systems, such as Intel 486-based systems and Sun IPX systems. The CPU requirements increase in two cases, though:

- **When the load on the system increases to high levels:** A DNS server with one request per second runs fine on a low-end system; when the number of requests increases, however, the CPU load goes up. Also, zone transfers are fairly CPU intensive, and a server pair (master and slave) with many zones requires more CPU power than a pair with only a few zones.

- **When features beyond the basics are used:** If you implement security features such as DNSSEC, which uses encryption, the CPU requirements increase exponentially because encryption requires lots of processing power. Other, advanced DNS features require more CPU power than does a standard DNS server.

Room to Move: Bandwidth

The network bandwidth consideration is a simple one. If you have a busy DNS server, it requires more bandwidth than a less busy server. This bandwidth requirement is carried all the way to the network backbone. For example, if you have a busy DNS server with a 100 Mbps connection to the switch but only a 1.54 Mbps T-1 Internet connection, the T-1 becomes a bottleneck and user requests are slow.

You can often solve the network bandwidth consideration in a corporate environment by simply adding a slave DNS server at remote sites. For example, if a master DNS server at the head office has a slow network connection to a branch office, you should place a slave server at the branch office. Rather than have all DNS requests travel to the head office, only zone transfers take place over the slow connection. Even more of an advantage can be gained if the branch office server is also a caching DNS server with an Internet connection because those requests are served locally rather than from the head office.

Maintenance Free?

Many Internet DNS servers have been poorly maintained, have changed hands many times, are fairly old, or are just generally not well administrated. Factors such as these contribute to DNS servers that are quite literally a mess. Maintainability is an important factor in designing a DNS server because the server administrators must be able to easily troubleshoot and make changes to the system. A system that is messy can contribute not only to difficulty for the administrator but also to mistakes that can cause problems or even total outages.

You must make a number of considerations for designing an easily maintained DNS server. The simplest DNS server with only a handful of zones doesn't require a large amount of planning; even in this case, though, you may find it hard to judge where you will be in a year or several years when the server may still be in place. If no planning was done in the beginning and a large number of zones are added, the server becomes difficult to maintain over time. You can keep the DNS server organized in many ways, including separating configuration and zone files into sections and even using `include` statements to divide the DNS configuration into multiple files. This strategy is useful if you have a large number of zones.

There Is No Free Lunch

Working in various environments, we have seen DNS server hardware from good-quality, name-brand Unix servers to "beige box" PCs with their covers missing and their hard drives hanging by their cables. Needless to say, your choice of hardware makes a huge difference in the reliability of your DNS services. DNS is often seen as an unimportant service and is relegated to some castoff, secondhand computer or a cheap system. Now, more than ever, high-quality, name-brand hardware is reaching low price points — as low as $1,000. You may be able to purchase a cheap PC for a little less than that, but the tradeoff in reliability usually isn't worth the price difference.

Appendix A

Using the DNSCMD Utility

In This Chapter

▶ Installing DNSCMD

▶ Using DNSCMD for various tasks

*I*n several chapters in this book, we describe the configuration of a Microsoft Windows Server running the DNS Server service. Also, we spend considerable time on the topic of the DNS Microsoft Management Console (MMC) snap-in. In addition to the graphical method of administering a DNS server, as shown elsewhere in this book, Microsoft has made available a command-line tool named DNSCMD that can also be used to configure the Microsoft DNS Server service.

You don't need to install the DNSCMD utility on the DNS server. You can use DNSCMD from a remote system, such as a Windows 2000 or Windows XP workstation or another Windows 2000, Windows .NET Server, or Windows NT 4.0 system. This tool is particularly handy if you're in charge of numerous servers because you can use it from just about anywhere and effectively accomplish DNS management tasks.

The DNSCMD utility is useful to skilled administrators because they can use it to troubleshoot and configure Windows-based DNS servers. Where DNSCMD truly shines, though, is in the area of scripts. If you're skilled at using a scripting language, such as Perl, you can write scripts to automate many of the administration functions of a DNS server. You can use a scripting language to build a Web-based front end using DNSCMD at the back end to make administration easier or even allow users to administer their own zones. With a utility like DNSCMD, the possibilities are virtually endless.

Installing the DNSCMD Utility

If you have decided that DNSCMD is a tool worth using, you first need to install it. DNSCMD is on the Windows 2000 or Windows .NET Server CD in the \support\tools\support.cab folder. The support.cab file is shown in Figure A-1. On a Windows 2000, Windows XP, or Windows .NET system, you can simply double-click the CAB file, and it opens automatically.

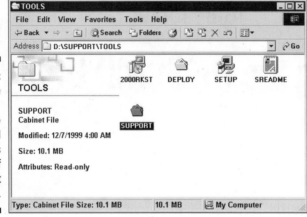

The
support.
cab
compressed
file contains
a number of
support
tools.

After you have opened the support.cab file, locate the dnscmd.exe file, as shown in Figure A-2. Double-click the dnscmd.exe file, and you're prompted for a location in which to save the file. The best location for the DNSCMD utility is in a folder that is in your default path, such as C:\WINNT, although you can place it anywhere you want. Select the directory from the list and click OK. The file is copied to that folder.

Figure A-2:
The
DNSCMD
executable
file is in the
support.
cab cabinet
file.

Now that the DNSCMD utility is installed, you can begin to use it. Although it's a simple utility to use, it has a wide array of available options.

Using the DNSCMD Utility

Using the DNSCMD utility is simple. Open a command prompt window by either choosing Run from the Start menu, typing CMD, and clicking OK or choosing Programs⇨Accessories⇨Command Prompt from the Start menu. From the command prompt, type **dnscmd** and press Enter. The results shown in Figure A-3 serve as an overview of all the DNSCMD features. As you can see, DNSCMD is a powerful tool with many options.

You can also use any of the DNSCMD commands in this section on a remote server by adding the server name to the command in this format:

```
DNSCMD <server> <command>
```

```
C:\WINNT\System32\cmd.exe                                      _ 8 X
C:\>dnscmd

USAGE:  DnsCmd <ServerName> <Command> [<Command Parameters>)]

        <ServerName>:
                                  -- local machine using LPC
                IP address        -- RPC over TCP/IP
                DNS name          -- RPC over TCP/IP
                other server name -- RPC over named pipes
        <Command>:
                /Info             -- Get server information
                /Config           -- Reset server or zone configuration
                /EnumZones        -- Enumerate zones
                /Statistics       -- Query/clear server statistics data
                /ClearCache       -- Clear DNS server cache
                /WriteBackFiles   -- Write back all zone or root-hint datafile(s)
                /StartScavenging  -- Initiates server scavenging
                /ResetListenAddresses -- Select server IP address(es) to serve DNS reque
sts
                /ResetForwarders  -- Set DNS servers to forward recursive queries to

                /ZoneInfo         -- View zone information
                /ZoneAdd          -- Create a new zone on the DNS server
                /ZoneDelete       -- Delete a zone from DNS server or DS
                /ZonePause        -- Pause a zone
                /ZoneResume       -- Resume a zone
                /ZoneReload       -- Reload zone from its database (file or DS)
                /ZoneWriteBack    -- Write back zone to file
                /ZoneRefresh      -- Force refresh of secondary zone from master
                /ZoneUpdateFromDs -- Update a DS integrated zone by data from DS
                /ZoneResetType    -- Change zone type Primary/Secondary/DSintegrated

                /ZoneResetSecondaries  -- Reset secondary\notify information for a zone
                /ZoneResetScavengeServers-- Reset scavenging servers for a zone
                /ZoneResetMasters -- Reset secondary zone's master servers
                /EnumRecords      -- Enumerate records at a name
                /RecordAdd        -- Create a record in zone or RootHints
                /RecordDelete     -- Delete a record from zone, RootHints or Cache d
ata
                /NodeDelete       -- Delete all records at a name
                /AgeAllRecords    -- Force aging on node(s) in zone
        <Command Parameters>:
                -- parameters specific to each Command
                dnscmd <CommandName> /? -- For help info on specific Command
C:\>
```

Figure A-3:
The options available for the DNSCMD utility.

Gathering information

One cool use for DNSCMD is to retrieve information about the status of one of your DNS servers. A number of DNSCMD commands serve this purpose.

Although the tools `NSLOOKUP` and `DIG` are useful, the `DNSCMD` command is far more powerful because it interfaces directly into the DNS server application instead of having to use the normal DNS request channels, like `NSLOOKUP` or `DIG`. In this section, we explore some command options you use when you issue the `DNSCMD` command from within the command-prompt environment (a DOS window).

/Info

The `DNSCMD /Info` command shows server information, as shown in Figure A-4. Although much of the information is for the most part meaningless to anyone who isn't a Microsoft engineer or a true DNS guru, some of it is indeed useful to just about anyone who needs to work with the DNS server in question. Much of the information shown by using the `/Info` command is set in the DNS server Properties dialog box when you right-click the server in the DNS snap-in and choose Properties.

Starting from the Server info section at the top of the results, you can see the server name followed by the server version, although the server version number doesn't represent a standard version number, as in `Windows 2000`. The `DS container` field represents the container in the Active Directory in which the DNS server resides if it's part of an Active Directory implementation.

Figure A-4: The DNSCMD /Info command shows information about the server.

```
C:\WINNT\System32\cmd.exe                                        _ | 8 | X
        ptr            = 00075B30
        server name    = dns2
        version        = C2000005
        DS container   = <null>
 Configuration:
        dwLogLevel              = 00000000
        dwDebugLevel            = 00000000
        dwRpcProtocol           = FFFFFFFF
        dwNameCheckFlag         = 00000002
        cAddressAnswerLimit     = 0
        dwRecursionRetry        = 3
        dwRecursionTimeout      = 15
        dwDsPollingInterval     = 300
 Configuration Flags:
        fBootMethod                = 3
        fAdminConfigured           = 1
        fAllowUpdate               = 1
        fDsAvailable               = 0
        fAutoReverseZones          = 1
        fAutoCacheUpdate           = 0
        fSlave                     = 0
        fNoRecursion               = 0
        fRoundRobin                = 1
        fLocalNetPriority          = 1
        fStrictFileParsing         = 0
        fLooseWildcarding          = 0
        fBindSecondaries           = 1
        fWriteAuthorityNs          = 0
 Aging Configuration:
        ScavengingInterval         = 0
        DefaultAgingState          = 1
        DefaultRefreshInterval     = 168
        DefaultNoRefreshInterval   = 168
 ServerAddresses:
        Addr Count = 2
                Addr[0] => 192.168.0.128
                Addr[1] => 192.168.209.3
 ListenAddresses:
        NULL IP Array.
 Forwarders:
        NULL IP Array.
        forward timeout = 5
        slave           = 0
Command completed successfully.

C:\>
```

The next section, Configuration, shows information about the configuration of the DNS server, including logging and debugging levels in addition to retry and timeout information for recursion.

In the section that displays configuration flag information, the output is some of the most interesting information revealed. It shows the settings typically managed by the DNS snap-in. You can view information such as whether recursion is allowed and whether DNS round robin is enabled. If you look through the list of flags in the Configuration Flags section and then look through the DNS server configuration with the snap-in, you see the correlation between the two tools.

In the Aging configuration section, you see how aging and scavenging are configured on the server. The ServerAddresses item shows the IP addresses configured on the server, and the ListenAddresses option shows which IP addresses are configured to listen for DNS requests. If ListenAddress is set to NULL IP Array, as shown in Figure A-4, all addresses shown in the Server Addresses section are used. The Forwarders section shows any servers configured on the Forwarders tab of the DNS server configuration and the forward timeout value. Forwarders and the forward timeout are used whenever a DNS query cannot be resolved locally.

/Statistics

Part of the DNSCMD /Statistics output is shown in Figure A-5.

Figure A-5: Some command output.

```
C:\WINNT\System32\cmd.exe
Record Sources:
    RR File                   =        42
    RR File Free              =         0
    RR DS                     =         0
    RR DS Free                =         0
    RR Admin                  =         0
    RR Admin Free             =         0
    RR DynUp                  =         0
    RR DynUp Free             =         0
    RR Axfr                   =         0
    RR Axfr Free              =         0
    RR Ixfr                   =         0
    RR Ixfr Free              =         0
    RR Copy                   =         0
    RR Copy Free              =         0
    RR Cache                  =         0
    RR Cache Free             =         0

UDP Sockets:
    PnP Socket Delete         =         0
    Recvfrom Failure          =         0
    ConnResets                =         0
    ConnReset Overflow        =         0
    GQCS Failure              =         0
    GQCS Failure wCntxt       =         0
    GQCS ConnReset            =         0
    Indicate Recv Fail        =         0
    Restart Recv Pass         =        64

TCP Connections:
    ConnectAttempt            =         0
    ConnectFailure            =         0
    Connect                   =         0
    Query                     =         0
    Disconnect                =         0

SkwanSec Hacks:
    Verified Old Sig          =         0
    Failed Old Sig            =         0
    Big TimeSkew Bypass       =         0

Command completed successfully.

C:\>
```

The /Statistics command shows a huge number of statistics regarding the DNS server. Some of the more interesting indicate

- ✔ When the server was started
- ✔ The number of queries received and responses sent
- ✔ The total number of queries and the number for each record type
- ✔ The number of queries handed off to the recursion process (not answered locally)
- ✔ The number of notify messages sent and zone transfer requests made as a master server
- ✔ The number of notify messages received and zone transfers performed as a secondary server
- ✔ The number of referrals from WINS
- ✔ The number of dynamic updates
- ✔ Security statistics, such as invalid TSIG keys
- ✔ Directory Server activity
- ✔ Memory usage statistics
- ✔ Error counts

As you can see, the output of the /Statistics command is engrossing (or just plain gross). Although this information can seem a bit overwhelming at first, you can use it to gain useful insight into what your server is doing. You can also use statistical information to see how specific record types are affecting your server's memory performance because the memory usage statistics are granular. The output of this command is especially useful on a high-traffic server on which you need to squeeze out every last possible drop of performance.

Use the more command to view the output of the /Statistics command page by page or else it scrolls off the screen and probably even out of the scroll buffer of your command prompt window. You *pipe* the output of the command by using the pipe character (|) like this:

```
dnscmd /statistics | more
```

You can also send the output of the command to a file by using the redirection character (>), such as in this line:

```
dnscmd /statistics > dnsstats.txt
```

You can also filter the output of the /Statistics command. Type **dnscmd /statistics ?** to see the list of filters you can use.

/EnumZones

Use the `DNSCMD /EnumZones` command to view a list of all zones in the server, as shown in Figure A-6. Any zone configured on the server appears on the list. The term file indicates that the zone is being stored in a zone file. Zones stored in Active Directory are indicated by `DS` in this field. A `Rev` identifier indicates a reverse lookup zone, and a blank field indicates a forward zone.

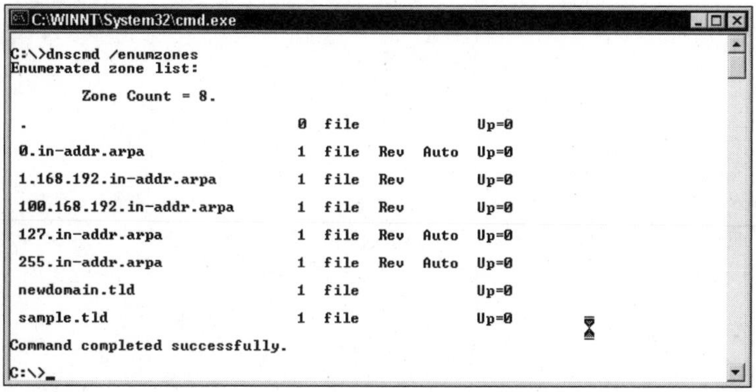

```
C:\WINNT\System32\cmd.exe
C:\>dnscmd /enumzones
Enumerated zone list:

        Zone Count = 8.

 .                                 0  file              Up=0
 0.in-addr.arpa                    1  file  Rev  Auto   Up=0
 1.168.192.in-addr.arpa            1  file  Rev         Up=0
 100.168.192.in-addr.arpa          1  file  Rev         Up=0
 127.in-addr.arpa                  1  file  Rev  Auto   Up=0
 255.in-addr.arpa                  1  file  Rev  Auto   Up=0
 newdomain.tld                     1  file              Up=0
 sample.tld                        1  file              Up=0
Command completed successfully.
C:\>_
```

Figure A-6: Listing all zones on a DNS server.

You can filter the `/EnumZones` command in one of two ways. The first filter is based on the zone type and uses the options `/Primary`, `/Secondary`, `/Cache`, and `/Auto-Created`. The second filter is based on whether the zone is a forward or reverse zone and makes use of the `/Forward` and `/Reverse` options. You can use these two filters together, but only one option from each of the two groups. For example, you can use `/Primary` and `/Forward` together, but you cannot then add `/Secondary` because one option from the first (zone type) group is already in use. Note that when you're using either filter, system-created zones, such as `127.in-addr.arpa` and `255.in-addr.arpa`, are not shown on the list.

/EnumRecords

Now that you know how to view a list of all zones on the server, you can use the `/EnumRecords` command to view records in a particular zone. Use the following command, as shown in Figure A-7:

```
DNSCMD /EnumRecords <zone name> <node name>
```

Specifying a node name of @ shows all records in the zone, and specifying a specific node name shows all records with that name.

Figure A-7:
Viewing the
records in a
zone.

The /EnumRecords command also has a number of filters you can apply. You
type DNSCMD /EnumRecords with no zone name to see a list of the available
data options. Using these options, you can filter based on record type and
view additional information about a record.

/ZoneInfo

The DNSCMD /ZoneInfo <zone name> command shows configuration information about a zone, as shown in Figure A-8. The zone configuration information is a reflection of the zone Properties dialog box that's displayed when
you right-click a zone in the DNS snap-in and choose Properties.

```
C:\WINNT\System32\cmd.exe

C:\>dnscmd /zoneinfo sample.tld
Zone query result:
Zone info:
        ptr             = 00075420
        zone name       = sample.tld
        zone type       = 1
        update          = 0
        DS intergrated  = 0
        data file       = sample.tld.dns
        using WINS      = 0
        using Nbstat    = 0
        aging           = 0
          refresh interval  = 168
          no refresh        = 168
          scavenge available = 3522959
        Zones Masters
        NULL IP Array.
        Zone Secondaries
        NULL IP Array.
        secure secs   = 0
Command completed successfully.

C:\>
```

Figure A-8:
Viewing
zone
information.

Like the /Info command, the /ZoneInfo command is useful for looking at
the configuration of a particular zone at a glance. The output can also be
parsed by scripts, as we mention at the beginning of this appendix. Included
in the output are the zone name and type, data filename, scavenging information, and identity of any master or slave servers for the zone. You can also

see whether dynamic updates are enabled and whether it's Active Directory integrated. Masters appear if the zone is a slave, and slave servers appear if the zone is a master and has slave servers configured.

Changing the server configuration

Viewing the DNS configuration information is all well and good, but you need a tool that can make changes too. Fortunately, DNSCMD comes though with this functionality in abundance. It has a variety of commands for configuring the server, including those to configure the server in addition to the zones and records maintained by the server. The DNSCMD command can essentially replace the DNS snap-in, but it can prove to be more difficult to use because it lacks the intuitive interface of the DNS snap-in. Not to worry: After you master DNSCMD, you find that it can be more efficient and definitely advantageous if you need to add DNS management abilities to a scripted application. This section examines the DNSCMD options that relate to the operation of the DNS server.

/Restart

```
DNSCMD /Restart
```

This command simply stops and restarts the DNS server in a manner similar to the way you use the Services control panel to restart the DNS Server service.

/Statistics

```
DNSCMD /Statistics
```

In addition to the ability of this command to gather information, as we explain a little earlier in this chapter, it has a configuration option. By typing DNSCMD /Statistics /Clear, you can wipe out the existing statistical information and start from scratch. This command can be useful if you want to view statistics for a specific period or if you want to evaluate the effect of a configuration change on the server's operation. You can reset the statistics and then sample them at specific intervals, which is especially useful for scripted statistics-gathering for analysis.

/ClearCache

```
DNSCMD /ClearCache
```

This command simply clears the DNS server's cache. You may need to clear the DNS server cache if you know that your server is caching a stale or incorrect record and don't want to wait until the TTL of that record expires. Using the /ClearCache command doesn't require you to restart the DNS service, the traditional method of clearing the cache.

Clearing the DNS server's cache using /ClearCache isn't the same as clearing the DNS client's cache using the ipconfig /flushdns command, as described in Chapter 6, in the section about looking at resolvers and what they do for DNS. If a stale DNS record is in the server cache, you first need to run the DNSCMD /ClearCache command to clear the server cache then run the ipconfig /flushdns command on the workstation. The stale entry is then removed from both systems and a new DNS request retrieves the correct record.

/WriteBackFiles

```
DNSCMD /WriteBackFiles
```

This command writes any data that has been changed and is stored in memory to only the appropriate zone files. You can use the DNSCMD /Write BackFiles <zone name> command to write data for only a specific zone. When you make configuration changes or zone transfers, the data isn't instantly written to the zone file. Using this command forces the data to be written to the files.

/StartScavenging

```
DNSCMD /StartScavenging
```

This command forces the scavenging process to begin on a DNS server on which scavenging is enabled. This command clears from the server any records marked as stale by the aging process. Scavenging is typically a scheduled event, but by using this command you can force the scavenging process to start at any time. This command is particularly useful if you're experiencing trouble with resolution and you suspect that the aged record is contributing to the issue.

/ResetListenAddresses

```
DNSCMD /ResetListenAddresses
```

Use this command to set the addresses on which the DNS server listens for DNS requests as shown by the DNSCMD /Info command. You can use the /ResetListenAddresses command in two ways:

- Used with no input, it sets the server's listen addresses to all configured IP addresses on the system.
- Used in the following form, the listen addresses are set to those specified:

```
DNSCMD /ResetListenAddresses <IP Address>
```

You can specify as many listen addresses as you want, separated by spaces, but they must be addresses configured on the system in the network configuration. They're shown in the `ServerAddresses` section when using the `DNSCMD /Info` command.

/ResetForwarders

```
DNSCMD /ResetForwarders
```

This command configures the DNS servers used as forwarders for the current DNS server. Forwarders are used when the current DNS server cannot provide a response from its local database. If recursion is enabled, the forwarders are contacted first and if they fail, the recursion process begins. Recursion is disabled, and if the forwarders cannot provide a response, the resolution process fails.

If you use the `DNSCMD /ResetForwarders` command with no additional parameters, the server is configured with no forwarders. If the server has existing forwarders (as shown by `DNSCMD /Info`), they're removed. To add forwarders, use this command:

```
DNSCMD /ResetForwarders <IP Address>
```

The IP specified address can be either a single address or a group of addresses separated by spaces. You can use two options with the `/ResetForwarders` command:

- `/Slave`: Indicates that the server is a slave.
- `/TimeOut <value>`: Sets the forwarder's timeout to something other than its default value of five seconds.

/Config

```
DNSCMD /Config <zone name> <property> <value>
```

One of the most powerful `DNSCMD` commands, the `DNSCMD /Info` command shows a number of configuration flags and values. You can set most of them by using the `/Config` command. The optional zone name is used for configuring zone options, as discussed in the following section. You display a complete list of properties by typing the command `DNSCMD /Config /?`, as shown in Figure A-9.

As mentioned, the configuration changes made using the `/Config` command are reflected by the `/Info` command. You can view the results of the changes you have made by typing `DNSCMD /Info`. The value you specify for `/Config` can either be decimal or hexadecimal if you prefix it with `0x`.

```
C:\WINNT\System32\cmd.exe                                        _ |8| X
USAGE:   DnsCmd <ServerName> /Config [<ZoneName>!..AllZones] <Property> <Value>
         Server <Property>:
                        /RpcProtocol
                        /LogLevel
                        /EventlogLevel
                        /NoRecursion
                        /ForwardDelegations
                        /ForwardingTimeout
                        /IsSlave
                        /SecureResponses
                        /RecursionRetry
                        /RecursionTimeout
                        /MaxCacheTtl
                        /MaxNegativeCacheTtl               ⧗
                        /RoundRobin
                        /LocalNetPriority
                        /AddressAnswerLimit
                        /BindSecondaries
                        /WriteAuthorityNs
                        /NameCheckFlag
                        /StrictFileParsing
                        /UpdateOptions
                        /DisableAutoReverseZones
                        /SendPort
                        /NoTcp
                        /XfrConnectTimeout
                        /DsPollingInterval
                        /DsTombstoneInterval
                        /ScavengingInterval
                        /DefaultAgingState
                        /DefaultNoRefreshInterval
                        /DefaultRefreshInterval
         Zone <Property>:
                        /SecureSecondaries
                        /AllowUpdate
                        /Aging
                        /RefreshInterval <Value>
                        /NoRefreshInterval <Value>
         <Value>:  A DWORD value;  Use 0x prefix to indicate hex value.
             Note some server and zone DWORD properties must be reset as
             part of a more complex operation.
             Use zone "..AllZones" to apply operation to all zones.
             See dnscmd help for more information.
Command completed successfully.
C:\>_
```

Figure A-9:
Listing all
available
properties
you can
configure.

Changing the zone configuration

Just as you can use DNSCMD to configure the DNS server globally, you can use
the command to configure individual zones. DNSCMD can replace all the functionality of the DNS MMC snap-in. This section peruses some command
options for DNSCMD that let you tinker with the zone settings.

/Config

```
DNSCMD /Config <zone name> <property> <value>
```

We describe this command in the preceding section in reference to global
server configuration, but you can also use it to configure an individual zone
by specifying the zone name:

Typing DNSCMD /Config /? displays in the Zone <Property> section (refer
to Figure A-9) the available properties for zone configuration. View the zone
properties by using the DNSCMD /ZoneInfo command discussed earlier in
this appendix, in the "Gathering information" section.

/ZoneAdd

```
DNSCMD /ZoneAdd <zone name> /Primary /File <filename>
DNSCMD /ZoneAdd <zone name> /Secondary <IP Address> /File
        <filename>
DNSCMD /ZoneAdd <zone name> /DsSPrimaryDSPrimary
```

The DNSCMD /ZoneAdd command adds a zone to the DNS server and can be used in one of three ways to add either a primary zone, a secondary zone, or an Active Directory-integrated zone. The DNS server must be integrated with Active Directory in order to add an integrated zone. The three commands look like this:

Adding a primary zone requires only a filename in which the zone data is stored. Adding a secondary zone requires at least one IP address of the zone master server, although you can specify more than one address separated by spaces. The filename is optional, and you can leave out the /File parameter. Adding an Active Directory–integrated zone requires no parameters. After you have added the zone by using this command, you can begin adding records to the zone.

/ZoneDelete

```
DNSCMD /ZoneDelete <zone name>
```

As you may have guessed, the /ZoneDelete option removes a zone from the DNS server. This command removes the zone from the DNS server; if it's an Active Directory–integrated zone, however, it remains in the directory server. To remove an integrated zone from both the DNS and the directory server, append the /DsDel option to the command. By default, you're prompted by the command for confirmation to delete the zone. If you don't want to be prompted for confirmation (if you were running the command from a script, for example), add the /f option.

/ZonePause and /ZoneResume

```
DNSCMD /ZonePause <zone name>
DNSCMD /ZoneResume
```

These commands pause and unpause (or resume) a zone. A paused zone doesn't respond to queries until it's unpaused. This functionality is useful for temporarily disabling a domain without disabling the entire server.

/ZoneReload

```
DNSCMD /ZoneReload <zone name>
```

This command reloads a zone into memory whenever its zone file or its information in the directory server (in the case of an integrated zone) has been changed. If you're manually editing zone files or the directory, you must run this command to have the changes become effective in the DNS server. The old data continues to be supplied to clients until the reload occurs.

/ZoneWriteBack

```
DNSCMD /ZoneWriteBack <zone name>
```

This command, which is identical to the /WriteBackFiles <zone name> command, commits to the zone file any changes made to the zone in memory.

/ZoneRefresh

```
DNSCMD /ZoneRefresh <zone name>
```

To force a zone transfer of a secondary zone from the master server, issue this command. The specified zone must be a secondary zone. When the command is run, a full zone transfer is performed, which is particularly useful when you know that the master zone has been changed and the data in the secondary DNS server is stale. If the stale data is pointing to an invalid server, the refresh is important. Using the DNS NOTIFY command on your DNS server makes obsolete the requirement to refresh secondary zones.

/ZoneUpdateFromDs

```
DNSCMD /ZoneUpdateFromDs <zone name>
```

This command is similar to the /ZoneRefresh command except that the zone information is reloaded from the directory server. This procedure is applicable only to Active Directory–integrated zones. The command is used whenever the zone data has been changed directly on the directory server.

/ZoneResetType

```
DNSCMD /ZoneResetType <zone name> <type>
```

This command changes a zone to a specified zone type. The zone type options are shown in this list:

- /Primary /file <filename>
- /Secondary <IP Address> /File <filename>
- /DsPrimary

Just like with the /ZoneAdd command, the /Primary option requires a filename for the zone file; the /Secondary option requires at least one master server IP address, but can accept more than one and doesn't require the /File parameter; and the /DsPrimary option requires no parameters.

The /ZoneResetType command also has two other options:

✔ The /OverWrite_Mem option overwrites the DNS data with the data stored in the directory server.

✔ The /OverWrite_Ds option overwrites the data stored in the Directory Server with the data in the DNS server.

/ZoneResetSecondaries

```
DNSCMD /ZoneResetSecondaries <zone name> <security>
        <IP Address> <notify options> <notify IP>
```

Using this command changes the secondary DNS servers for a master zone. The command in this form sets the secondary DNS server configuration for the specified zone.

The options for security are shown in this list:

✔ /NoXfr: No zone transfers are allowed.

✔ /NonSecure: Zone transfers to any host are allowed.

✔ /SecureNs: Zone transfers are allowed to any host with an NS record in the zone file.

✔ /SecureList: Zone transfers are allowed to any host in the list specified by <IP Address>, which must be separated by spaces.

The default security setting for a zone is /NonSecure. The notify options are shown in this list:

✔ /NoNotify: No notify messages are sent.

✔ /Notify: Notify messages are sent to all secondary DNS servers.

✔ /NotifyList: Notify messages are sent to only the hosts specified in <notify IP>, a list that must be separated by spaces.

The default notify setting is /Notify. As you may notice, these configuration options are the same ones available on the Zone Transfers tab in a zone's Properties dialog box in the DNS snap-in.

/ZoneResetMasters

```
DNSCMD /ZoneResetMasters <zone name> <IP address>
```

Similar to /ZoneResetSecondaries only for secondary zones, this command changes the master servers for the zone. The <IP address> option must contain at least one IP address for a master server, and multiple IP addresses must be separated by spaces.

/ZoneResetScavengeServers

```
DNSCMD /ZoneResetScavengeServers <zone name> <IP address>
```

This command configures which servers are allowed to scavenge the zone. If no IP address is specified, all servers that host the zone — master or slave — can scavenge it. If an IP address or list of addresses is specified, any of the specified servers can scavenge the zone.

/AgeAllRecords

```
DNSCMD /AgeAllRecords <zone name> <node>
```

Use this command to timestamp the records in a zone and enable aging. If you omit the <node> option, the entire zone is timestamped and aging is enabled. With the <node> option enabled, only the specified node is affected. Adding the /Tree option to the command causes the entire tree below the specified zone or node (all subdomains) to be affected also. You can append the /f option also if you don't want to be prompted for confirmation, such as when the command is integrated into a script.

Configuring records

The DNSCMD command provides a number of options for working with various record types. You can add and remove records by using this utility.

/RecordAdd

```
DNSCMD /RecordAdd <zone name> <node> /Aging <TTL>
         <record type> <value>
```

This command adds a record to a specified zone. The record name is specified by <node>, and the record type must also be specified. For each record type, the required value data is different, as shown in Figure A-10. When you're adding a record, reference the command's help system by typing DNSCMD /RecordAdd /? to ensure that you provide the correct values.

The /RecordAdd command has two optional parameters:

✔ The /Aging option enables aging on the record, which is disabled by default.

✔ The <TTL> option for the record is set to the TTL in the SOA record for the zone by default; by specifying a value for <TTL>, however, you can override the SOA value.

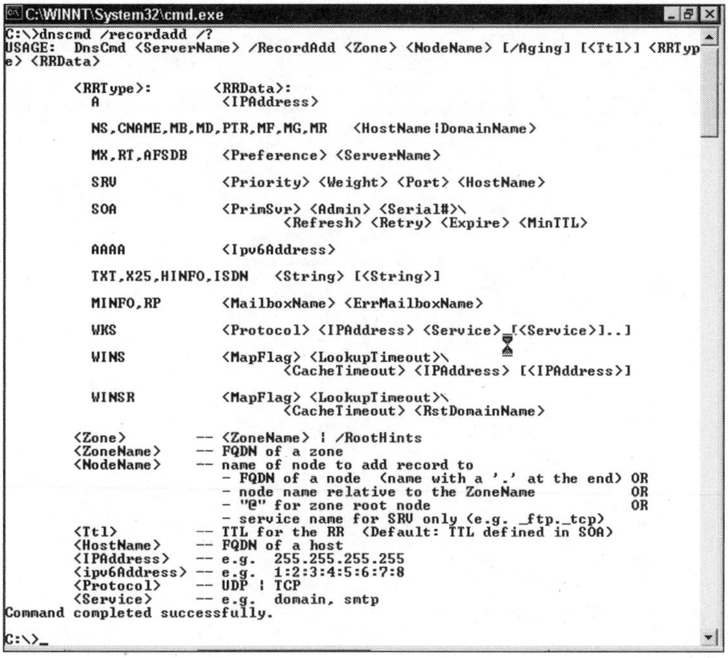

Figure A-10:
The help
information
for this
command
shows the
values
required for
each record
type.

/RecordDelete

```
DNSCMD /RecordDelete <zone name> <node> <record type> <value>
```

The /RecordDelete command removes a specific record from a zone. The record specified by the node, the record type, and the record value are deleted from the specified zone. As with the /RecordAdd command, you use the DNSCMD /RecordDelete /? command, as shown in Figure A-11, to determine what data is required for the value. You can also append the /f option to the command if you don't want to be prompted to delete the record.

/NodeDelete

```
DNSCMD /NodeDelete <zone name> <node>
```

The /NodeDelete command is one of the most useful commands DNSCMD provides. Using this command deletes from the specified zone all records belonging to the specified node, which saves you from having to delete each record individually when a node is completely deprecated.

Adding the /Tree option causes nodes in subdomains and subdomains with the specified node name to be deleted, and appending the /f option eliminates the prompt for confirmation.

```
C:\WINNT\System32\cmd.exe                                            _ 8 X

C:\>dnscmd /recorddelete /?
USAGE:  DnsCmd <ServerName> /RecordDelete <Zone> <OwnerName> <RRType> <RRData> [
/f ]

        <Zone>      -- <ZoneName> ! /RootHints ! /Cache
        <ZoneName>  -- FQDN of a zone
        <OwnerName> -- name of node to delete records from
                       - "@" for zone root OR
                       - FQDN of a node (DNS name with a '.' at the end) OR
                       - single label for name relative to zone root ) OR
                       - service name for SRV only (e.g. _ftp._tcp)
        <RRType>:       <RRData>:
          A                 <IP Address>
          NS,CNAME,MB,MD,PTR,MF,MG,MR  <HostName>

          MX,RT,AFSDB          <Preference> <ServerName>

          MINFO,RP            <MailboxName> <ErrMailboxName>

          TXT,X25,HINFO,ISDN        <String> [<String>]

          SRV             <Priority> <Weight> <Port> <HostName>

          WKS             <Protocol> <IPAddress> <Service> [<Service>]..]

          AAAA                <IPv6 Address>

          ATMA                <ATM address>

          WINS                <MapFlag> <LookupTimeout>

                              <CacheTimeout> <IPAddress> [<IPAddress>]

          WINSR               <MapFlag> <LookupTimeout>
                              <CacheTimeout> <RstDomainName>

        /f  -- Execute without asking for confirmation
        <RRData> not specified
                 -- delete all records with of specified type

    Tip:  you can view the RRData format by enumerating the records
          at the node. ( use 'Dnscmd <server> /EnumRecords ... )

Command completed successfully.

C:\>_
```

Figure A-11:
This command shows the values required for each record type.

Appendix B

Using Webmin for BIND Administration

*T*he *Webmin* open source application provides a Web front end for the administration of many common Unix services. In addition to providing you with the ability to manage service through a Web browser, Webmin has a flexible feature set because it was built as a modular application. A *modular* application makes use of subapplications, or *modules,* to add functionality. If you need to make a change to a given module, you can typically modify that module without having to alter the overall operation of the master, modular, application. Although a wide variety of Webmin modules are available, if you need a module that isn't available, you can develop it yourself or have it custom developed.

Webmin runs on almost all Unix systems, from widespread Linux and Mac OS X to the mammoth commercial Unix systems, such as Sun Solaris and IBM AIX. You can also run Webmin on Microsoft Windows under Cygwin, a Unix-like abstraction layer that allows the operation of Unix code on Windows-based systems. The only requirement beyond the basic operating system (Windows or Unix) is that you have the Perl 5 support files installed on your system. You can find a specific list of supported operating systems at www.webmin.com/support.html.

Get In with Webmin

Depending on the operating system you're using, you can use one of two installation methods:

- ✔ **RPM/Sun Solaris packages:** For use with supported Linux and Unix systems
- ✔ **Source code:** For all other supported operating systems

Using packages

Installing Webmin from packages is the best option for most users because it's a fairly simple process. If you have ever installed any software from packages, you should get no surprises here. If you're working with a Sun Solaris system, you need to use the PKGADD command to install the appropriate package. If you're a Linux aficionado, you use the RPM command to install the proper RPM package. Of course, before you can use either command to install anything, you need to go get the package. You can download these packages from the Webmin Web site, at www.webmin.com. After you get to the Webmin home page, click the Downloading and Installing link, locate your package, and start the download. The Downloading and Installing page is shown in Figure B-1.

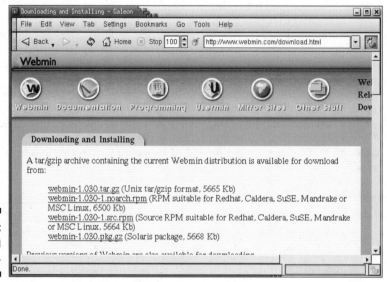

Figure B-1:
Downloading
Webmin.

As you can see in the figure, four options are available on the Webmin download site. The first option is intended for anyone needing the Webmin source code. If you're compiling Webmin from source code, download this file. The remaining files listed are packages of various types, including the RPM binary files, source code in RPM format, and Solaris packages. The sample system we use is Mandrake Linux (which supports RPM), so we downloaded the RPM binary files. After you have the RPM binary files, you can install Webmin by opening a console window, changing to the directory where you downloaded the RPM package and then executing the command `rpm -Uvh webmin-1.030-1.noarch.rpm`. Replace the `rpm` filename with the name of the RPM package you have downloaded.

You can use the command `rpm -ivh` in place of `rpm -Uvh`; they both install packages. The `rpm -i` command is most commonly used for installing packages, but if an earlier version of a package is already installed and `rpm -i` is used, the earlier version isn't removed and you're left with two separate installations. Using the `rpm -Uvh` command, however, installs a package exactly like the `rpm -i` command if no existing version of the same package is used. If an older version of the package exists, though, it gets upgraded and the old package is removed instead of being left in place, like `rpm -i`.

Figure B-2 shows the results of the `rpm -Uvh` command. As you can see, Webmin has been installed and started and is now running on the local system on `port 10000`. You should be able to connect to Webmin from a Web browser at this point. We describe the use of Webmin later in this appendix.

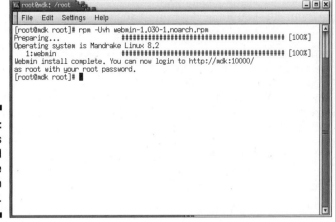

Figure B-2:
RPM has been used to install the Webmin package.

Starting at the source

If you're using an operating system that doesn't support Solaris or RPM packages or you want to have an installation specifically optimized for your system, you need to install Webmin using the source code. Installing from source code is more difficult than an installing from packages (refer to the preceding section, "Using packages") because it requires more steps and a little more knowledge; in some cases, however, it's necessary. Because more steps are involved and you must compile the installer, you should avoid this process unless absolutely necessary.

To install Webmin, follow these steps:

1. **Download the Webmin source code.**

   Go to the Webmin site, at www.webmin.com, and click the Downloading and Installing link. From that page, as shown in Figure B-1, download the webmin-***.tar.gz source file, where *** is the current version.

2. **Unpack the source code in the directory of your choice.**

   First, move the file to the directory in which to unpack. Which directory you use doesn't matter that much because a new subdirectory is created and the source is unpacked into it.

3. **Unzip the source code by typing the command** gunzip webmin-1.030.tar.gz.

   This command produces a file named something similar to webmin-1.030.tar.

4. **Unpack this file by typing the command** tar xvf webmin-1.030.tar.

   The result is a new subdirectory named webmin-1.030 (or whatever version of Webmin you're using) that now contains the source code for the Webmin application.

You can now configure, compile, and install the Webmin source code as a functioning application. Change to the new Webmin source subdirectory and read the README file. It contains installation information and other important information. Installing Webmin from the source code is fairly simple: Just run the file setup.sh. You're prompted for some information:

- The location of the Webmin configuration files
- The location of system log files
- The path to the Perl binaries
- Your Web server port number

✔ A user name and password for the Webmin service

✔ Whether you want the Webmin service to start when the system boots

Although you can accept the defaults for most of these options, you must set a password for the login name and select whether Webmin should start on bootup. After the setup script finishes, Webmin should be installed and running.

"How Do I Use This Thing?"

As its name implies, *Webmin* (short for *Web* ad*min*istration) is a Web-browser-based tool that you can access from anywhere by loading the appropriate server name or IP address and port number into a Web browser session. To use this tool, you connect to your Webmin server from a Web browser, as shown in Figure B-3. You simply use `http://localhost:10000` from the local system or `http://ipaddress:10000` from a remote system.

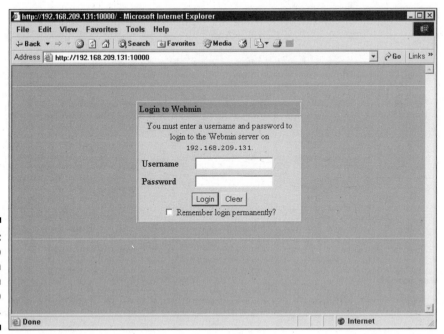

Figure B-3:
Connect to Webmin through any Web browser.

After you have connected to Webmin, enter the username and password you specified during the setup process or use the user root with your root password if you installed from the RPM file. The Webmin console opens, as shown in Figure B-4. You can also enable the Remember login permanently check box and have Webmin remember your username and password. If you will be accessing the Webmin tool from various locations or you're using the root account for authentications, it isn't a good idea to have Webmin remember your logon information.

Making Webmin play with BIND

After you have connected to the Webmin service, you need to complete some basic configuration before it becomes truly useful.

1. **Click the Servers button at the top of the Webmin console.**

   The Servers page opens, as shown in Figure B-5. The Servers page shows installed Webmin modules for working with various types of applications.

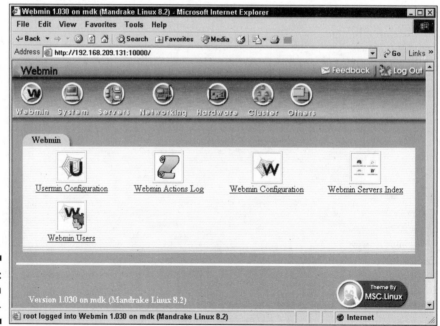

Figure B-4:
The Webmin console.

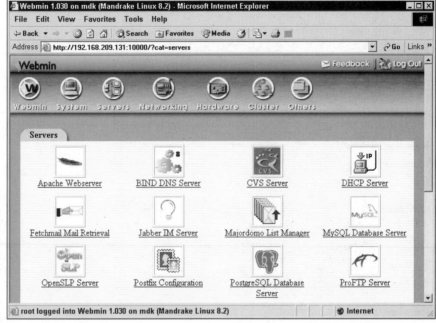

Figure B-5:
The Webmin
Servers
page shows
the installed
Webmin
modules.

Although the modules shown are installed by default, you can install many other Webmin modules later. A Webmin *module* is simply a Perl script built in such a way that the Webmin service can use the module to perform some kind of task. A discussion of how to add and build modules for Webmin is way beyond the scope of this book, but if your interest is piqued, you can check out the helpful documentation on the Webmin Web site, at www.webmin.com.

2. Click the BIND DNS Server module.

You probably see an error message, as shown in Figure B-6, unless your BIND files are all in the location expected by Webmin.

The Webmin module is for BIND 8 because no BIND 9 module is available yet. The module does support BIND 9, but not all BIND 9 options are available.

3. Regardless of whether you receive the error, click Next on the Module Config tab to enter the BIND module configuration, as shown in Figure B-7.

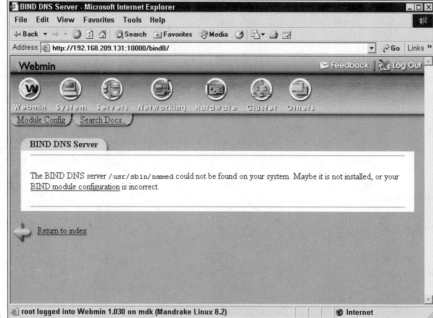

Figure B-6:
The
Webmin
BIND con-
figuration is
incorrect,
and Webmin
cannot find
the BIND
files.

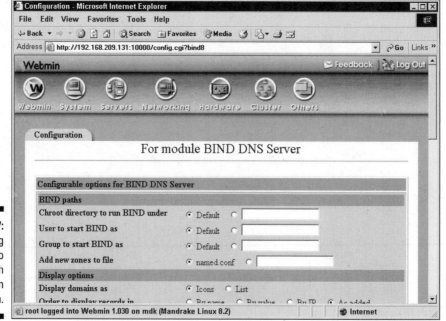

Figure B-7:
Configuring
Webmin to
work with
BIND on
your system.

4. **Browse through the options in the module configuration.**

You can leave most options at the default settings unless you know that your configuration is specifically different from the defaults that are displayed. In the Module Configuration Controls section (labeled BIND paths options), you can see configuration options for starting BIND, including the startup user, group and default configuration file.

The next section, Display options, controls how BIND information is shown in Webmin. If you tweak these options, you can customize the look and feel of your Webmin/BIND session. Of the displayed options, the most important are Display domains as and Order to display records in. If you have only a few zones, the Icon and As added default settings, respectively, are sufficient. As you add more zones, though, the default becomes cluttered and you will probably have a difficult time finding the zone you're looking for. You may want to change the settings to List and By name, respectively, to make a large number of zones easier to view.

In the Zone file options section, you configure the way new zone files are created and existing zone files are modified. In most cases, the default settings are fine, unless you want to customize the way your zone files are structured.

The last section shown in Figure B-8, System configuration, is the most important section for initially configuring the module. The first two settings are the location of the named.conf file and the BIND binary file. Because these files are fairly important, you have to ensure that the path information is correct for your system. Note that the error message shown in the figure was caused by an incorrectly named executable location.

In the System configuration section, you must specify where to find the whois command and specify the command used to reload zones. Whois is normally in the path by default, but you must change the command to reload zones, ndc by default, to rndc for BIND 9. Note also that you must have already configured RNDC with a key in the rndc.conf and named.conf files (refer to Chapter 8). You can leave the PID option as the default, but you have to ensure that the command to start the BIND option is correct for your system. You may need to change it to point to the BIND executable if you're not using a startup script or if BIND is starting in a script with a number of other applications.

When all your settings are in place, click the Save button at the bottom of the page. Your changes are saved and the module page opens, as shown in Figure B-9.

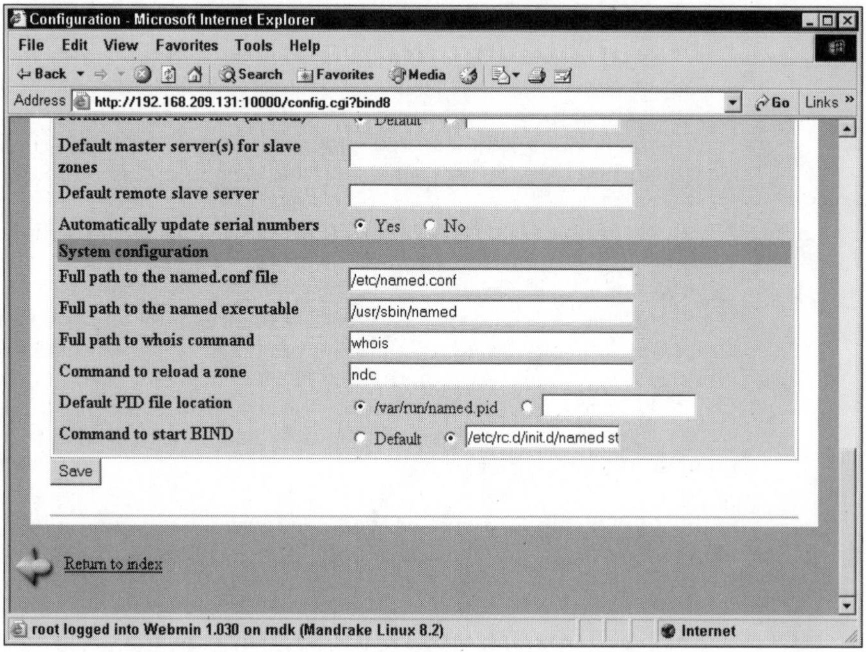

Figure B-8:
Setting system-specific information, such as file locations.

One of the first things you can do with the Webmin module is start the BIND server if it isn't running. At the bottom of the module page is a button labeled either Apply Changes or Start Name Server, as shown in Figure B-9. If the button is labeled Start Name Server, click it to start BIND. If BIND starts successfully, the page refreshes and the button changes to Apply Changes. If BIND is unsuccessful in starting, a specific error is shown, indicating (if you're lucky) the source of the problem.

Exploring the BIND module

The BIND module configuration module page has two sections:

- ✔ **Global server options:** In this upper section, you set the configuration options that affect the entire BIND server. These include all options that would normally be manually configured in the named.conf file under any directive other than zone, such as the options, key, or controls directives.

- ✔ **Existing DNS zones:** In this section, as its name suggests, you configure existing zones and add new zones to the server. You configure all options that would normally be in zone directives in the named.conf file.

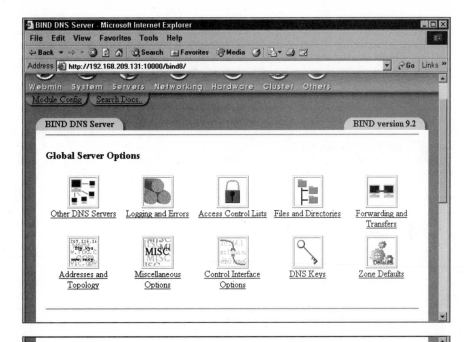

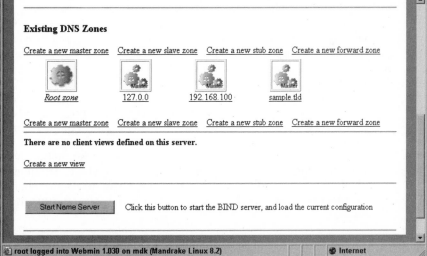

Figure B-9:
You manage
the name
server from
the BIND
module
Webmin
page.

Webmin doesn't replace the named.conf file. Instead, Webmin is just a graphical front end to a process that edits the named.conf file transparently in the background. If you make a change in the named.conf file with Webmin and then check the file again, you can see the changes Webmin made.

Global server options

Whenever you make changes to any of the configuration options on any of the configuration pages, click the Save button at the bottom of the page to ensure that the changes are committed. Don't use the Back button in your Web browser because the information that's displayed may be cached locally and not reflect the true status of the monitored service.

After you finish making configuration changes to your DNS server, you must click the Apply Changes button at the bottom of the BIND module page. This action restarts the DNS server and causes the changes to take effect.

In the Global Server Options section, a number of icons refer to a specific type of configuration for the server. The first option is Other DNS Servers, as shown in Figure B-10. On this page, you configure the other DNS servers to which, or from which, you will be making zone transfers. You don't need to configure every other server to which this server will be exchanging zones — only those that require configuration other than the default. You first specify the IP address of the server, and then you can configure settings for it.

Although it may sound like a quote from a 1990s Keanu Reeves movie, the `Ignore bogus server?` option instructs BIND to ignore all zone transfers from this server. You can use this option when you have a malicious or improperly configured or otherwise "bogus" DNS server attempting to complete a zone transfer with your server. The next option allows you to select whether zone transfers should be done in batches or one zone at a time. The Maximum transfers option controls how many zones can be transferred in a batch. Finally, the Use DNS keys option allows you to select a defined key to be used for zone transfers with this server.

The next set of options is Logging and Errors. The Logging and Errors page, as shown in Figure B-11, shows the existing logging channels, or logging parameters, and allows you to define new logging channels. In most cases, the defaults are acceptable; if you have large logs or want to keep your DNS logs separate from your other system logs, however, you can configure a logging channel. You can add a new channel by clicking Add a new channel and filling out the necessary information. Click the Save button to save the new logging channel.

The Access Control Lists configuration option, as shown in Figure B-12, is fairly straightforward. As we describe in Chapter 11, an access control list (ACL) is essentially an alias for a list of names or addresses that can be referenced anywhere else in the BIND configuration by the ACL name. For example, you can place all internal networks in an ACL named `internal` and use `internal` as the value for a control statement or other access control rather than specify all the addresses or networks each time.

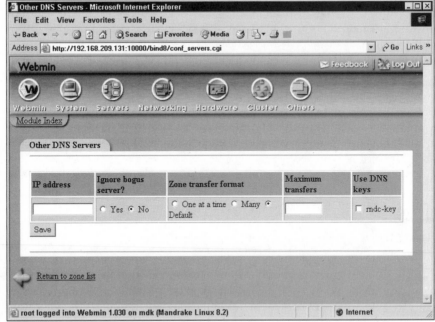

Figure B-10:
Setting configuration options for specific servers with which zone transfers will be made.

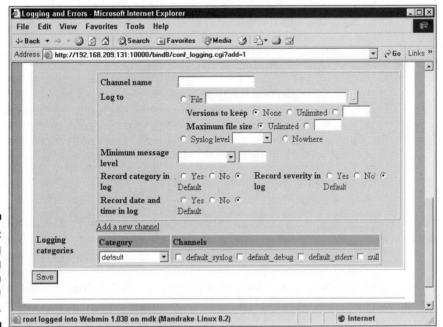

Figure B-11:
Configuring logging behavior on the BIND server.

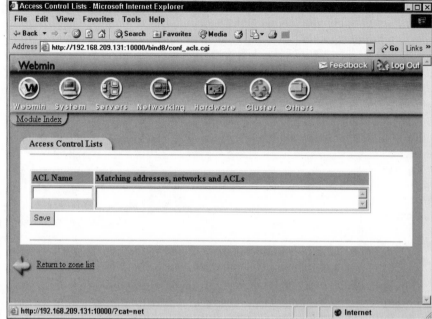

Figure B-12:
Defining an
ACL in the
BIND con-
figuration.

The Files and Directories page is shown in Figure B-13. This page allows you to painlessly specify files for statistics and database output files, the PID file, and an alternative zone transfer utility. Defaults are specified, so if you have no need to specify a new location for storing the kind of affected information, have no fear: You don't have to touch a thing!

Figure B-14 shows the Forwarding and Transfers page. As you may guess, this page is used to configure forwarders for the DNS server in addition to managing the global zone transfer options. To add a forwarder (it's used if the name isn't resolved from the local zones), simply enter the IP address of the server or list of servers in the Servers to forward queries to box. You can then tell BIND how to behave in the event that resolution help is needed. If you select the Yes option, the local server performs a recursive lookup to resolve the address if the forwarder fails. If you select No, the server doesn't perform a recursive lookup and sends back to the client an error indicating that the name resolution attempt failed.

The zone transfer options are similar to those on the Other DNS Servers page except for the Maximum zone transfer time, which determines the longest amount of time a zone transfer can take. Using the Zone transfer format option, you can select whether zones are transferred in batches or individually, and using the Maximum concurrent zone transfers value, you can control how many zones can be transferred in a single batch.

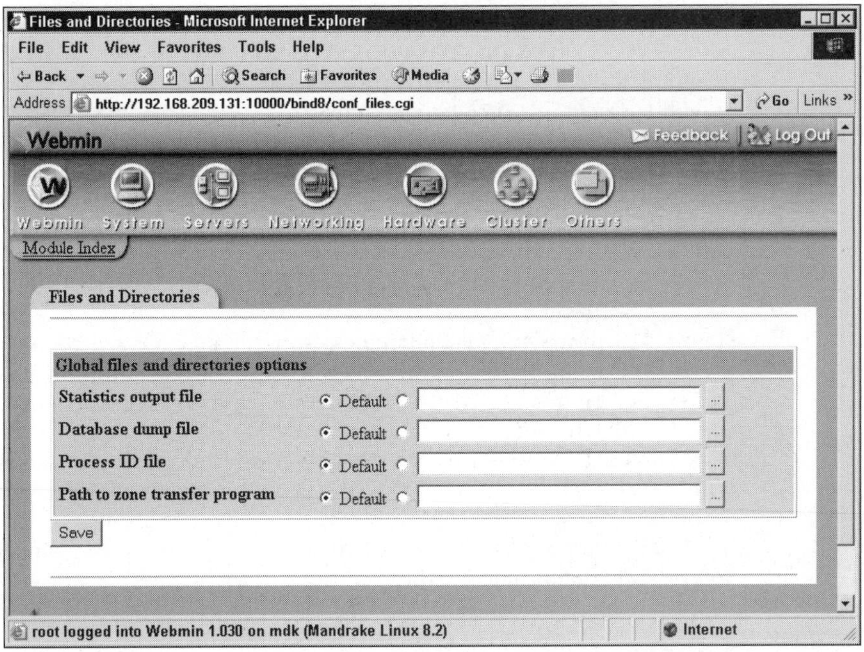

Figure B-13:
Specifying
filenames
other than
the defaults
for specific
output files.

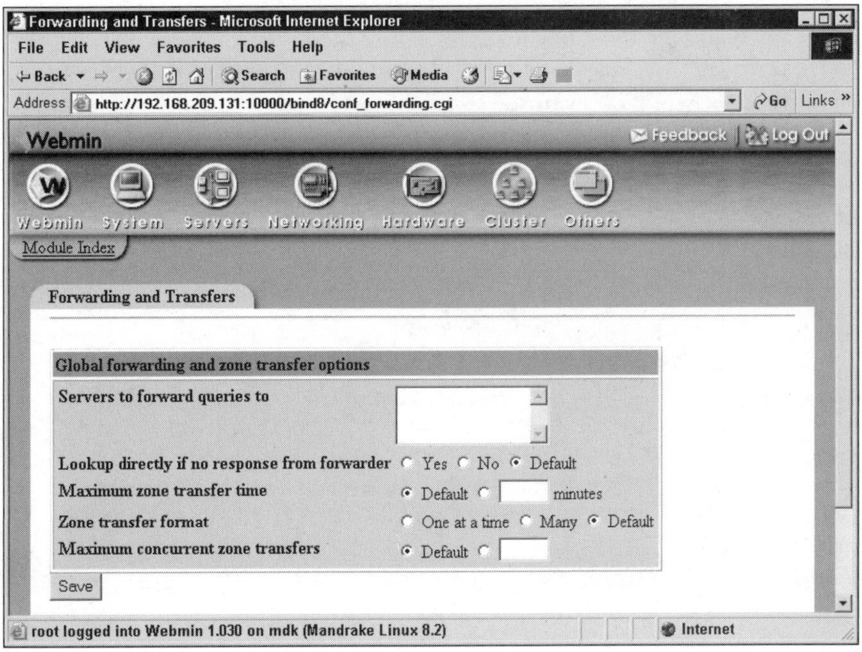

Figure B-14:
Configuring
forwarders
and global
zone
transfer
options.

From the next page, Addresses and Topology, you can set the port and addresses on which the server listens for queries, as shown in Figure B-15. By default, the server listens on all IP addresses assigned to the server and the default DNS port. You can also configure the source IP address and port to use for all DNS queries that originate from the configured server. This ability is particularly useful if you need to configure a firewall to allow outgoing queries for recursion and you want to open only a single IP address and port. Use the Nameserver choice topology box to list a number of name servers and the order in which they're queried. Closer servers are placed at the top of the list, and more remote servers are placed lower on the list.

Figure B-16 shows the Miscellaneous Options page. On this page, you get access to the configuration options that defy normal categorization (the "rebellious" options). The first four options are orderly, advanced options used to limit the amount of memory and disk space used by the BIND application. The next group of options are advanced timing options. The last four options are switches used to disable recursion, disable the fetching of glue records, allow multiple CNAME records for one name, and set the authoritative flag on responses. Unless you're completely sure of the consequences, you probably should leave these options undisturbed.

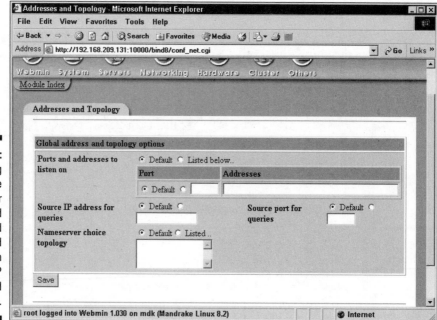

Figure B-15:
Determining how the server should respond and send queries on the IP address and port levels.

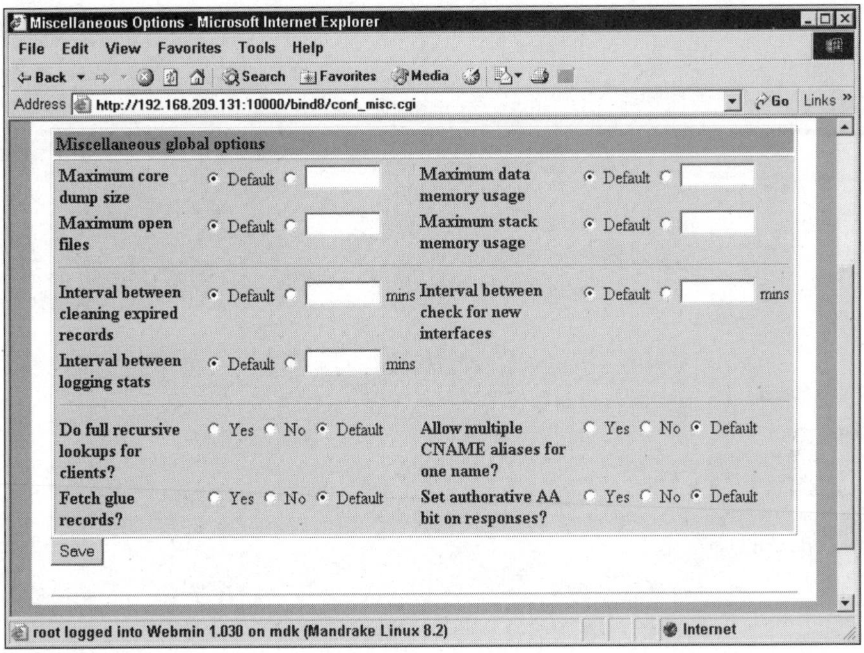

Figure B-16:
Configuring
advanced
global
options for
the server.

Using the next feature, Control Interface Options, you can determine who can control the server.

Controls are one area in which Webmin cannot support BIND 9. The BIND 9 controls are based on RNDC and keys, and the BIND 8 controls are based on NDC and IP addresses. You shouldn't use the Control Interface Options page to configure controls in BIND 9 until the module is updated to support BIND 9.

The DNS Keys page lets you add, modify, and remove keys from the server. As shown in Figure B-17, you can add a key by simply specifying the key name, hash algorithm, and key value. These keys are used for zone transfer and dynamic update authentication and for controls in BIND 9.

Zone Defaults, as shown in Figure B-18, is the last global configuration page in Webmin. You use it to set the default settings for zone files created with Webmin. Every zone file you create using the new zone features described in the following section are assigned these values by default. The settings include default values for items such as the SOA record, although one of the more interesting features is the Template records section. By using this section, you can set a series of template records that are added to each zone as it's created. For example, some common uses are the creation of a www or mail record in each domain. When you leave the value field set to From form, you're prompted to specify the values for the records when the zone is created.

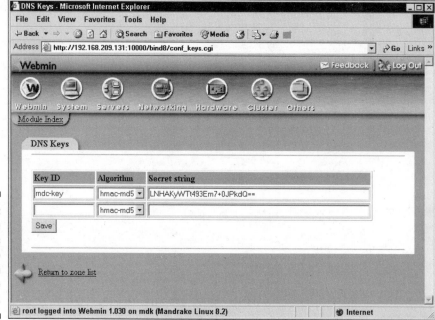

Figure B-17:
Using the
DNS Keys
page to
work with
keys on the
server.

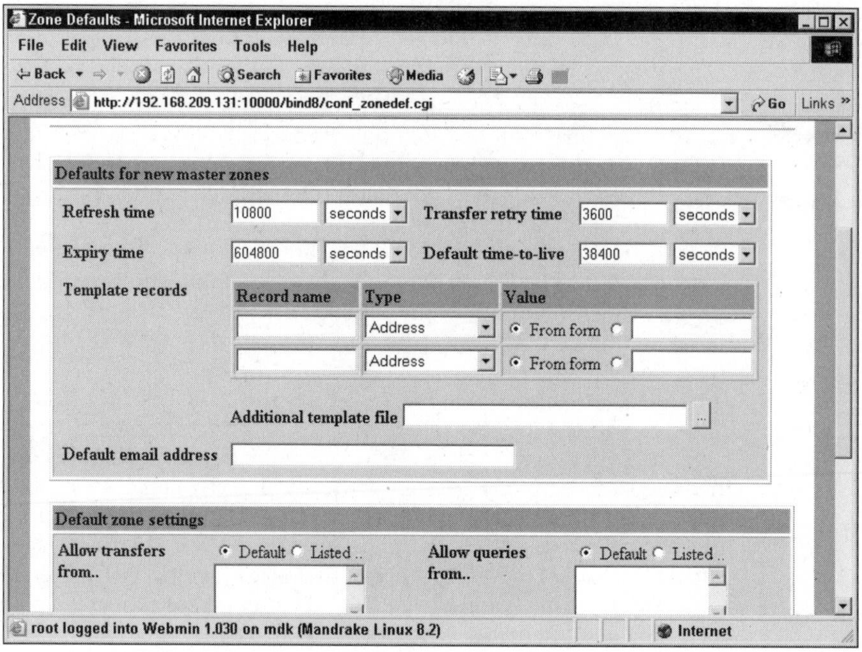

Figure B-18:
From this
page, you
can set
options that
are used
whenever a
new zone is
created.

In the Default zone settings section, you can set the options that are normally set in the zone directive in the `named.conf` file, including servers allowed to perform zone transfers and hosts allowed to query the zone. You can set strict name checking in zones and responses and enable the DNS `NOTIFY` feature.

Existing DNS zones

The Existing DNS Zones section of the BIND module has two uses: modifying and removing existing zones and adding new zones. Working with an existing zone is simple: You locate the zone and click it to open the Edit Master Zone page, as shown in Figure B-19. At the top are the various record types that can exist in the zone with the number of that record that exists in the zone in parentheses.

By clicking any of the record types, you can add or modify a record of the selected type, as shown in Figure B-20. Add a record by entering the relevant information and clicking the Create button. You can also have the reverse lookup record added automatically by selecting that option. This step saves you from the work of adding the record manually, which is typical in BIND. To edit an existing record, click its name on the list. You can then make changes on the Edit Address page and click Save or click the Delete button to remove the record.

The Edit Zone Parameters page simply allows you to modify information in the zone's SOA record if you want it to be different from the information configured on the Zone Defaults global configuration page. The Edit Zone Options page is the same for only the zone options, such as allowed hosts for zone transfers, dynamic updates, notifications, and queries.

On the Edit Records File page, you manually edit records in the zone. Note, however, that the syntax isn't checked and the zone serial number isn't incremented automatically. The Record Generators page, as shown in Figure B-21, is more interesting, though.

On this page, you can create a series of records using a set pattern. In some environments, a series of host names is used — such as `host1`, `host2`, and `host3` or `ws1`, `ws2`, and `ws3`, for example — and these host names are often associated with IP addresses. Note that the brand-new Record Generators feature may not function properly yet.

The last option on the Edit Master Zone page is the Delete Zone button, at the bottom of the page. Clicking this button removes the zone. You're prompted before the zone is deleted, though.

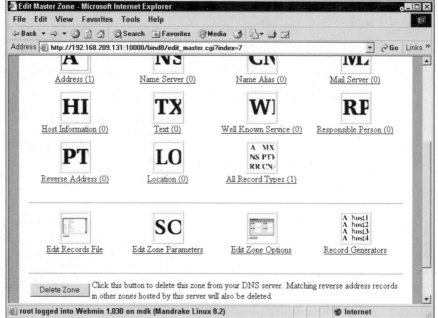

Figure B-19:
From the Edit Master Zone page, you can modify an existing zone.

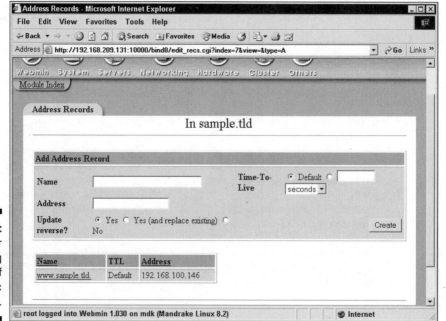

Figure B-20:
Adding or modifying records of a specific type.

Figure B-21:
Adding a
series of
records
auto-
matically.

You can also use the Existing DNS Zones section to add a zone to the server. To create a zone, click one of these options:

- Create a new master zone
- Create a new slave zone
- Create a new stub zone
- Create a new forward zone

The following example shows the creation of a master zone. Selecting the Create a new master zone option opens the Create Master Zone page, as shown in Figure B-22.

Creating the zone is as simple as filling in the blank fields, changing any of the defaults you need, and then clicking the Create button. If any template records were defined on the Zone Defaults page earlier with the From form option selected for the record value, that value is taken from the IP address for template records field. After the zone has been created, the Edit Master Zone page is displayed, as shown in the preceding section.

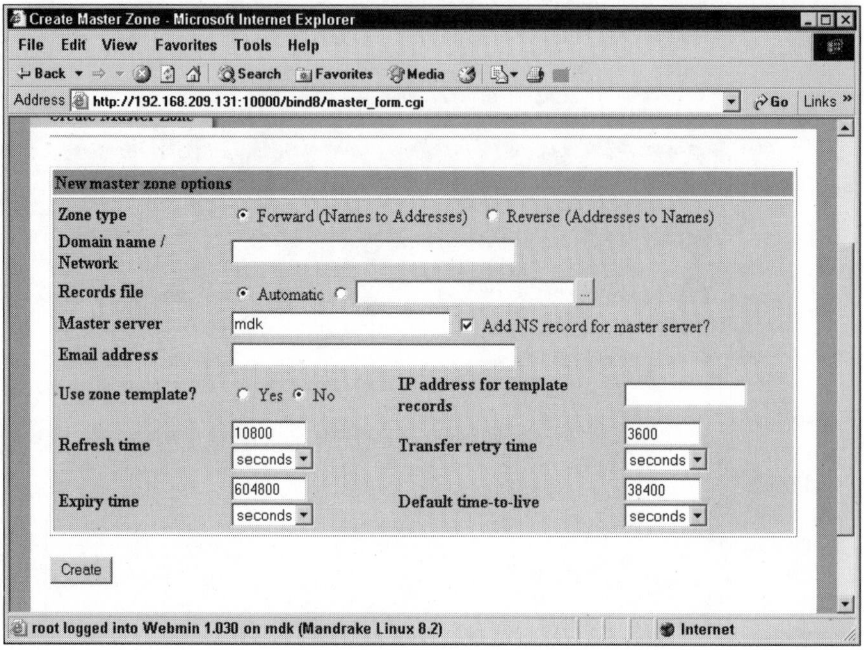

Figure B-22:
Using
Webmin to
create a
new zone
on the
server.

You can also use Webmin to create views on the DNS server by clicking the
Create a new view option on the BIND module page. Unfortunately, a description of views is outside the scope of this book.

Appendix C

Other DNS Server Applications

*I*n *DNS For Dummies,* we provide thorough coverage of the main DNS server applications for both Microsoft Windows and Unix. The vast majority of Windows DNS servers run the Microsoft DNS Server service, and, similarly, the vast majority of Unix DNS servers run some version of BIND (although this book covers BIND 9, the latest version). Aside form being associated with the various operating system products, these DNS applications are available for free, after you have purchased the appropriate operating system.

We would be remiss, however, if we didn't inform you that a number of other DNS servers are available for both Windows and Unix. This appendix gives you a brief overview of some of the more common servers.

Windows-Based DNS Servers

Although most Windows-based DNS servers use the DNS Server service, included for free with all versions of the Windows server operating systems, several DNS server applications are available. They usually offer an advantage of speed, additional functionality, or security, but the advantage, again, is usually in one area, and functionality is sacrificed in others. For example, some third-party DNS servers for Windows may be more secure, although often they're less configurable or lack the ability to perform at the level available with the Windows DNS server. In some cases, though, using a third-party DNS server may be useful in your environment. Regardless, not a large number of Windows-based DNS server applications are available, for a few reasons — primarily that Windows isn't commonly used as a DNS server platform and the DNS Server service typically provides enough functionality and performance for applications in which Windows is used as a DNS server platform.

Get 'em in a BIND

Although we cover BIND Version 9 on Unix in this book, BIND is also available for Windows — and is free. You can download BIND from the Internet Software Consortium (ISC) Web site (`www.isc.org`) in a compiled binary format for Windows. The Windows version provides functionality identical to that of the Unix version.

As we tell you a little earlier in this appendix, BIND on Windows functions identically to the Unix version. BIND uses the same `named.conf` file and zone files for configuration and even uses the `RNDC` command to control the server (refer to Chapter 8). Also included with the Windows version of BIND are the same utilities that are in the Unix version, such as `DIG` and `NSLOOKUP`, in addition to the `RNDC` and `DNSSEC` utilities for managing security keys. All this combines to make the Windows version of BIND a great option for a user who needs to integrate a Windows DNS server into an existing Unix environment. Although some people may snicker at the notion of a Windows DNS server being used where Unix-based systems are available, Windows DNS Server can serve as a low-cost DNS server on an intranet environment if the Windows server is present and available for use.

Incognito DNS Commander

Incognito Software (`www.incognito.com`) makes the feature-rich DNS Commander, which provides both a DNS server back end so that the DNS Server service isn't required, and a rich, graphical front-end interface that makes administration, especially of large sites, much easier. Incognito also says that DNS Commander is secure and provides high performance. DNS Commander is a good choice if you host a large number of zones on a Windows DNS server.

Simple DNS Plus: Keep it simple and then some

Simple DNS Plus (`www.jhsoft.com`) is a fairly basic DNS server application for Windows. It doesn't have a feature-rich GUI, but it it's meant for smaller DNS implementations that host only a few zones or are used for caching DNS. Simple DNS Plus is a good choice for a small-office or home implementation of DNS on a Windows system, especially if you want to host your own Web site. Simple DNS Plus even supports Active Directory. In addition, Simple DNS

Plus can run on Windows 9*x* and Windows NT, Window 2000, and Window XP workstation systems on which the Microsoft DNS Server service isn't supported.

Unix DNS Server Applications

The choices for a DNS server application under a Unix operating system are much more varied than under Windows. Unix-based DNS servers are much more common than Windows-based servers because most DNS servers are run by ISPs that commonly use Unix as a platform for most applications. Unix-based DNS servers vary from stripped-down, high-speed applications to feature-rich applications meant for large DNS implementations.

TinyDNS (djbdns)

TinyDNS (`www.tinydns.org`, `cr.yp.to/djbdns.html`), also referred to as djbdns, is a basic DNS server written by D. J. Bernstein, the author of the Unix mail-transfer agent qmail. The qmail mail application is well-known for its incredible speed and high security, and djbdns was written under the same premise. Because of the way these programs were written, you're unlikely to find a security flaw in them. djbdns was essentially written in response to the large number of security flaws in earlier versions of the BIND DNS server.

TinyDNS is fairly simple to install if you're familiar with how to compile software in Unix. Download the source code from the TinyDNS Web site and use the `make` command to compile the software in accordance with the installation directions. TinyDNS is then configured with the included configuration utilities. TinyDNS doesn't have a large number of features by default, but you can use patches to add to TinyDNS most of the features available for other DNS servers. Although this strategy may result in a relatively large amount of work, the result is a lean, fast, and secure DNS server, as opposed to the monolithic design of BIND, in which everything is included by default.

Incognito DNS Commander

Incognito DNS Commander (`www.incognito.com`), also listed earlier in this appendix, in the section "Windows-Based DNS Servers," is also available for Linux and Sun Solaris. DNS Commander has a number of advantages over the other DNS server applications available for Unix — primarily, its graphical interface. The main type of environment in which this functionality is useful is at a large ISP where the maintenance of BIND or the TinyDNS configuration is arduous because of the large number of zones or records. Many companies build their own Web-based interfaces to the BIND configuration files using such scripting tools as Perl. DNS Commander, however, provides this functionality out of the box, although it comes at a price. In addition, Incognito claims to be faster and more secure than BIND.

Index

• O •

FOR DUMMIES®

The easy way to get more done and have more fun

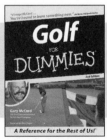
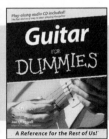

FOR DUMMIES®

A world of resources to help you grow

TRAVEL

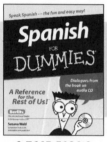

0-7645-5453-0

0-7645-5438-7

0-7645-5444-1

Also available:

America's National Parks For Dummies
(0-7645-6204-5)

Caribbean For Dummies
(0-7645-5445-X)

Cruise Vacations For Dummies 2003
(0-7645-5459-X)

Europe For Dummies
(0-7645-5456-5)

Ireland For Dummies
(0-7645-6199-5)

France For Dummies
(0-7645-6292-4)

Las Vegas For Dummies
(0-7645-5448-4)

London For Dummies
(0-7645-5416-6)

Mexico's Beach Resorts For Dummies
(0-7645-6262-2)

Paris For Dummies
(0-7645-5494-8)

RV Vacations For Dummies
(0-7645-5443-3)

EDUCATION & TEST PREPARATION

0-7645-5194-9

0-7645-5325-9

0-7645-5249-X

Also available:

The ACT For Dummies
(0-7645-5210-4)

Chemistry For Dummies
(0-7645-5430-1)

English Grammar For Dummies
(0-7645-5322-4)

French For Dummies
(0-7645-5193-0)

GMAT For Dummies
(0-7645-5251-1)

Inglés Para Dummies
(0-7645-5427-1)

Italian For Dummies
(0-7645-5196-5)

Research Papers For Dummies
(0-7645-5426-3)

SAT I For Dummies
(0-7645-5472-7)

U.S. History For Dummies
(0-7645-5249-X)

World History For Dummies
(0-7645-5242-2)

HEALTH, SELF-HELP & SPIRITUALITY

0-7645-5154-X

0-7645-5302-X

0-7645-5418-2

Also available:

The Bible For Dummies
(0-7645-5296-1)

Controlling Cholesterol For Dummies
(0-7645-5440-9)

Dating For Dummies
(0-7645-5072-1)

Dieting For Dummies
(0-7645-5126-4)

High Blood Pressure For Dummies
(0-7645-5424-7)

Judaism For Dummies
(0-7645-5299-6)

Menopause For Dummies
(0-7645-5458-1)

Nutrition For Dummies
(0-7645-5180-9)

Potty Training For Dummies
(0-7645-5417-4)

Pregnancy For Dummies
(0-7645-5074-8)

Rekindling Romance For Dummies
(0-7645-5303-8)

Religion For Dummies
(0-7645-5264-3)

Available wherever books are sold. Go to www.dummies.com or call 1-877-762-2974 to order direct

FOR

DUMMIES®

Helping you expand your horizons and realize your potential

GRAPHICS & WEB SITE DEVELOPMENT

0-7645-1651-5

0-7645-1643-4

0-7645-0895-4

Also available:

Adobe Acrobat 5 PDF
For Dummies
(0-7645-1652-3)
ASP.NET For Dummies
(0-7645-0866-0)
ColdFusion MX for Dummies
(0-7645-1672-8)
Dreamweaver MX For
Dummies
(0-7645-1630-2)
FrontPage 2002 For Dummies
(0-7645-0821-0)

HTML 4 For Dummies
(0-7645-0723-0)
Illustrator 10 For Dummies
(0-7645-3636-2)
PowerPoint 2002 For
Dummies
(0-7645-0817-2)
Web Design For Dummies
(0-7645-0823-7)

PROGRAMMING & DATABASES

0-7645-0746-X

0-7645-1626-4

0-7645-1657-4

Also available:

Access 2002 For Dummies
(0-7645-0818-0)
Beginning Programming
For Dummies
(0-7645-0835-0)
Crystal Reports 9 For
Dummies
(0-7645-1641-8)
Java & XML For Dummies
(0-7645-1658-2)
Java 2 For Dummies
(0-7645-0765-6)

JavaScript For Dummies
(0-7645-0633-1
Oracle9i For Dummies
(0-7645-0880-6)
Perl For Dummies
(0-7645-0776-1)
PHP and MySQL For
Dummies
(0-7645-1650-7)
SQL For Dummies
(0-7645-0737-0)
Visual Basic .NET For
Dummies
(0-7645-0867-9)

LINUX, NETWORKING & CERTIFICATION

0-7645-1545-4

0-7645-1760-0

0-7645-0772-9

Also available:

A+ Certification For Dummies
(0-7645-0812-1)
CCNP All-in-One Certification
For Dummies
(0-7645-1648-5)
Cisco Networking For
Dummies
(0-7645-1668-X)
CISSP For Dummies
(0-7645-1670-1)
CIW Foundations For
Dummies
(0-7645-1635-3)

Firewalls For Dummies
(0-7645-0884-9)
Home Networking For
Dummies
(0-7645-0857-1)
Red Hat Linux All-in-One
Desk Reference For Dummies
(0-7645-2442-9)
UNIX For Dummies
(0-7645-0419-3)

Available wherever books are sold.
Go to www.dummies.com or call 1-877-762-2974 to order direct